High
Growth
Handbook

**Stripe
Press**

Ideas for progress
San Francisco, California
press.stripe.com

To my lovely wife Jennifer and son Liav. Suddenly, everything is possible again.

To my fantastic parents and my amazing sister, thank you for all the support and belief over the years.

P.S. To any children born in the future, sorry you are not in this dedication. You would be in here if you already existed.

INTERVIEWS WITH

Sam Altman
Marc Andreessen
Patrick Collison
Joelle Emerson
Erin Fors
Reid Hoffman
Claire Hughes Johnson
Aaron Levie
Mariam Naficy
Keith Rabois
Naval Ravikant
Ruchi Sanghvi
Shannon Stubo Brayton
Hemant Taneja

Thank you to the founders and entrepreneurs I have worked with over the last decade either formally or informally. Your dedication, creativity, curiosity, energy, and hope to have a lasting impact and to make the world a better place has been inspiring.

Countless people contributed their thoughts, revisions, and feedback on early versions of parts of this book.

Thanks to the entrepreneurs and investors who allowed me to interview them, and whose perspectives have added immeasurably to this book. Sam Altman, Marc Andreessen, Patrick Collison, Joelle Emerson, Erin Fors, Reid Hoffman, Claire Hughes Johnson, Aaron Levie, Mariam Naficy, Keith Rabois, Naval Ravikant, Ruchi Sanghvi, Shannon Stubo Brayton, and Hemant Taneja: Thank you for making this book smarter than I could have done on my own.

Thanks to Stripe for believing in this project and committing to it early on. Thanks to Brianna Wolfson for managing the book project, Tyler Thompson for creative direction, Kevin Wong for interior layout, Christina Bailey for transcribing the interviews and early edits, and Dylan Tweney for editing the manuscript.

ELAD GIL

High
Growth
Handbook

PRAISE FOR HIGH GROWTH HANDBOOK

"Elad Gil is one of Silicon Valley's seriously knowledgeable and battle-tested players. If you want the chance to turn your start-up into the next Google or Twitter, then read this trenchant guide from someone who played key roles in the growth of these companies."

—Reid Hoffman, cofounder of LinkedIn,
   coauthor of the #1 NYT bestsellers *The Alliance* and *The Startup of You*

"This book is packed with key frameworks for building your company, as well as inside knowledge gleaned from helping some of the most important new companies in tech. I have benefited from Elad's advice at Instacart and this book codifies many of those learnings in book form."

—Apoorva Mehta, cofounder and CEO of Instacart

"Elad eschews trite management aphorisms in favor of pragmatic and straight-shooting insights on complex topics like managing a board of directors, executing functional re-organizations with as little trauma as possible, and everything in-between."

—Dick Costolo, former CEO of Twitter and serial entrepreneur

"Armed with observations gathered scaling some of the most successful and important companies of Silicon Valley, Elad has no-nonsense, highly applicable advice to any operator transitioning a company from the proverbial garage to the next stage and beyond."

—Max Levchin, cofounder and CEO of Affirm, cofounder and CTO of PayPal

"Elad first invested in Airbnb when we were less than 10 people and provided early advice on scaling the company. This book shares these learnings for the next generation of entrepreneurs."

—Nathan Blecharczyk, cofounder of Airbnb, Chief Strategy Officer, and Chairman of Airbnb China

"Elad is one of the best connected and respected early stage investors in the Valley—he invested in Minted when we had fewer than 50 employees and his advice was critical to us in growing our business to where we are now, in the low hundreds of millions in sales. In his book, he crystallizes all of these learnings for the next generation of companies."

—Mariam Naficy, cofounder and CEO of Minted

"Elad is one of the most experienced operators in Silicon Valley having seen numerous companies hit their inflection point. His advice has been key for Coinbase as we go through hypergrowth, from hiring executives to improving M&A."

—Brian Armstrong, cofounder and CEO of Coinbase

"Elad jam packs every useful lesson about building and scaling companies in a single, digestible book. My only gripe is that he didn't write this when we were in the early days of Box as it would have saved my ass countless times."

—Aaron Levie, cofounder and CEO of Box

ABOUT THE AUTHOR

Elad Gil

Elad Gil is an entrepreneur, operating executive, and investor or advisor to private companies such as Airbnb, Coinbase, Checkr, Gusto, Instacart, OpenDoor, Pinterest, Square, Stripe, Wish, and others.

He is cofounder and chairman at Color Genomics. Elad was CEO of Color from 2013 to December 2016.

Previously, he was the VP of Corporate Strategy at Twitter, where he also ran various product (Geo, Search) and other operational teams (M&A and corporate development). Elad joined Twitter via the acquisition of Mixer Labs, a company where he was cofounder and CEO. Mixer Labs ran GeoAPI, one of the early developer-centric platform infrastructure products.

Elad spent many years at Google, where he started the mobile team and was involved in all aspects of getting that team up and running. He was involved with three acquisitions (including the Android team) and was the original Product Manager for Google Mobile Maps and other key mobile products.

Prior to Google, Elad had product management and market-seeding roles at a number of Silicon Valley companies. He also worked at McKinsey & Co.

Elad received his Ph.D. from the Massachusetts Institute of Technology and has degrees in Mathematics and Biology from the University of California, San Diego.

How to use this book

Many of the sections of this book started life as blog posts on my website, blog.eladgil.com, where I've been writing since 2007.

It's not meant to be read straight through, like a novel or a class curriculum. This is meant to be an active reference—a book you can flip through to find useful guidance on specific topics when you need some perspective or advice.

I've included many interviews from entrepreneurs with proven track records. Although I have worked at some of the fastest growing companies in Silicon Valley history, my experience is far from exhaustive. Sometimes it just helps to have different perspectives. I'm honored to include these experts' perspectives, even when—especially when—it doesn't jibe completely with my own. You might find it fun to skip between interviews and read one after the other—there are some great stories and valuable advice embedded within.

When there are online references that might prove useful, I've included a footnote pointing to my website, where you can find more direct links to these resources.

For those links, additional resources, and updates, visit growth.eladgil.com.

High Growth Handbook
© 2018 Elad Gil
growth.eladgil.com

First published in 2018 in hardcover
in the United States of America
by Stripe Press/Stripe Matter Inc.

Stripe Press
Ideas for progress
San Francisco, California
press.stripe.com

Printed by Hemlock in Canada
ISBN: 978-1-7322651-0-3

Third Edition

Table of contents

CHAPTER 7: PRODUCT MANAGEMENT

CHAPTER 8: FINANCING AND VALUATION

Welcome to the High Growth Handbook

A lot has been written about the early stages of establishing a technology startup, from fundraising and searching for product/market fit to early team building and M&A exits. But what happens next? Very little tactical advice exists about scaling a company from 10 or 20 employees to thousands.

Startup survival numbers explain this discrepancy. While thousands of startups are founded each year, most die or are bought well before they reach the high-growth stage (sometimes called "hypergrowth," "scaling," or "breaking out"). As a result, while many people have experience starting a company, very few have experience scaling one.

Just as there are common patterns that early-stage companies follow, later-stage high-growth companies also face similar issues over and over. Every high-growth company eventually needs to tackle the same set of challenges around organizational structure, late-stage fundraising, culture, hiring executives for roles the founders don't understand, buying other companies, and more. Since most founders are dealing with these issues for the first time—and navigating many of them simultaneously—hypergrowth tends to feels like a hyperstressful roller coaster.

Since 2004, I've participated in nearly every stage of the startup life cycle, as either an operator or an investor. I joined Google somewhere between 1,500 and 2,000 employees and left when it was at 15,000, close to four years later. I then started a company,

Mixer Labs, that Twitter acquired when Twitter was around 90 people. As a vice president at Twitter, my job was to scale the company from 100 to over 1,000 people. I left two-and-a-half years later, when Twitter hit roughly 1,500 employees, and then stuck around as an advisor to the CEO and COO for another year, by which point the company had reached roughly 2,500 people. At Twitter, I was involved at various times with product, platform, internationalization, user growth, M&A, recruiting, organizational process, culture, and other aspects of scaling.

I am also an investor in a number of breakout or high-growth companies: Airbnb, Coinbase, Gusto, Instacart, OpenDoor, Pinterest, Stripe, Square, Wish, and others. In some cases I have helped companies in meaningful ways, in others I have been a mere observer along for the ride.[1]

I have found that the same patterns unfold across various high-growth companies. Founders, CEOs, and executives consistently come to me with similar questions and issues as they scale their companies.

I'm writing this book to answer those questions and capture the key lessons of my experiences. In parallel, I have been publishing a blog for a long time—and many of the chapters here started as blog posts, and I will keep adding to it over time.

---

[1]   While I try to be helpful to all companies I invest in, different companies need different levels of help at various points in their lifetimes.

Visit growth.eladgil.com for updates, additional material, and links to many online resources and articles mentioned in the following pages.

The advice presented here is meant to be painfully tactical and to avoid the platitudes you will get from investors who have never run or scaled a company. My hope is that the book will be helpful to founders, CEOs, and employees who are facing hypergrowth and scaling for the first time.

All startup advice is only useful in context, and I am a firm believer that the only good generic startup advice is that there is no good generic startup advice. So take what is written here with a grain of salt—it is very much one person's experiences, not a rulebook for what is correct for every company in every context.

If the high-growth stage at your company feels like a chaotic, scary, stressful shitshow, don't worry. It feels that way for everyone the first time around. Buckle up and enjoy the ride!

Elad
@eladgil

An interview with Marc Andreessen

Marc Andreessen is a cofounder and general partner of the venture capital firm Andreessen Horowitz. He co-created the highly influential Mosaic internet browser and cofounded Netscape, which later sold to AOL for $4.2 billion. He also cofounded Loudcloud, which as Opsware sold to Hewlett-Packard for $1.6 billion. Marc holds a BS in Computer Science from the University of Illinois at Urbana-Champaign, and serves on the board of a number of Andreessen Horowitz portfolio companies as well as the boards of Facebook and Hewlett-Packard Enterprise.

It's a thrilling thing to build a new product, then watch as consumers actually pick it up. But achieving product/market fit also marks the beginning of a challenging time for a lot of founders. You've poured your energy into getting here—now what?

Few people have as much insight into this make-or-break moment as Marc Andreessen. As a repeat founder himself and one of Silicon Valley's most influential investors, he's seen firsthand that the decisions startups make at this juncture are some of the most consequential they will ever make. I spoke with Marc to get his top recommendations for how startup leaders can turn early success into lasting relevance.

Elad Gil:

After you've achieved product/market fit, what do you think are the most important determinants of a company's success? You have your first product working, everything is scaling, everything seems to be going great, but now it's time for you to do these three things. What are those things in your mind, or what are the most common issues people run into?

Marc Andreessen:

I think there are three big categories. Once there's product/market fit, then the main thing becomes taking the market—which is to say, figuring out how to get the product to the entire market, how to get dominant market share; because most tech markets tend to end up with one company with most of the market share. And that company tends to be all the value that gets created in that sector, from a return standpoint. That company also tends to have all the resources to do everything else that they want to do, including build new products.

So winning the market is the big thing. The thing that is so essential that people need to understand is that the world is a really big place. The good news is that markets are bigger than ever. There are more consumers on the internet than ever before. There are more businesses that use software than ever before. There are more sectors of the economy where this stuff all matters. And so the markets are bigger than before.

But that means that the challenge of building an organization, a model, and a distribution capability that can actually get the product to all the customers is an intense challenge. And of course the personality type of the technical founder who creates a breakthrough product, they don't necessarily intuitively understand that that next part involves taking down the market.

That's number one. Number two is getting to the next product. We are in a product cycle business. Which is to say that every product in tech becomes obsolete, and they become obsolete pretty quickly. If all you do is take your current product to market and win the market, and you don't do anything else—if you don't keep innovating—your product will go stale. And somebody will come out with a better product and displace you.

So you do need to get to the next product. Of course that's a punishingly hard thing to do. It was hard enough to get to the first one, and to come up with the second one is often even harder. Although the consistency between these two tasks is this: If you do take the market, you tend to have the financial resources to be able to invest heavily in R&D. And you also develop M&A currency, so you can then go buy the second product if you have to. It gives you another option to get to the second product.

"If you don't keep innovating—your product will go stale. And somebody will come out with a better product and displace you."

—Marc Andreessen

Elad: And that can also use your established distribution that you can just plug into, which is nice.

Marc: Exactly. In fact, the general model for successful tech companies, contrary to myth and legend, is that they become distribution-centric rather than product-centric. They become a distribution channel, so they can get to the world. And then they put many new products through that distribution channel.

One of the things that's most frustrating for a startup is that it will sometimes have a better product but get beaten by a company that has a better distribution channel. In the history of the tech industry, that's actually been a more common pattern. That has led to the rise of these giant companies over the last fifty, sixty, seventy years, like IBM, Microsoft, Cisco, and many others.

But then the third thing you need to do is what I call "everything else," which is building the company around the product and the distribution engine. That means becoming competent at finance, HR, legal, marketing, PR, investor relations, and recruiting.

That's the stuff that's the easiest to put to one side—for a little while. If you've got a killer product and a great sales engine, you can put that other stuff aside for a while. But the longer you put that stuff aside, the more risk that you develop and the more you expose yourself to catastrophic failure through self-inflicted wounds.

Of course, the obvious one that we're all seeing right now in this environment is HR. The number of companies in the Valley that put HR off to the side and decided it wasn't important and are now dealing with some level of catastrophe—either a public catastrophe or one that's in the making—that's a pretty high percentage of companies right now. And it's totally unnecessary. If they had taken HR seriously starting at an earlier point, they probably would have been able to fight a lot of their issues. But for whatever reason they decided it wasn't important. So HR has to be taken seriously.

Then there's legal. We see cases in the Valley where companies have just decided that laws are optional, felonies are fine. And at some point, not having a general counsel who's able to explain to the CEO where the line is, that becomes a big issue.

And obviously finance. There are companies that blow themselves up financially that don't have to, with wildly out-of-control cost structures or horribly screwed-up pricing or whatever.

Elad: A common question for a lot of founders, especially first-time founders, is when should they actually hire an HR leader or somebody in the HR function or a GC [general counsel] or somebody for finance? Is that at a certain round of financing? Is it at a certain revenue level? Is it at a certain number of people? When should you start adding those different functions?

Marc: It's somewhere between 50 to 150 people. It's somewhere in there. If you don't start layering in HR once you've passed 50 people on your way to 150, something is going to go badly wrong.

I think there's actually an explanation for that. It's because 150 is the Dunbar number, the number of people you can directly know. So somewhere between 50 to 150 people, everybody doesn't know everybody. There are people running around who other people have never met. When you were 5 or 10 or 20 people, it was one big happy family and everybody knew everybody—well, maybe it wasn't, but at least everybody knew everybody. And the CEO had direct one-on-one relationships with everybody in the company. Once you get to 50+, that's just no longer the case. At that point there's a necessary impersonality of the professional relationships in the company. And then HR catastrophes emerge, because people trip the line from proper professional behavior in a workplace to improper. There are just too many people running around interacting.

Elad: Let's focus on each of these three points. When it comes to taking down the market, can you talk a little bit more about the primary things that people should be doing? And what do people tend to miss, or where do they tend to screw things up?

MAJOR GOOGLE ACQUISITIONS

DoubleClick
Added to the backbone of Google's
AdWords network

YouTube
One of the largest destinations on the
internet

Writely
This became Google Docs and, later, G Suite

Where2
Became Google Maps

Android
The biggest mobile operating system by
number of users. Need I say more?

Marc: I think the single biggest thing is that every market has early adopters. There are early adopters for everything, and it's kind of amazing that that's the case. But there are always people. There are people on product sites every day looking for the next new consumer thing to try. There are even early adopter CIOs. There are Fortune 500 CIOs who pride themselves on discovering the next new whatever it is—the new relational database, AI, whatever it is. They're all over it.

And a lot of product/market fit is the fit with the early adopters. And so you get these extremely enthusiastic people, who in a lot of cases have sought you out as the vendor, saying, "Wow, your thing is really cool. Can I please use it?" And that's your sign of product/market fit.

The problem is, the early adopters are only ever a small percentage of the overall market. And so a lot of founders, especially technical ones, will convince themselves that the rest of the market behaves like the early adopters, which is to say that the customers will find them. And that's just not true.

In the consumer world, it's not true because people have plenty of existing things they can spend their time on. They have to be convinced to try the next new thing. And so whether you want to call that marketing or growth hacking or user acquisition or whatever you want to call it, there's some distribution function there, for all these things, that's critical.

And then for sure for B2B. Most businesspeople in the world, most CIOs or whoever is going to buy technology in a business, don't wake up in the morning and say, "Gee whiz, can I go find the next hot thing to take a chance on?" That's not how businesspeople live their lives. And so there needs to be some distribution capability to get to them.

Again, the danger there is a market share thing. If you stick to the early adopters, you'll get 5% of the market, but you're not going to get 95% of the market. And that means, sort of by definition, somebody else is going to go get 95%.

One of the things you see crystal clearly in VC is how much competition emerges whenever anything works. Every single time we say, "Oh, this startup is unique. There's some unique product here and there's not going to be competition," invariably six months later there are 20 venture-backed competitors doing the exact same thing. And so at some point, if the early

"If you don't start layering in HR once you've passed 50 people on your way to 150, something is going to go badly wrong."

—Marc Andreessen

guys don't get to the other 95% of the market, somebody else is going to go take it away. And whoever has 95% of the market, number one they're going to get all the value. All the investment returns, all the employee compensation flows to that company. And then number two, that company then accretes resources so they can work backward. In a lot of cases, they end up buying the company that got the early adopters for a small percentage of their equity, and then they just take the whole thing.

Elad: You mentioned three or four tactical things that startups can do to stay viable. One is product iteration and building products that serve more of that market. Second, you really emphasize building up distribution. Third is M&A, which seems to be really underutilized in Silicon Valley today, at least in terms of the next generation of companies. If you have a $10 or $20 billion market cap, you should be buying things. One thing you didn't mention, but I'd love to hear more on, is moats—in other words, building defensibility into what you're doing. As you think about those four different factors, how do you rank them or think about common failure modes?

Marc: I am shocked by the absence of M&A relative to what I would expect in the environment. And I would say there's no question that the big new tech incumbents are not buying enough stuff just on the math. I think it's just kind of obvious. In the old days, their predecessor companies were far more aggressive at building up their positions for M&A. And honestly, the Fortune 500, the big public companies, are not nearly as aggressive as I think they're going to be.

I think this is a temporary lull. I think five years from now we're going to be having a very different conversation, because it's just going to become obvi-

"Give me a great product picker and a great architect, and I'll give you a great product."

— Marc Andreessen

ous that this is an underutilized thing. And I do think that that could be a very effective weapon, therefore, for somebody who really figures this out and does it aggressively in the right way.

Cisco is one of the great case studies in the Valley. It's a very successful, very big, very established company, and a very large percentage of that has been M&A. And then obviously Google. Probably an under-told part of the Google story is how M&A built Google. People, I think, don't even necessarily remember the number of things that Google bought that turned into what you think of today as Google-originated products.

As far as defensibility, I think you construct defensibility through some combination of product innovation and distribution building. You construct it. You obviously want as much defensibility as you can get in your product, and so you try to get as far out ahead as you can. It's the idealized Peter Thiel model of "build something nobody else can build." Or the SpaceX model of "go get all the talent."

The problem with that is true defensibility purely at the product level is really rare in the Valley, because there are a lot of really good engineers. And there are new ones every day, whether they're coming out of Stanford or coming in from other countries or whatever. And then there's the issue of leap-frogging. The next team has the opportunity to learn from what you did and then build something better. So I think pure product defensibility is obviously highly desirable, but it's actually quite difficult.

I think the distribution moats end up being at least as important. At some point, whoever has the distribution engine and gets 100% of the market, at some point that engine itself is a moat. Again, that might be an enterprise sales team for a SaaS company, or it might be the growth team at a consumer company.

One interesting question I have is: Would you rather have another two years' lead on product, or a two years' lead on having a state-of-the-art growth effort? I think the answer for a lot of consumer products is actually that you'd rather have the growth effort.

The other big missing variable in all of this is pricing. I've talked in public about this before. What I don't hear from companies is, "Oh, we don't think we have a moat." What I hear from companies is, "Oh, we have an awesome moat, and we're still going to price our product cheap, because we think that's somehow going to maximize our business." I'm always urging founders to raise prices, raise prices, raise prices.

First of all, raising prices is a great way to flesh out whether you actually do have a moat. If you do have a moat, the customers will still buy, because they have to. The definition of a moat is the ability to charge more. And so number one, it's just a good way to flesh out that topic and really expose it to sunlight.

And then number two, companies that charge more can better fund both their distribution efforts and their ongoing R&D efforts. Charging more is a key lever to be able to grow. And the companies that charge more therefore tend to grow faster.

That's counterintuitive to a lot of engineers. A lot of engineers think there's a one-dimensional relationship between price and value. They have this mental model of commerce like they're selling rice or something. It's like, "My product is magical and nobody can replicate it, and I need to price it like it's a commodity." No, you don't. In fact, quite the opposite. If you price it high, then you can fund a much more expensive sales and marketing effort, which means you're much more likely to win the market, which means you're much more likely to be able afford to do all the R&D and acquisitions you're going to want to do. And so we always try to snap people into a two-dimensional mindset, where higher prices equals faster growth.

Elad: That's an awesome insight. I feel like there's two really key notes that you brought up that typically aren't talked about. One is distribution moats. I think people emphasize network effects and data effects way too much, and I've never seen a real data effect, at least recently. And then second is charging more equals faster growth. Those are really key things that people really don't talk about or think about.

Marc: I think network effects are great, but in a sense they're a little overrated. The problem with network effects is they unwind just as fast. And so they're great while they last, but when they reverse, they reverse viciously. Go ask the MySpace guys how their network effect is going. Network effects can create a very strong position, for obvious reasons. But in another sense, it's a very weak position to be in. Because if it cracks, you just unravel. I always worry when a company thinks the answer is just network effects. How durable are they?

To your point on data network effects, I would just say that we don't see it very often. We see a lot of claims, and very little evidence. The reality is, there's a lot of data in the world, and a lot of ways to get data. We have not seen very many data moats that actually make sense, even in science. Deep learning is the latest area where people think there's data network effects. The problem is there's innovation in deep learning to actually do deep learning on small data sets now. So even the science strains underneath that in a way that's undermining it. So that's risky.

Elad: I'd love to talk a little bit about getting the next product in the product cycle. How do you start iterating and how do you come up with your v2 or your new product area? And how do you think about percent investment in core adjacent versus completely new areas? Google had a 70-20-10 framework. Do you think frameworks like that work?

Marc: I don't really like the numeric version of the answer because it's kind of what big, dumb companies do. They say, well, we invest R&D as a percentage. But anybody who's actually worked in R&D knows it's not really a question of money. It's not really a question of percentage of spend. It's who's doing it.

What I've always found is this: give me a great product picker and a great architect, and I'll give you a great product. But if I don't have a great product manager, a great product originator—it used to be called a product picker—and I don't have a great architect, I'm not going to get a great product.

Elad: Google's framework, by the way, was percentage of people. So it was 70% of human resources versus financial. But fair enough.

Marc: But it's kind of the same thing. I mean, it's a fine concept, but it begs the question: Who are the people?

I would take more of a micro-view of it. Which is: Okay, how many great product pickers do you have, people who can actually conceptualize new products? And then how many great architects do you have, who can actually build it? Sometimes, by the way, those are the same person. Sometimes it's a solo act. And sometimes that's the founder.

As you scale, you need more of those people. But I always think it's a matter of, okay, how many of those people do you have or can you go get? Or, back to acquisition, how many of those can you acquire? And then basically that's the number of products you can be working on. You organize R&D around that, in my view. You want to have a relatively flat R&D structure. You basically want to have autonomous teams, where each team is guaranteed to have a great product person and a great architect. And that's the model.

This is why I always ask people, okay, let's just do an inventory of how many of those people you think you have. And even at really, really big companies, it's not a large number. Even at giant companies there might be ten or twenty of each, maybe. And then you build the rest of the engineering organization around those people, including all the rest of the stuff that you do for recruiting and onboarding and all that other stuff. But at the core of it, who do you actually have who can conceptualize new products, and who do you actually have who can build it?

If it's the founder, fair enough. But you need to construct the organization so that the founder has the time to continue to do that. So that gets to all the questions around when you need an outside CEO or when you need a COO. And then, even the founders who can do that themselves eventually run out of time. And the challenges get bigger. So how do they attract and retain people who can pick up some of that work for them?

Elad: If it does get distributed, do you have any perspective on whether it should be a general management, verticalized structure versus a matrixed one?

Marc: I generally think matrixed is death, so I'm always pushing companies to go to a flat structure of independent teams. I'm really on the Jeff Bezos program on that, the two-pizza team thing.[2] I think hierarchies kill innovation for the most part. And I think that matrixes are just lethal in most cases. There are exceptions, but in most cases, you need original thinking and speed of execution, and it's really hard to get that in anything other than a small-team format, in my view. ■

This interview has been edited and condensed for clarity.

---

[2] Jeff Bezos favors product innovation teams with five to seven people—no more than can be fed with two pizzas. See eladgil.com. [*https://www.fastcompany.com/50661/inside-mind-jeff-bezos*]

CHAPTER 1

The role
of the CEO

CHAPTER 1

The role of the CEO

THE ROLE OF THE CEO: MANAGING YOURSELF

In most business books, the role of the CEO boils down to a small number of key responsibilities. The CEO:

- Sets the overall direction and strategy of the company and communicates this direction regularly to employees, customers, investors, etc.
- Hires, trains, and allocates company employees against this overall direction while maintaining company culture.
- Raises and/or allocates capital against this overall direction.
- Acts as chief psychologist of the company. Founders are often surprised by the extent to which people and organizational issues start to dominate their time.

Many books emphasize the first two points—corporate strategy and culture setting. However, you will find that in practice you have little time in a high-growth, rapidly scaling company to think deeply about those points until you hire a strong executive team and manage your own time properly.

Instead of covering strategy-setting and big picture stuff, I want to instead cover three key tactical duties of a CEO that often go under-discussed: how to manage yourself, your reports, and your board of directors.

First and foremost: managing yourself. Because if you fail at that, you're headed for burnout—and both you and your company will suffer.

PERSONAL TIME MANAGEMENT

As your company scales, the CEO role will need to scale with it. The demands on your time will grow nonlinearly, and more and more people will ask for your time, including members of your team, your customers (especially if you run an enterprise company), and various external stakeholders such as investors, the press, other entrepreneurs, etc. As CEO, you will need to find a way to get leverage on your time—and learn to say no a lot.

Key components of personal time management include:

- Delegation.
- Auditing your calendar regularly.
- Saying no more often.
- Realizing your old way of operating will no longer work.
- Finding time for the things you care about in life.

DELEGATE

There are a few good ways for first-time managers to learn to delegate:

1. **Hire an experienced manager to run a team and watch how she does it.** You will notice she probably tends to hold regular 1:1s (to stay in sync with her team) while also trying to give the most rope to the team members who run most independently. The very best executives tend to be a combination of a router (i.e., they send items on to other people for execution and end meetings with few to no action items for themselves), a strategist, and a problem solver (i.e., someone who can identify when the team is off track and dive in to help).

2. **Trial and error.** Try delegating and try again until it works. This will be part of any approach you take. You need to build some pattern recognition for when someone is starting to flail (they seem overworked and rumpled, they're late to every meeting, etc.) or when people have more slack in their time. You will learn to iterate on the size of responsibilities, teams, or projects you give someone and build confidence in their skills as they continue to add to their stack.

3. **Get a formal or informal mentor.** Ask a board member, angel, fellow entrepreneur, or executive you trust to mentor you on management and delegation. Alternatively, assemble a set of CEOs whose companies are at the same stage as yours, and meet them regularly for dinner so you can compare notes—you can learn a lot from your peers.

4. **Get an executive coach.** Most of these are bad (since any random person can dub himself an executive coach without any basis for it). But some are quite good and can help you think through how to increase your effectiveness, including proper delegation.[3]

---

[3] One way to find a good executive coach is to ask other entrepreneurs who they have used. Alternatively, you can find a semi-retired executive, one who has successfully driven large teams, to mentor and coach you.

However you choose to learn this skill, you'll also need to watch out for key signs that you are not delegating the way the CEO of a high-growth company needs to:

- You tend to leave meetings with many action items for yourself.
- Someone now "owns" an area you used to run, but after 4-8 weeks you find you are still doing most of the work or weighing in on every decision, however small.
- You feel the need to jump in on every email thread or attend every meeting across the company.

You can also over-delegate and abdicate all responsibility for, or involvement in, areas that are crucial to the success of the company. I have seen at least one CEO go into hard-core avoidance mode or get distracted by the external spotlight. This approach can cause many problems for the company, but it is less common, so I do not address it in depth here.

The biggest reasons CEOs don't delegate:

- They don't know how.
- They don't have lieutenants they can trust or who have the right skill sets to operate at scale. See the section in this book on hiring executives to address this issue.
- They are stuck in a work mode that made sense for a smaller company but doesn't for their fast-growing organizations.

The latter can be addressed in part by auditing your calendar and asking yourself, "Do I really need to do this? Or can someone on my team do it instead?" When in doubt, force yourself to delegate. You can even set a weekly goal for the number or percentage of meetings you stop attending or items you start delegating.

AUDIT YOUR CALENDAR WEEKLY, THEN MONTHLY

I encourage you to go through your calendar once a week and add up where all your time is going. (Once you become proficient at this kind of auditing, bumping that down to once a month or once a quarter should be sufficient.) If your involvement is not uniquely crucial to the success of a task, or an item is not core to your personal life, you should figure out how to off-load it. In most cases, that will boil down to simply learning how to say no, which we'll talk about next.

Often when I help high-growth CEOs audit their calendars, we find a few common types of meetings they should skip 90% of the time:

- **First-round interviews.** You don't need to be part of every first-round interview for every candidate. You can still talk to people in later rounds or as a final sell. Executive hiring is different and as CEO you may need to actively reach out to candidates. More on executive hiring in a later chapter.

- **Sales or partnership meetings.** Who can go on your behalf? I am not advocating you skip all such meetings, but some you can probably skip. Note: Silicon Valley product- or engineering-centric founders can often have the opposite problem of not talking to their customers enough. If you are a technical founder selling to enterprises, you will need to make the time to meet with customers regularly.

- **Every internal engineering, product, and sales meeting.** When do you really need to be there? Who can you delegate to? You can also move from a lot of point meetings (attending every engineering or product sub-team meeting) to a simple process that brings everyone to you for important decisions ("Weekly product synch with the CEO").

- **Random external meetings.** See "Learn to say no" below.

If you identify areas that consistently consume your time, but should no longer require the CEO, you can either delegate to someone on your team or hire someone to take them on. Hiring is often easier said than done if you are swamped, but you must force yourself to carve out the time.

If done right, after 4–8 weeks of self-auditing you will start to open up time to focus on strategy and the other key components of your company. You need to be focused on the most important things—not on everything. You also need the ability to take a step back and look at the big picture. If you spend all your time on the tactical brass tacks, you will steer the company in the wrong direction (or people will self-direct in the wrong direction).

LEARN TO SAY NO

One of the most important things you will do as CEO is learn to say no to those things that are not the best use of your time. Just as at some point you stopped taking out the trash and ordering food for your startup, there are other items you should stop doing or push back on.[4] For example:

- **Items for your calendar audit.** As mentioned above, you can skip things like first round interviews and many of the internal meetings you used to attend. Note that I am not advocating that you abdicate all involvement or responsibility. However, debating the nuances of database schema may or may not be the right thing for you to be involved with (unless your company sells a database product).

- **6am customer or partner meetings.** If your East Coast contacts will meet with you at 9am ET, they will also meet with you at noon ET. Don't take every meeting at any time—that will just exhaust you and not really help progress. While doing whatever

---

[4] I still occasionally tidy up around the office and encourage others to do so. People should feel ownership of their own environment. But there comes a point when the CEO shouldn't be doing this all the time.

- it takes for your customers continues to be crucial, you need to create limits so you don't burn yourself out. I have seen a number of CEOs continue to act like they are in scrappy startup mode years after product/market fit—often resulting in burn out.

- **Every press opportunity.** Do you really need to talk to Dog Life Monthly Webzine for their "SaaS entrepreneurship" issue?

- **Every event.** Choose the one or two highest-impact events to attend or speak at in a given quarter. You do not need to be everywhere. Be selective about the events you attend to free up time for other items.

- **Excessive networking.** Networking is a crucial part of being an entrepreneur, but take a look at your calendar: If large blocks of time are taken up each week with meeting other entrepreneurs or investors, you are probably not being focused enough with your time. Put networking into consolidated blocks so the switching cost is low, and focus your outreach on things that are actually meaningful to your company or to you personally.

- **Unnecessary fundraising.** Fundraising is a necessary side effect of having a company that needs capital to scale, but it's also hugely distracting. Some people seem to fundraise for no reason other than they think they should. Or because "a VC approached us, so we figured we may as well talk." Only fundraise when you are ready to do so and it supports a set of objectives for your company.

A big part of the transition from "hungry, no product/market fit CEO" to "high-growth CEO" is realizing that the amount of downtime you have will continue to collapse. You will need to say no to things that you would have readily accepted before.[5]

REALIZE YOUR OLD PATTERNS OF WORK CAN NO LONGER APPLY

When you go from a small startup to a larger one, one of the unexpected transitions is that the sorts of tasks that you can uniquely do to make your company successful change. While you may be an excellent programmer, if your team now has 50 or 500 engineers, it is unlikely that writing code is the best thing you can contribute as CEO. Similarly, your old patterns of personal and professional time management will break down as more people either need, or simply want, your time and attention. It may be painful, but to scale your organization and move ahead as CEO you will likely need to let go of certain parts of your prior roles that you enjoyed or thought were important.

---

[5] Read the original post on entrepreneurial seductions and distractions at eladgil.com. [*http://blog.eladgil.com/2013/05/entrepreneurial-seductions-and.html*]

"A common trigger of founder burnout is finding yourself working on things that you hate."

—Elad Gil

TAKE VACATIONS AND TIME OFF

One of the mistakes I made in my first two-and-a-half years as CEO of Color Genomics was that my vacations often were not real vacations. On my first anniversary trip with my wife, I spent half a day on the phone with a potential major partner. (Incidentally, the partnership did not work out.) On subsequent trips and vacations, I was constantly online, on the phone, and effectively trying to work full time while supposedly out of the office. This was also true for weekends—I was working every day of every one. This path can only lead to burnout, and I now try to truly unplug when away.

A CEO's energy levels dictate those of the team. You should find time to take vacations and truly be offline—otherwise you will lose energy, burn out, and potentially give up. This means once a year you should take a real one- to two-week vacation, and every quarter you should take a three-day weekend. If you are working every day, I strongly suggest that you start enforcing a personal no-work day at least once a week. Burning out will not help you or your company deal with all the stresses of scaling.

In ways big and small, you need to remember to take time for yourself. If you have a significant other, make sure at least one night a week is held for date night—and really do something together that night. Similarly, schedule exercise in the morning at least three times a week. One way to enforce this is to hire a personal trainer or schedule workouts or runs with a friend. That peer pressure will ensure that you actually make it happen.

WORK ON THINGS YOU CARE ABOUT

A common trigger of founder burnout is finding yourself working on things that you hate. Some product-centric founders end up having to spend endless hours on managing people, sitting in meetings discussing sales compensation plans, sales pipelines, marketing plans, HR issues, and other items that bore them to tears. Mark Zuckerberg famously delegated big swaths of Facebook to Sheryl Sandberg in order to free up more time to focus on product and strategy.

If you end up working long hours on things you fundamentally couldn't care less about, you should consider hiring one or more executives (or a COO) to do all those things on behalf of the company. As a founder and CEO, you do not need to be excellent at everything or enjoy everything. Rather, you need to build the competency within the company so that the company collectively is excellent at these other functions.

When you take care of yourself, you'll be much better equipped to tackle the next key leadership tasks of a CEO: managing your reports (next section) and managing your board of directors.

THE ROLE OF THE CEO: MANAGING YOUR REPORTS

There are a few key elements to managing your team of reports. A lot has been written about this topic already, so rather than write something for the sake of writing, here are some relevant links and brief suggestions.

1. **You should hold regular 1:1s with your team.** Ben Horowitz has great advice on how to hold 1:1 meetings in a pair of posts.[6]

2. **Once you are at about 30 people, you should hold a weekly staff meeting.**
   - Schedule a regular weekly time.
   - Review key metrics.
   - Be ready with a set of key topics for discussion on broader company or product strategy or key issues a functional area faces. Different members of the staff can present on a specific key topics or issue each week. Note: this is not meant to be an opportunity for team members to give an in-depth update once a week—it is a forum for discussion of metrics and strategy.
   - Remember the purpose of the meeting may be more for your reports then for you. While you have context on what every executive is doing, the other executives will not otherwise have clarity into their peers' organizations. The weekly staff meetings are meant to create a forum for knowledge sharing and issue raising, relationship building, collaboration, and strategy.

---

6 See links on eladgil.com. [*https://a16z.com/2012/08/18/a-good-place-to-work/ and https://a16z.com/2012/08/30/one-on-one/*]

3. You should start to add skip-level meetings as one way to stay in touch with the broader organization. As companies scale, the CEO often starts to lose touch with what is happening in the company. Information starts to get filtered by middle managers or hires from big companies, who view their job in part as shielding the CEO from "unimportant" information. The problem is that they may wind up shielding you from ideas that you consider quite important to know.

In a skip-level meeting, you meet with employees who work for your reports or are further down in the organizational chart. Often extremely bright junior people may have their fingers on the pulse of the market, or may be alert to key new ideas or information. You'll benefit from hearing from them, and these promising people will also benefit from learning how you think about your company, product, market, and culture.

Skip-level meetings help you:
- Create open lines of communication.
- Identify and nurture new talent.
- Get new ideas from people at the front lines of the company.

One key is to hold skip-level meetings without your reports feeling threatened. If a person's manager shows up to what is explicitly a skip-level meeting, there is likely something wrong with that manager or their management style. It is also up to you to clearly articulate to your report that you hold skip-level meetings with numerous people at the company so that they do not feel threatened or concerned.

DECISION-MAKING AND MANAGING EXECUTIVES

An interview with Claire Hughes Johnson

Claire Hughes Johnson is the Chief Operating Officer of Stripe and a board member at Hallmark Cards. Previously, she was a Director of Online Sales and Operations and Vice President of Google Offers and Google X, where she led operations for that company's self-driving-car initiative. Johnson holds a bachelor's degree in English literature from Brown University and master's degree in strategy and marketing from Yale School of Management.

When Claire Hughes Johnson joined Stripe as COO in 2014, the company had 165 employees. Now that number has grown to over 1,000. Along the way, the technology startup has entered into partnerships with giants like Amazon and launched next-generation products like Atlas, which guides internet companies through incorporation.

In our interview, we talk about how to manage your reports, how the org chart should be structured, and how to build functional processes that will help your company scale. We also address strategic planning and how founders should be allocating their time as the company grows.

Elad Gil:
Urs Holzle, who was an early SVP at Google, literally wrote, "A Guide To Urs" about the interaction approaches that work best for him. So if you needed to interact with him or you wanted things from him, you knew what to do. And apparently that really helped streamline how people worked with him. Do you think every founder or exec should write such a guide, or is that only for specific instances?

Claire Hughes Johnson:
I think it's a best practice. When I came into Stripe, I had a similar document. I wrote a document back when I was at Google called, "Working with Claire." And when I first got to Stripe, I adapted it slightly, but it was pretty relevant. I shared it with everyone who was working with me closely, but I made it an open document. It spread quite quickly through the organization. It made sense, because I was new, I was in a leadership role, people wanted to understand me. And then people started asking, "Well, why don't we have more of these?"

It's been a little bit of a viral, organic adoption, and now a lot of people at Stripe have written their own guides to themselves. I've even had folks who are not managers but are on my team write me these guides to them. And it's been super insightful. So I'm a huge fan.

I think that founders should write a guide to working with them. It would be one of the pieces I'm describing, to clarify the founder's role: "What do I want to be involved in? When do I want to hear from you? What are my preferred communication modes? What makes me impatient? Don't surprise me with X." That's super powerful. Because the problem is, people learn it in the moment, and by then it's too late.

Elad: Another thing that I've seen a lot of companies do as they scale is implement more day-to-day processes. Because there's a huge difference between running a 100-person company and a 1,000-person company, particularly if you have a large product and engineering org. Are there two or three things like that that you view as the most crucial processes as a company starts to grow, and that help free up executive time?

Claire: Yes. I would say that it's a combination of what I would call "operating structures," which are things like documenting your operating principles and processes. Operating structures are not tied to any one particular process, but instead explain, "This is what we expect of ourselves, in terms of how we work." And when you document things like that, new leaders, new managers, new people in the organization can say, "Ah, this is what's important. Let me adapt my behavior as we scale to follow along in this structure."

"I think that founders should write a guide to working with them."

— Claire Hughes Johnson

And then you have things like launch processes or what-have-you. One thing I've observed is that you can't make too many things at a company mandatory. You really have to be judicious about the things that you're going to require, because there just can't be that many. There's probably something related to performance and feedback. There's probably something related to whatever your planning process is. And then there's a few day-to-day tactical things, like a launch review. But you can't have that many and you can only have one at each level.

As you scale, you realize, "Huh, I really need more of these." And the danger is getting too process-y instead of outlining the objectives so people understand, "Okay, we're doing this for this reason." It's almost like you want to provide more context versus trying to exert more control. Because maybe in a very autocratic, hierarchical, bureaucratic structure you can exert control and you can micromanage. But most successful, high-growth, fast-moving companies are instead an environment of smart people who are all trying to optimize and do the right thing. They need some structural boundaries, but you can't over-constrain them. And that's why you want to have some high-level metrics that everyone's steering toward, operating principles, a documentation of plans, and then a set of processes that you follow.

So for us, yes, if your launch is not on the product launch calendar, that means it's not going to happen. You better get it on the calendar. And in order to get it on the calendar, you have to follow some steps. But you can only have a few of those.

As your company grows, how you communicate information has to evolve, too. Don't forget as you build these structures and establish a few processes that you need to have new communication approaches. Because not everyone is in the room anymore. What does everyone have to read? Where is all the documentation? Where is the source of truth? How do you use your all-hands meetings? How do you use emails from the leadership team? You have to think about all of that.

Elad: Yeah, that actually happened really early on at Color. We started asking that everybody send out meeting notes as part of every meeting, so there was transparency in terms of who attended, what was discussed, etc. And one early person pushed back. It was an example where literally a week into it he was saying, "Oh my god, you were right. We should have been doing this all along." There was a lot of resistance and a perception that it was micromanagement or it was us trying to track everybody in a nefarious way. But it was really just trying to open up communication.

Claire: Right, and just saying, "This is about context and communication, not about control" is so important. You literally have to state the obvious and make sure people know that.

Elad: How do you think the org structure maps to decision-making?

Claire: That's a great question. For starters, I think that there's no such thing as an optimal org structure. If you're searching for one, yeah, good luck. There are certain sets of things that can be very functionally related to certain org leaders, so you can use org structure as a decision-making proxy to a point. But you really have to be careful that people don't make false assumptions about who is responsible for a given decision.

At Stripe, for example, we make a lot of decisions jointly as a group. You're just not going to find one person you can go to, which I think can be frustrating internally. But in fact, if you believe in the wisdom of crowds or the fact that a smart group of people is going to make a better decision than one person alone, it's a good thing. But that means you have to set expectations within the organization that they're going to have to take the time to make sure that smart group of people is informed.

My answer would be that you can map decision-making to org structure to a point. Then it goes back to being explicit about how certain types of decisions are going to be made. "Hey, if we're making a major pricing change, everyone on the leadership team needs to agree." Be transparent to the org about whose role and responsibility it is to make those calls.

Otherwise, it just starts defaulting to the founder, which is not healthy for scale. I do know some executive teams who write up "roles and responsibilities" docs that they share internally. One part of those documents could be clarifying the things for which each person is the primary decision-maker. And if they're not the primary decision-maker, where do you go? That helps organizations know how to adapt as things scale.

Elad: What decisions do you think should not be made by a group? There are a variety of different models; some orgs are very consensus driven, and some are almost dictatorial depending on who's in charge. Are there specific things that you think should always just be owned by an individual? Or do you think it really depends on the context? What should the CEO not delegate, in other words?

Claire: I would say that there's a difference between a CEO or founder facilitating a group discussion to get opinions from people and making a group decision. And they might need to say, "Okay, ultimately, I'm the one who's going to make this decision."

Sometimes that gets confused, though, because the group thinks they're the decision-maker and that the goal is consensus. When really the goal is, "Let's hash it out together. We may not all agree. One person will be the decision-maker, and then we will all commit to it." If you don't clarify what kind of decision this is, then groups really struggle because their expectations are not set correctly.

When I'm leading through a tough decision, I try to say, at the outset, "I want all of your opinions, but I'm going to be the one who ultimately makes the decision." Or in some cases, I will say, "I don't know if I'm the right decision-maker. I need help exploring what the decision vectors are, and I need all of your help. And then I will let you know how we're going to make the decision once we've talked about it." If you don't give people that guidance, which is I think a common mistake, you're likely to run into trouble.

Ultimately, there will always be decisions that the CEO and the founder have to own, with a lot of input from the process and the system. Hiring a significant new leader for the company, for example.

One thing I've been talking a lot about with our engineering team is that usually your company's plans and incentives and metrics structures aren't built to stop things, or to stop and redo things. So if there is a need to pay down some technical debt or make a really hard call on stopping a project, you need a leadership voice, or even a CEO, to say, "Hey, we're just not doing this anymore." Because the org is always oriented toward making it work. I think decisions to stop or to retrench or to rebuild usually have to come from a leader if not a leadership team.

Elad: That makes a lot of sense. The one other failure mode that I've seen, which is in some sense maybe unexpected, is when a founder or CEO hires a more experienced senior exec—a COO or a CFO, for example—and they're so impressed by that individual's expertise that they effectively abdicate. They step back from the things that they're really good at or the decisions that they're actually uniquely geared for.

"As your company grows, how you communicate information has to evolve, too."

— Claire Hughes Johnson

Claire: And that's not a great signal to the org, because they think, "Wait, do they not care about some of these things anymore?" I think you're absolutely right. That balancing is really important and it goes back to the beginning of this conversation, which was about having a clear understanding of who's doing what and how you're going to work together.

Elad: Do you have any thoughts or advice for founders who are navigating growing orgs and new demands for strategic planning?

Claire: It's easy to say these things and it's hard to take the time to do them. I would just recommend that people make the time to do these things, because it's really valuable time. As a leadership team at Stripe, we spend a lot of time just with ourselves, talking about what we need to do and getting aligned.

And one last thing: Don't get too comfortable. Because if you are succeeding in scaling, you're not going to be able to use everything you came up with for the next phase. Getting your organization used to the fact that it's an iterative process and that you're a learning organism and actually celebrating that is much better than resisting. You can almost start viewing yourself as a failure if you have to change these things, and that's not true. It means you're succeeding and you need a new thing. Sometimes companies are afraid to reinvent for their next stage, and I really hope people know that it's a very reasonable thing to do.

Elad: It's interesting because on the employee side of that, getting re-orged every three to six months because the company is growing so quickly can feel very chaotic and uncertain.

Claire: That's exactly right. So how do you manage expectations and actually celebrate some of what is chaotic about what you're going through? That's my advice: figure out a way to get ahead of that and get people ready for inevitable changes so that you don't have fears or concerns that are unfounded.

Elad: There's a lot of confusion around how to approach strategic planning and decision-making as startups scale. What are the different levels at which companies should be planning? How do these different levels come together, and how frequently should a company do them?

Claire: I think this is definitely an area that needs to evolve as companies evolve and as they scale. If you're pre-product/market fit, you probably need a different cadence, one that's a little bit more agile as you're finding traction. It might focus more on the short term: "Okay, here are some milestones we need to get through in order to start testing and proving that we can have product/market fit."

Whereas once you have traction with some core product, you should fairly quickly be able to get to key targets or metrics that matter as indicators of progress. You should be able to say, "Here are our short-, medium-, and long-term goals to really build this out." Because usually once you initially get traction you still have a lot of work to do to take advantage of it and to expand on it.

There is a balance between focusing too much on either the short term or the long term. The key to me is having two documents. The first—at Stripe, we're calling them charters—articulates the long-term view of why this team or this product or this company exists, what its overarching strategy is, and what success would look like over even a three-to-five-year period. And then the second is a shorter-term plan: "Okay, in the near term, then, what are we trying to get done?" That can look like a results-based management model or an OKR—objectives and key results—model. But it's some way that a team can say, "This is where we're going long term. And on a quarterly basis, this is where we're focusing. We're hoping to move X and Y metrics."

If you're working on an early-stage product, even within a company that has a more mature product, that shorter-term plan looks different. You probably don't know what X and Y metrics are yet. You're still in the milestone mode. Any planning process needs to accommodate product life cycle, if you will. You want to establish buckets that the company understands to capture each of the product stages you have.

At every stage, though, you want to find a balance between that long-term charter ("Why do we exist?") and the short-term plan ("What are we going to do?").

Elad: How do you think about iterating on each of those? For example, should the long-term charter be refreshed annually? Semi-annually? What's the cadence for that document versus the cadence for your goal-setting or OKR document?

Claire: I think a charter needs a re-look roughly annually. And the goal-setting and OKRs is probably more like quarterly or bi-annually, depending on what kind of product you have. One thing that we do annually now—in addition to the charters—is set company metric targets for the coming year. We're adjusting the plans against those targets every quarter too.

Elad: How far ahead do you think your charter or strategic plan should go?

Claire: One thing that I have really thought about is the set of what I'm going to call "founding documents" that are really important for any company to have, especially as you get beyond, say, 50 or 100 people. That includes your mission statement and your vision, but also your overarching long-term goals. When we wrote that document for Stripe, I thought of as it the three-to-five-year plan. But we just called it long-term goals publicly in the company. And if you read those goals again today—and I worked on them, the leadership team worked on them, three years ago—they're still the same. And I don't think they're actually going to change even in three to five years. They're our long-term goals.

Then the other thing you have is your operating principles or your values or whatever vocabulary you choose. You need to codify a set of principles and behaviors and then cohere to them, culturally. And those founding documents shouldn't change very often. We refresh those operating principles every year, but they don't change that meaningfully. I don't think founding documents should change frequently.

When it comes to a given product or area of the business, then the longest you're probably going to project out is three years. Because things are changing so rapidly when you're at a growth stage that you can't really go much past that. We have a finance plan where we try to look three years out so we can test some of our assumptions. But we'd be pretty hard-pressed to make that meaningful in a five-year period.

Elad: Who do you think should own generation and implementation of charters and OKRs? When I was at Twitter, for example, I was asked to help implement OKRs across the company, and at the time the company was 500 people. So it needed Dick Costolo, who was CEO at the time, to pound the table for us. Because, at that scale, unless you have the leader of the company reminding everybody, things like that just aren't going to happen. It was so late in the evolution of the company.

At what scale people should adopt these different processes? And then who do you think should own them on an ongoing basis?

"You need to codify a set of principles and behaviors and then cohere to them, culturally."

— Claire Hughes Johnson

Claire: I think adopting some planning framework early will serve a company well. I was giving a talk recently at a startup, and they asked what operating processes I thought should be in place when. I told them that I'm not going to tell you which operating processes you should put in place. But I will tell you that you need them, and you need them sooner than you realize.

The analogy I drew was to games, or sports. I said, "You know why playing a game is fun? Because it has rules, and you have a way to win. Picture a bunch of people showing up at some athletic field with random equipment and no rules. People are going to get hurt. You don't know what you're playing for, you don't know how to win, you don't know how to score, and you don't know what the objectives are."

Everyone was nodding along—and this is a 40-person startup—but I could tell that they're struggling, because they don't really have any core goals. They're definitely in a product/market-fit, find-our-way mode, so I don't think they should have anything too heavy. But organizations need constraints and objectives to optimize against, so that people can actually independently make decisions.

When I first came to Stripe, we didn't have OKRs or even the charter or the planning process we have today. We had six company goals and that was it. And what we did in my first couple of quarters was just push the goals process down a little bit into teams. And that was pretty good for about 6–8 months. That helped us get people at least to know what different teams were up to. But earlier than you think, you need these structures, and you have to choose which ones make sense for you. Ultimately, our early approaches weren't totally right—either for Stripe as a business or maybe we grew out of them—but we were building the muscle of stopping to plan and think ahead, of creating objectives and measuring progress, and that is the main thing you need: the organizational capability from an early stage.

And then in terms of who should own it, really leaders need to own it. This needs to be something that waterfalls and has accountability all the way down through the company. And I do think the leadership team, including the CEO, has to be quite involved. I don't think they have to lead the process every time, but they have to be visible participants.

That's my view: you need planning structures earlier than you think, and they should proceed all the way from the top down.

Elad: One challenge is if you have one or two people on the executive team who haven't worked in large organizations before, sometimes you'll end up with resistance in the executive team itself to adopting these processes. Then six months after they've been adopted, they'll say, "These are great. I wish we'd always done these." But it's often quite painful early on.

On this topic more generally, where do you think founders should continue to be involved over time, and where do they often fail to delegate? I'm curious if you've seen common patterns across different companies. Are there things that people often need to let go? Or, alternatively, maybe things they shouldn't let go, but where processes would allow them to distribute decision-making so the important stuff bubbles up to them?

Claire: I'm a big self-awareness advocate, and I would say there are two things you've really got to spend a good amount of time on as a founder or CEO and a leadership team. The first one is, what are things that only the founder/CEO can do and which are existential to the company? What must they spend time on? One of those is often recruiting additional leaders. Others would be, in most companies, articulating the product vision and setting cultural standards.

Figure out what those are, and figure it out quite transparently with the rest of the leadership team. Then do a big self-awareness exercise across that leadership team, in terms of skills, capabilities, past experience, strengths. See if you can deploy the group against your needs and objectives, and be really ruthless about what the CEO and founder has to be involved in. Part of that will be them weighing in on what they want to be involved in versus what they have to be involved in. And ideally, you want that documented, their preferences on how they'd like to be involved and their role description in terms of where they have to be involved.

Instead, though, this stuff often goes way too organically and becomes opportunistic. "Oh, we hired this person. They have this background so we'll have them do this." You've really got to think through it as a group and you've got to connect it to the company's strategy and products. ■

This interview has been edited and condensed for clarity.

Working with Claire: an unauthorized guide

First of all, I'm really excited to be working with each of you and your teams.

Operating approach
- Bi-weekly or weekly 1:1s. We'll try to keep the times consistent so you can plan. I'm a big fan of a joint 1:1 doc to track our agendas, actions, goals, and updates.
- Weekly team meetings, as appropriate—I view these as both update and decision-making/work review forums. I expect people to be prepared and to participate, even though we'll have to manage video conferences and time zones.
- Quarterly planning sessions—it's my hope we make these happen with strong pre-work and good follow-up afterward with our teams and partners (internal or external).
- It's possible that we'll have some Stripe separate business review-type meetings and we can work hard to keep work manageable between these and planning sessions. Stay tuned.
- Speaking of 1:1s
  - We'll do a career session at some point in our first few months of working together—your history, why you've made choices you have made, what your ambitions are for the future, etc. These help me know where you are in terms of personal development interests and ambitions with respect to longer-term plans.
  - Personal goals—I believe in the two of us reviewing the top 3-5 personal goals you have each quarter or so (these are the things that you personally spend your time on, not your team plans, which I know you also spend time on…). We can discuss them each Q and then mark out a plan on how we make sure you get the time, space, and support to

accomplish what you need. I do these every 3–6 months and will share mine with everyone, also.

- Your teams
    - Please add me to emails (fwd as FYI or add me) or documents that might be helpful for me to see as a way to understand the team and day-to-day work.
    - As work is ongoing or a team member does a great job on something, forward it or link from our 1:1 doc. I like to see WIP and I am happy to meet with folks who have done great work so they can walk me through it—your discretion.
    - Finally, I look forward to personally meeting everyone on your team and let's keep an eye to make sure I've done that over the next few months.

MANAGER HANDBOOK

Management style
Collaborative
- I'm very collaborative which means I like to discuss decisions and options and whiteboard big stuff in a group. I will rarely get stuck in one position or opinion but the downside is that you won't always get a quick judgment out of me—I need to talk it through and see some ideas/data/options. Due to this bias, I can sometimes be slow to decide and if you need a decision quickly, make sure I know it.

Hands-off
- I'm not a micro-manager and I won't sweat your details *unless* I think things are off track and if I do, I'll tell you my concern and we can work together to make sure I understand and plan together on how to communicate better or right the situation. That said, when I am new to a project/team I often get into the work alongside people so I can be a better leader—I will get involved in details and be more hands-on early on in a new initiative and just be warned on that. It's how I will know how to help if you need me later.
- I expect you are making decisions a lot without me and if you come to me I'll usually put it back on you with, "What do you want to do?" or "What should you do?" and just help you decide. That said, if there is a big one brewing, I'd love to know about it and I'm always here to talk it out. I like to know what's going on with you and your team.

Accountable and organized
- I take action items really seriously and I expect you to know what yours are, when they are due, and get them done. I don't like chasing them but I do notice when things slip—it's fine to renegotiate deadlines but I'll be annoyed if it's the day after the deadline....

- I dislike being caught last-minute with people working hard on something we could have gotten ahead of—please help anticipate big work efforts and let's be in front of them together. Similarly, I want us to be ruthless in priorities while we are resource-constrained. I need you all sane…and me too.

Data-driven

- I like data and dashboards so there is one, objective (ideally) way to measure progress and results but I dislike being bogged down in data and torturing the numbers. Let's review consistent information on what really matters and use data to get insight, not to lull ourselves into thinking we know what's going on or to try to find answers that might involve going with our gut.
- I also like to make agreements on "how we do things" that we then agree to vary/make exceptions on as a group versus everyone inventing their own process/frameworks.
- If we're discussing something and you know of or can imagine data that would be useful to our decision, bring it up. (See below—sometimes I go into intuitive mode and I should be analyzing first.)

But intuitive?!

- I'm also intuitive about people, products, and decisions which means I'm happy to handle situations when I don't have a lot of facts or data. You're thinking uh-oh, she's going to jump to conclusions, but I've worked hard in my career not to be that person. Ultimately, I think I have a good gut but I'm not wedded to it. *Your* job is to get my sense of something and argue it out with me. I love a good fight to a better outcome.
- I use my intuition a lot with talent management and I've been told I am a good "read" on people. Again, I work hard not to judge or jump to conclusions but I will put forward hypotheses about your team members and your job is to make sure I really know the people.
- I always like to know what's going on personally with people so I can see the whole picture. I am a believer that we are "whole selves," not work selves and home selves and it will help me know you and your team better if I know context. If something hard is going on with someone on your team, I'd love to know and be there to support you/them.

Strategic

- I try to think about where things will end up and the straightest line to get there but I'm pretty flexible along the way. If there is swirl I usually think to myself: "What's the big lever here?" "What problem are we trying to solve?" "Why do we need to solve it?" "When do we need to solve it?" "What information do we need and when will we get it?" and I expect you to do the same. Every day I try to think about what's the most important thing I can do and do that above all else. But sometimes I get buried under email and fail!

By the way, I am often overly generous with my time and say yes too often to things. If you see this, please flag it to me. Although I love meeting with people, I sometimes don't spend enough time on the strategic stuff because I am working on other things. Help keep me honest.

User oriented
- I put this last because I think of my key leverage as more about scale than individual customer work, but I'm always interested in sales status, customer issues, customer stories, and meetings with users, especially when I'm traveling.

Communication
1:1S
- Use 1:1s for items better discussed verbally and items that can wait for our weekly check-in. Email takes a *ton* of time, so use it wisely.
- If we don't have a 1:1 for a while, feel free to email or ping, of course.

Email
- I read fast but I have slight carpal tunnel in my left arm and I don't love writing super long emails, nor do I think they're very productive, although watch me break this rule on occasion!
- I will read every email I get in a day but I don't respond just so you know I read it—I'll only respond if you ask me something directly or I have a question. Thus, assume I did read the email within 18 hours, but if you think I owe you a response please resend or ping me and I won't be offended.
- I *love* fyi emails when you send me something you saw, a customer anecdote, an article, some data, or something someone on your team did and if you write fyi in the subject or in the fwd I'll know it's for my information but *not* requiring response or urgent reading and I'll do the same for you. FYI = no response required.
- If you add me to a team email celebrating something that I somehow missed, I know that's the signal to weigh in usually with "yay!", so go ahead but don't overuse it or in my experience people will think it's meaningless.

Chat/ping
- If it's urgent/impt/timely or super short feel free to ping any time, even when I am "red."
- Short questions on ping are fine but I might be inconsistent in response times since I am often in meetings.
- If it's a long topic and not time sensitive, maybe just wait for our 1:1.

"I like a good laugh and to have fun with the people I work with."

—Claire Hughes Johnson

Overall, I like more communication rather than less and I like to know what's going on with you and your team and that helps me do a better job for you. I don't view that as micromanagement but if you feel like I am too much in the weeds, please tell me. Finally, I don't believe I will create a lot of email volume and I'll be the first to recommend we do a quick in-person sync to resolve something versus a long email exchange. Or better yet, you can be the first to recommend it, and I'll be the second.

I also like plans that are documented. I don't care if it's slides or docs or spreadsheets but I expect detailed work has been done when needed and if you have WIP or plans, I love to be included early and often in their development *but* I'll generally only weigh in when asked or on final review, even if I have draft access.

Feedback
I like it. I like to give it and I like to receive it, particularly constructive. We're in this to get better together. We'll have a quarterly official session but I'll try to be timely when I observe or hear something and please do the same. I also like to know how and what your team is thinking and feeling and I will do skip levels, office hours, etc. Remember, whatever I hear or see, I have your back and I'll tell you when I'm concerned. Anyone who vents to me about you is going to get my help to tell you directly.

Management and people
I care a lot about you, your people, and all of your development. Please make sure we're touching base on your team, building our teams' skills as individuals and as teams constantly, and that I know when there are superstars and challenges so we can help people together.

Results
Let's get good ones and know we did. Measure measure measure :)

Humor
Finally, I like a good laugh and to have fun with the people I work with.

Hope this was helpful and, again, I look forward to working together.

You are all welcome to add to this document and make it a little more "authorized!" :)

UNEQUAL COFOUNDERS

One of the big myths in Silicon Valley is that cofounders should be equal.[7] However, if you look at the most successful tech startups of the last 50 years, many of them had a dominant cofounder. This includes:[8]

Amazon. Jeff Bezos.

Apple. Steve Jobs famously split equity unequally with Wozniak.

Facebook. Although Zuck had multiple cofounders, the website used to be called "A Mark Zuckerberg production" and he had many times as much equity and power as his cofounders.[9]

Instagram. Kevin Systrom was the dominant founder.

Intel. Robert Noyce led the company for seven years and then Gordon Moore for 12 years.[10]

Intuit. Scott Cook was the dominant founder.

LinkedIn. Reid Hoffman had multiple cofounders but was really dominant in terms of equity and control (despite hiring a CEO to take over pre-Jeff Weiner).

Microsoft. Paul Allen stepped down after a few early years, leaving Bill Gates as dominant founder.

Netflix. Reed Hastings took over as CEO from Marc Randolph early in the life of Netflix.

THE CHANGING COFOUNDER DYNAMIC

If you have multiple cofounders, one of the biggest executive transitions that will happen is a change of influence and role for one or more of your cofounders. At many early startups multiple cofounders weigh in on every decision. As a company grows you will need to define the boundaries of decision-making and roles more tightly.

There are basically three end points for most cofounder dynamics:
- Some cofounders may move to individual contributor roles and are happy there (Steve Wozniak at Apple).
- A cofounder may remain as a key executive and help drive the success of the company as CTO, president, VP product, or another role
- One or more cofounders may leave if they feel they do not have enough influence at a company, if they want the CEO role and know they will not attain it in the short run, or if there is a mismatch between their skills and the role they want to play. Some may also leave due to family circumstances—a sick family member or needing to move for a spouse.

The change in cofounder status is driven either by *(i)* the need for there to be a single strategic direction and view point driving a company as it scales or *(ii)* the cofounder getting out of their depths or competencies relative to the scale of the company. As you grow employee headcount, people need to know who to go to for final decisions or the company will slow down and grind to a halt. You need to allocate resources to the areas of greatest need and value. In parallel, your cofounder may or may not have the skills and experience to play the role they want in the future of the company.

To manage the cofounder transitions:
1. **Think through what roles your cofounder would optimally play for the next 12–18 months of the company.** What functional role should the cofounder play (CTO versus VP Eng or an individual contributor on

---

7　See eladgil.com. [http://blog.eladgil.com/2012/02/how-to-choose-cofounder.html]

8　A number of private companies also do not have equal co-founding relationships or equity splits, but since these companies are not yet public it is harder to talk openly about them.

9　See link on eladgil.com. [https://www.buzzfeed.com/amygrindhouse/a-mark-zuckerberg-production-1qq?utm_term=.qfbBY8oxEV#.su1OnjRzW7]

10　An underreported phenomenon is the number of times one cofounder is replaced by another as CEO. This happened at Intel, Logitech, and other companies.

engineering)? What cultural role should they play (interview every candidate? Something else)? What are other ways you want them to be involved (public speaking or events that fit their knowledge or that you do not attend? Certain types of deals or partnerships?) And what input and decisions should they play a role in what are the key types of topics you should be discussing with them ongoing)? Remember that this will be an ever-evolving story as the company scales, so you do not need to think too far ahead—12 to 18 months may be enough.

2. **Ask your cofounder to think through what they want to do.** And have them write a job specification for themselves.

3. **Have a discussion.** You and your cofounder need to resolve differences between what the cofounder wants to do and what you as CEO think they should do. This will most likely be a series of conversations if there is a mismatch.

4. **Enlist an advisor, investor, or board member you both trust to do the right thing for the discussion.** If you and your cofounder are unable to resolve the role change together you many need to enlist a third party for mediation and help.

5. **Once you reach agreement.** What are the things you can do for your cofounder to help them succeed in this new role? Do they need a management coach?

Remember at all times that your cofounder took an early bet on the idea or company just like you did, and that they are a major equity holder (and potentially board member) of the company. While a lot of emotion is tied up into cofounder relationships (like any long term partnerships), it is critical to the success of your company that you find a solution.

If you and your cofounder are unable to reach agreement, you will likely need to negotiate the exit of that cofounder from the company. In some cases this may be contentious. Alternatively, your cofounder may be relieved that the company has reached a level of growth and success that allows her to leave without hurting momentum. If a cofounder is not playing the CEO role, she may eventually feel disempowered and want to go work on something where she is the final decision maker.

Oracle. Larry Ellison was the sole founder.

Pinterest. Ben Silberman has driven the success of the company.

Salesforce. Marc Benioff.

Square. Jack Dorsey is primary cofounder.

Uber. Travis Kalanick was the primary force until recently.

WhatsApp. Jan Koum was the dominant founder and equity holder.

Most of these companies are examples where both power and equity splits between founders were unequal. In general, equal power sharing yields worse outcomes than having a dominant cofounder (or at least one who emerges as dominant once a company starts working). Founding a company is hard, and having a cofounder helps balance the work and stress of a startup. The key is to have clear decision making so that a single individual (the CEO) can set a clean path forward.

The set of counterexamples with more equal cofounding partnerships includes Google (cofounded by Larry Page and Sergey Brin, with a bit of a founder-like contribution by Eric Schmidt being hired as CEO early in its life). Having an equal cofounding relationship is not impossible, it's just rare among the most successful companies.

CHAPTER 2

Managing
the board

CHAPTER 2

Managing the board

"HIRING" YOUR BOARD OF DIRECTORS

If your cofounder is like your spouse, then your board members are like your mother-in-law and father-in-law. You are going to see them regularly, they are hard to get rid of, and they can have an enormous impact on your company's future.

The members of your board are among the most important people you will ever "hire" for the company. The best board members will play key roles in company strategy; sourcing, hiring, and closing senior executives and key hires; fundraising; operations; and governance. In mid-stage companies, they are often responsible for selecting/keeping/firing the CEO, and then holding that person accountable for deadlines, plans, and deliverables. Later in the life of a company, board members play more specialized roles through the various committees they may be part of. (I won't cover public boards here.)

Your board will typically be composed of a few key players: VCs who invested in your company, independent board members, and members of the founding team (aka "common seats," which usually include one or two founders, or rarely as many as three). If you have an external, non-founder CEO, he or she will also have a board seat (and in some cases an external non-founder COO will as well).

CHOOSING A VC PARTNER WHO IS RIGHT FOR YOUR BOARD

Most of your board members will be VCs who invested in your company. They may be brilliant strategists or operators, or alternatively just have a bunch of money that came bundled with a board role. I would always take a lower valuation in order to work with a board member or VC partner I really like, rather than a higher valuation and a lesser board member.[11]

Remember, when a venture capitalist invests in your company it is the fund investing, not the individual partner. This means that funds typically have the right to swap out the partner that sits on your company's board. While you may start off with a senior partner, you may someday find a junior, wet-behind-the-ears, brand-spankin'-new VC as your board member. This junior partner will probably start attending as a board observer[12] or just start showing up with the senior partner, who will say she wants to add "more bandwidth to your team from our firm." If you do well as a company, this will indeed be the case. However, if you do poorly, then the venture fund has someone less valuable they can swap in to save the senior partner's time. This junior partner will be less able to help you, and will effectively get trained by you and your other board members.

CHOOSING AN INDEPENDENT BOARD MEMBER

Your independent board members will typically be other operators or entrepreneurs with relevant functional experience (e.g., a former CFO) or industry experience. While some series A investors won't push for the independent seat to be filled for a while (or, in some cases, at all), others will push for a faster addition to the board. Please note: this will be one of the most important people you "hire"—and it will be hard to remove a director once you add one. Proceed carefully and deliberately through these critical steps:

1. Write a job spec. It bears repeating: this is one of the most important people you will hire. You should write up what you would optimally want in a board member by drafting a checklist or hiring spec. This should include:

- **Experience—which may include:**

  Operating experience. Do you want someone who has operated a company at a certain scale or has started a company herself? Can the prospective director share process or management best practices with you? What can you learn from him or her?

  Market experience. Is there specific domain or market expertise you care about at the board level? Is the prospective director in the information flow in ways that will give you a competitive advantage? Can she provide intros to people in the market who can help you?

  Functional experience. Do you want specific functional experience (e.g., an ex-CFO or VP International Sales)?

---

[11] See eladgil.com for a link to a story about Elon Musk and John Doerr. [*https://pando.com/2012/07/17/who-made-the-bigger-mistake-in-the-botched-series-c-for-tesla-elon-musk-or-john-doerr/*]

[12] See eladgil.com for a link to a useful Mark Suster post on board observers. [*https://bothsidesofthetable.com/rethinking-board-observers-the-role-of-the-silent-observer-eee4ccecac7d*]

Depending on your existing board and experiences as a founder, you may or may not care about market experience, functional experience, or operating experience. Or you may be willing to trade these off, as it will be hard to find the perfect person.

- **Involvement with other high-growth companies (optimally as a founder).** People who have not seen a company go from two people in a coffeehouse to a multi-thousand-person organization aren't used to all the bumps in the road that this entails. Things will always take longer and always be rougher than expected. Most startups face at least one moment, if not more, that feels like an existential crisis, where the company faces death from competition, excessive burn, government regulation, or other issues. And, unlike at a large established company, natural momentum won't necessarily exist. At an early-stage startup, each bit of execution is an act of sheer will, rather than an act of momentum. As your company matures, this will shift and eventually you may have too much momentum, with a large, difficult-to-steer ship of your own. This is of course many years down the line, and is in some sense a good problem to have. In the meantime, you need board members who understand this journey.

  Optimally, if there is just one independent board slot, the independent board member would be a current or former entrepreneur. Other successful entrepreneurs will be able to relate more closely to a founder's emotional state and provide advice based on their own experiences. They will understand the "newbie" nature of being a founder/CEO and be open to answering "stupid questions" without condescension or judgment. They will have firsthand knowledge of how to build a business and understand that the bumps along the way are inevitable.

  Finally, successful entrepreneurs can serve as a counterweight to the VC board members in a way that benefits the company, and hence also benefits the VC. If an entrepreneur board member is successful enough, the VC is unlikely to have much leverage over them—they already have lots of money, strong personal brands, and others who will work with them. The VC cannot exploit a power dynamic to force a truly independent board member to side with them on contentious board business.

- **Raw intelligence.** This is self-explanatory. Some folks, such as Marc Andreessen, Reid Hoffman, Mike Moritz, and Vinod Khosla, are known for their raw intellectual horsepower. Notably, the former two took board seats or made investments prior to becoming full-time VCs.

- **Business and strategic sensibility.** Ultimately a high-growth company board will face a number of core business and strategic questions. Will they help you navigate the strategic landscape, understand how to use M&A at scale as a tool, or have deep insights into product pricing or other aspects of running a business? Many founder CEOs also need input into team management and operations that a business-savvy independent may provide.

- **Entrepreneur-friendly orientation.** A number of VCs will suggest a "friend of the (venture) firm" as your independent board member. These people will often owe the VC more than they will ever owe your company, and when shit hits the fan they'll vote with the VC. In other words, the "independent" board seat will in reality be an investor board seat, and you will lose control of the company (see "Avoiding a VC crony" below). To avoid this, you ideally want an independent board member who is sympathetic to your aims as an entrepreneur, not just to the VCs' fiduciary duties.

  On the other hand, you do want to find someone the VC respects and will listen to. Optimally, the entire venture firm that backed you knows this potential independent board member. The best scenario is to find someone that your VC respects, but who you know is an entrepreneur at heart or who will at least be more entrepreneur-friendly. In the best case, you will have a preexisting, long-term relationship with this person, which will help you trust each other when the company inevitably hits a hard spot.

- **Respect of investors/VCs.** Part of the independent board member's role will be to remind VC board members that they should be voting in the company's best interest (rather than each investor's own best interest). He or she should have the confidence and insight to push back on the VCs when it makes sense to do so. The independent should help keep the VCs "honest." This does not mean the independent should rubber stamp the founder's every whim. Rather, he or she is there to do what is best for the company and to remind the VC members that their purpose should be the same.

  This is easiest to accomplish if both the VC and the founder respect the independent board member. Both of you should spend a lot of time with candidates for your board before adding them.

2. Agree on the spec with your investors. Once you have defined what you want, discuss it with your investors and get agreement on the spec. This helps you call bullshit on them (e.g., when they offer up a friend of the firm with no relevant background) and lets them call bullshit on you and keep you honest (e.g., when you suggest your best friend from high school).

3. Create the list of options. Make a prioritized list of people you would most like to add to the board. You can use an executive search firm which specializes in board members or ask your investors, advisors, or other entrepreneurs for suggestions. Your board members are optimally people that you wish you could hire for the company, that are truly out of reach otherwise.

4. Spend time getting to know the potential board members. You will get a lot of pressure from your investors to finalize the board, but don't be afraid to push back and make sure you take the time (many months) to find the right person. You would not rush to hire a crappy engineer "just to fill the spot." With a board member (who will be more of a pain to remove than a bad employee) this becomes even more important.

AVOIDING THE VC CRONY

Venture capitalists will often push cronies, or people who owe them, onto your board. Effectively they are trying to turn the "independent seat" into an additional seat that the VC controls. There are a few common ways to spot a VC crony:

• The VC has worked with her a lot in the past or sits on her board, or she is an executive the VC has placed in a company before.

• She has worked at multiple companies backed by the VC.

• She sits on a few boards with the same VCs.

• She does not have relevant experience, does not understand your product, or makes generic comments rather than insightful ones.

• She is likely to get placed in her next job by the VC (e.g., a VP of Sales who wants to become CEO).

You can decrease the likelihood of adding a VC Crony if you follow the steps on this post (and convince your VC to follow step 8 below).

Have some questions and topics ready to discuss with potential board members:

• Ask them to discuss key directions for the company. Do they align with the vision and approach you want to take? Do they have key insights or interesting feedback?
• Ask how they will help the company. Where will they pitch in? What are they good, or bad, at providing?
• Ask about their goals and aspirations. What do they want to do with their career or life? How does the role on your board impact this?
• Ask them to do something for you. Try to put them to work and see if they will help with something relevant to their experience. You could hire them as a consultant for a project in your area of expertise. Or, for a more lightweight test, ask them for an introduction to someone in their network, ask for their help and advice on structuring a deal, or have them spend some time advising you on a current strategic issue you're facing.

5. Check personal rapport and attitude. This is really important. You as the founder(s) should have great personal rapport with the independent board member. He or she should be someone you feel you can trust—who you would feel good about calling at midnight on a Friday—and someone you think will be able to help you grow the company and, ideally, grow personally. This board member should be someone who, if circumstances were different, you would be excited to start a company with.

When assessing a potential board member's attitude, there are a few things to avoid:

• **The condescending, gray-haired operating executive** who sees you as a "bunch of kids" and who views herself as part of the "adult supervision." This typically leads to unnecessary oratory by the board member or the founder getting fired as CEO and replaced by some visionless "operator."

• **The micro-manager** who confuses being on the board with being your boss.

• **People interested in the role for the potential financial reward** rather than the excitement of helping you build a business.

- **People who simply want to "join a board"** so they can increase their own personal stature or start to take more board seats themselves.

- **People who want to join your board so they can network** with, or get to know, your investor board members. (This can lead to disaster, as they will side with an investor over you to curry that investor's favor.)

- **The VC crony.** More on this in the sidebar. It is important and common enough to deserve its own section.

6. Check alignment of vision. Does the independent board member understand where you want to take the business? Is he or she aligned with that vision and direction? You want someone who will support that vision rather than second-guess it. Similarly, you want someone who will take a long-term view to building a great company (assuming that is your intent), rather than focus on a short-term flip.

Look at prospective board members' backgrounds: What has happened to the companies they have started or run? Did they sell early, and if so why? What other choices have they made in their careers, and how thoughtful are they in hindsight about those decisions?

7. Check references. What do people who have worked with your prospective board members think of them? Are they high integrity? What are they helpful at? If they are already on boards, what do the entrepreneurs they work with think of them?

8. Finalize who to add. Optimally you will take a "common nominates, preferred stock approves" approach to adding the independent board member. Just like with the Supreme Court—where the president nominates the justices and Congress approves the nominations—the balance of power lies with the nominator (thanks to Naval Ravikant for this analogy). Your VCs may have some great suggestions for board members (and you should definitely ask for their opinion). But ultimately you want to be driving the final "election," and to do that, your biggest point of leverage is in who you nominate.

Like any other member of your team, the independent board member may eventually lose their usefulness beyond a certain scale of company. A public company board tends to look and act differently from an early stage startup board. If you control the independent seat, you may want to change people out if their skills and insights lose relevance.[13]

---

[13] Many thanks to Josh Hannah, Naval Ravikant, Sam Altman, and David King for providing feedback on the original version of this material on choosing an independent board member. The original blog post is on eladgil.com. [*http://blog.eladgil.com/2011/12/how-to-choose-board-member.html*]

"Your board members are optimally people that you wish you could hire for the company, that are truly out of reach otherwise."

— Elad Gil

THE CHAIRMAN OF THE BOARD

Typically, the only real "legal" capability of a chair (depending on charter and state of incorporation) is the ability to call for a board meeting independently of the CEO (assuming the roles are split).

In early-stage startups, the title "chair" is pretty meaningless; most won't have a stand-alone chair.

In later-stage companies, the chair may play a board-coordination and influencer-leadership role, especially if the size of the board of directors has ballooned. For example, the chair may funnel feedback from the other board members back to the CEO in certain cases, or help with the agenda-setting and follow-up from board meetings. In these cases, you can think of the chair as the equivalent of the board's "tech lead"—i.e., someone who can set the tone and agenda of the board without direct management responsibility for it.

In most high-growth companies, the chair role is filled by the founder, who is also the CEO. If the CEO is not also the chair, this role is usually filled in one of two ways:

1. Often, the chair role is taken by a founder who is no longer active in the company's day-to-day operations but who has a large financial stake and/or in-depth knowledge that could be helpful to the company. For example, when Jack Dorsey stepped down from his first stint as CEO of Twitter, he assumed the chair mantle. Alternatively, if the board hires a professional CEO, an active founder may assume the chair role (and often is called "executive chair"—see below for more). For example, Jim Clark was Chair of Silicon Graphics when Ed McCracken replaced him as CEO.

If a founder is still CEO, it is very weird to have an additional operationally active, non-CEO founder as the chair. This usually suggests a power struggle between the two founders.

2. Sometimes a VC or early investor will take the chair role when he or she makes the investment. For example, Don Valentine (who started Sequoia Capital) was the chair of a number of companies he invested in, and Oren Zeev is the chair of Houzz, after being the first investor in that company's seed.

"Executive chair" is a title usually given to a chairman of the board who is actively engaged with the company on a day-to-day basis, but not fully operational (for example, an executive chair may not officially manage any functional areas or organizations). The executive chair will often be focused on one or more strategic areas for the company. When Eric Schmidt stepped down as CEO of Google, he took on the executive chair title and spent much of his time on government relations and overall corporate strategy for the company.

BOARD DIVERSITY

You want to fill your board with directors who share a common sense of purpose and who strongly support the mission and direction of the company. You want people who will stay calm and weather the inevitable storms, and who can provide operating advice, financial expertise, a deep network, or other skills. You want people who are high-performing and driven.

In parallel, building a team of directors with diverse backgrounds—in terms of ethnicity, gender, sexual orientation, and other factors—may help your company in many ways. That diversity can be a benefit when it comes to recruiting, providing role models or mentors for your team, and broadening the network and perspectives of the company.

Many technology company startup boards start without much diversity. Most venture capitalists are white and male. Since VCs often take the first external board seat at a company, most startup boards start off without much venture capitalist diversity. Similarly, many independent directors are the CEOs or top executives of large companies—many of which lack diversity in their highest ranks.

WAYS TO SOURCE DIVERSE BOARD CANDIDATES

There are several tactics—including a small number of emerging resources—that can help you find women, minority, or other board members:

"The makeup of your board should change as your company scales from a young organization seeking to develop a meaningful product to a more mature startup in high-growth mode."

—Elad Gil

1. **Get a diverse set of angel investors early on.** Build these relationships early in the life of the company, and by the time you need to add a board member you will already have numerous bridges to great independent board candidates. You will get to know their thinking firsthand and will be able to build relationships with them that allow you to convert them to board members later.

   For example, Color Genomics, which I cofounded, has over a dozen female investors. Color's first external board member was Susan Wagner, cofounder of BlackRock and a board member at Apple, BlackRock, and SwissRE. Sue started off working with Color as an angel investor, and we were lucky to eventually convince her to join our board after she got to know the company and its mission.

2. **Pitch diverse venture capitalists.** Pitch women and minority venture capitalists as part of each round of funding. This increases the likelihood you will have a more diverse board.

3. **Tell recruiters and investors what you are looking for.** If you hire a recruiting firm to help you with your board search, you can specify diversity as a criterion that is important to you. Similarly, your investors are often involved with the hunt for board members; ask them for help and introductions.

---

14 https://theboardlist.com/

4. **Check theBoardlist.** Sukhinder Singh Cassidy recently launched theBoardlist as a resource for suggesting and finding female board members.[14]

5. **Review "most powerful" lists.** There are numerous "top" and "most powerful" lists for women, African Americans, Latinos, and other groups. These can be segmented by geography or other factors. Go through these lists and find someone to introduce you to potential members.[15]

BOARD EVOLUTION OVER TIME

Setting up your board of directors is not a one-and-done endeavor. Your board's composition will no doubt change over time as members come and go—and at certain key junctures in your company's life cycle, you may need to nudge that evolution along.

The makeup of your board should change as your company scales from a young organization seeking to develop a meaningful product to a more mature startup in high-growth mode. At the early stages, certain board members may be valuable in your quest for product/market fit or your next round of funding. Later, though, you will need board members with operating experience, a network of potential later-stage executive hires, and broader strategic insights.

We'll talk more about how to ask private company board members to step down in the next section (TL;DR: It's hard to pull off). But whether you're building a board for the first time, or simply adding a new member, always come back to these "hiring" guidelines. Whatever your company's stage, bringing someone onto your board is a critical decision—one that can help the company, founders, and executives mature, or one that will cause frustrating headaches.

REMOVING MEMBERS FROM YOUR BOARD

Unfortunately, there are times when things just don't work out with a board member. This could range from board members being benign but useless (e.g., spouting generic advice that does not matter) to being actively destructive. I have heard of board members leaking information to the press, fomenting political factions among the staff under the CEO, derailing a company's financings, or pushing for strategic directions that make no sense. I have seen cofounders leave more than one company due to poor advice from board members, as well as board members who poach executives from one startup to join another of their portfolio companies.

While it is typically straightforward to remove a misbehaving employee, a poorly behaved board member may be harder to "divorce." In general, investor board members are harder to remove than independents.

---

[15] See eladgil.com for links. [*https://www.forbes.com/power-women/#750df0665e25 and http://savoynetwork.com/top100/*]

REMOVING VC BOARD MEMBERS

Once they join your board as part of a financing, investor board members are notoriously hard to get rid of, as they usually have contractual rights to the board seat written in their financing documents (i.e., your series A, or series B, C, etc., paperwork).[16] Removing a VC board member can generally only happen at a time of transition or leverage (a financing event, major change in company direction, IPO, etc). Additionally, the VC may have extra economics in the investment for taking the board seat, or view the seat as something that builds her stature in the broader world. So how do you get rid of a misbehaving board member? There are a few tactics you can try, depending on the stage of your company, the leverage you have as an entrepreneur, and your relationship to the VC and her firm.

1. Change the overall composition of the board to reflect the maturation of the company (and boot the VC off as part of this shift). The makeup of your board should change as the company scales from a young organization seeking to develop a meaningful product to a more mature startup in high-growth mode. At the early stages, board members may be valuable in your quest for product/market fit or your next round of funding. For example, board members may know of new distribution tactics or other strategies that are working in their portfolios, which they can share with you (e.g., "Facebook is suddenly working well for mobile app distribution"). However, if they lack operating experience, a network of potential later-stage executive hires, or broader strategic insights, it might make sense to replace them and other board members as your company starts to scale rapidly.

Once a company finds product/market fit and focuses on scaling, the skill set, network, and advice needed from a board member shifts as well. Similarly, as a company starts to plan to go public it will need to add more independent directors and more operators, as well as more specialized board members (e.g., a former CFO for the finance/audit committee).

When shifting into high-growth mode, you can ask multiple early board members to step off the board to help enable the transition to a successful later-stage or public company. This approach prevents any one request from being viewed as a personal criticism of any one board member—rather, you are changing the slate as the company matures. If an early board member can be especially helpful in your later stages, you can retain this board member or alternatively convert her to an independent seat.

While the request to step down as the company matures may be a logical one that should increase the value of the company overall, some may refuse—because they benefit from the stature of being on your board, for example, or want to protect their investment in your company until the company has a liquidity event. But if one or more of the other board members step down as part of an overall board reshuffle, it puts pressure on holdouts to comply as well.

---

[16] See eladgil.com. [*http://blog.eladgil.com/2011/03/how-funding-rounds-differ-seed-series.html*]

Alternatively, as a later-stage funding round occurs you can ask an early investor to step down so that you can create a seat for a later-stage investor. Many early-stage investors may refuse. However, you can point out that the investor coming in brings new and necessary skills, networks, or advice to the table. Remind existing members that there is a need to keep the board to a constrained size and also to start planning toward an IPO (assuming one is in sight in 18 months or less).

In general, simply asking an investor board member to step down is unlikely to work.

2. Buy them out. It takes 5–10 years for most companies to have a liquidity event. Many investors will be raising additional funds from their own limited partners (LPs) along the way, and they'll want to show a return to get the LPs to invest more in those future funds. This means you can offer VC board members an opportunity to sell a subset of their stake in your company in exchange for stepping off the board. This stock sale could happen either via a secondary event (see the chapter on late-stage financings) or as part of a later-stage primary funding round. If the investor does want to sell stock prior to a full liquidity event such as an IPO, you can make the following arguments for why a stock sale should be tied to her stepping off the board:

- If the VC is selling part of her stake, she is signaling about the upside of the company to the market and should step down.

- Board composition is reflective of ownership stake—i.e., the board is supposed to reflect share ownership. If the VC sells a subset of her position in the company, she will own less of it and therefore should no longer have a board seat.

- The company has now returned the VC's investment. The requirement for ongoing governance of her investment (which they have diversified out by selling) has decreased and she should step off the board.

3. Ask the VC firm to swap out your board member for another partner from their firm. This tends to work only if your company is working really well and the firm wants to maintain a positive relationship with you over time as the founder of a breakout company. Unless the VC partner you are trying to remove controls the whole firm, the firm may agree to swap out your board member for another one to maintain warm ties with you. (Thanks to Reid Hoffman for this insight.)

These conversations, by the way, can be very tough and very emotional. VC board members are humans too, and they may have a lot of ego or emotion wrapped up in a successful company. Even if they have done nothing to help the company beyond capital (and capital is indeed helpful), your VCs may still feel that they fundamentally contributed to the company's success. When making your case that they should step down, be firm, calm, and consistent.

"Once a company finds product/market fit and focuses on scaling, the skill set, network, and advice needed from a board member shifts as well."

— Elad Gil

REMOVING INDEPENDENT BOARD MEMBERS

Independent directors are generally easier to remove than investor board members. In some cases, you control the independent board seat and can simply ask the board member to step down (see below on "Independent board seat structures"). The simplest way is to explain why you want them to do so. Obviously, though, there are lots of reasons (ego, a difference of opinion, VC investor influence, etc.) that board members may not be willing to step down.

There are two types of independent board members: those whose primary relationship is to you, and those whose primary relationship (and sense of loyalty) is to the VC who invested in your company and helped bring them on board. The VC Crony probably owes a lot more to the VC than they do to you. Additionally, they will have a tendency to vote the way the VC wants or push for things the VC asks them to push for.

These VC Crony independents may be harder to remove, as your investor board members will have a disincentive to support their replacement on the board. In some cases you may need to negotiate with the VC directly for the removal of the independent. Alternatively, if you have a larger board with many members, they can help push for the removal of a non-performing independent.

INDEPENDENT BOARD SEAT STRUCTURES

There are a few ways an independent board seat may be modified (depending on your financing documents). The most common are:

- **A board vote.** Each board member can vote for or against the removal of a board member, and each vote is counted with the same weight.

- **Stock votes for the seat on an as-converted basis.** In this type of vote, each share of common and preferred stock counts as one vote. Everyone votes and you add it all up.

- **Mutual agreement by common shareholders voting as a class (i.e., the founders) and preferred shareholders voting as a class.** Each class of stock needs to agree to the change. In other words, a majority of common stock (usually just founder votes matter, since founders tend to control most common stock) AND a majority of preferred stock (e.g., investors) both need to agree to the change.

- **Common nominates, preferred approves.** VentureHacks has some of the best content out there on the board of directors and how to construct it.[17]

Depending on the structure above and your percent ownership as founders, you may or may not be able to remove an independent board member on your own. Sometimes you can just get one additional board member or a major holder of preferred shares to vote with you to change or remove a board member, but sometimes you need all the preferred board members to vote your way. If this is the case, removing a VC Crony may be impossible without trading something of value with the VC.

Once you have agreed to remove the board member, work with your lawyer to generate the proper legal documentation and board resolutions to make it all official.

---

[17] See eladgil.com. [*http://venturehacks.com/archives#board-of-directors*]

An interview with Reid Hoffman

Reid Hoffman cofounded LinkedIn, the world's largest professional networking service, in 2003. He led LinkedIn through its first four years and to profitability as Chief Executive Officer. Prior to LinkedIn, Reid served as Executive Vice President at PayPal, where he was also a founding board member.

Now a partner at Greylock Partners, Reid currently serves on the boards of Airbnb, Aurora, Coda, Convoy, Entrepreneur First, Gixo, Microsoft, Nauto, Xapo, and a few early stage companies still in stealth. In addition, he serves on a number of not-for-profit boards, including Kiva, Endeavor, CZI Biohub, and Do Something. Prior to joining Greylock, he angel-invested in many influential internet companies, including Facebook, Flickr, Last.fm, and Zynga.

Reid earned a master's degree in philosophy from Oxford University, where he was a Marshall Scholar, and a bachelor's degree with distinction in symbolic systems from Stanford University.

Reid Hoffman is one of the most respected and connected investors, entrepreneurs, and advisors in Silicon Valley. Lucky for us all, Reid has shared a small part of what he's learned, penning two bestselling books (*The Start-up of You* and *The Alliance*) and an ongoing series of essays on all things startup. Reid has more recently focused on "Blitzscaling" (i.e., the art of growing a company very rapidly), which is also the title of his forthecoming book on the subject of scaling companies. There is also a great series of videos on YouTube from the Stanford class he taught where you can watch lessons on this.

I jumped at the chance to hear his thoughts on boards of directors, CEO transitions, and other topics that founders and executives need to navigate amid the chaotic ups and downs of high-growth companies.

Elad Gil:
You've seen quite a few boards in action. What do you consider their primary function?

Reid Hoffman:

Fundamentally, a board is the in-depth control of what is being set for the future of the company. Now, some people say—and it's right in part—that the only responsibility of the board is to hire, fire, and compensate the CEO, because the CEO is what essentially expresses that forward strategy. The board cannot operate itself, so it's done by the selection of a CEO and agreement with the CEO and so forth. But there are still parameters. The CEO doesn't decide to say, "Oh, I'm just going to go and sell the company," or, "I'm going to go buy this other company," or, "I'm going to go deploy all my capital on X." They have to talk to the board about it.

Part of the reason that that conception of the board is incomplete is because a board is not just standing as judge and jury. It's actually people who are collaborating with you. It's also an extension of your team. The board is a team of people in dynamic collaboration with the CEO, who, in a startup company, is almost always a founder. If the two founders hired a CEO, that CEO is essentially a third founder. And actually, as you've read, my view of the key thing in hiring a CEO is to look at it as bringing on a later-stage co-founder.[18] That's actually the key thing that most people don't think about in a CEO hiring process that's really important to do.

When working with a board it comes down to saying, "Okay, what's the game we're playing?" Now, in all startups, the game we're playing is "default mortality." I use the metaphor that a startup is like throwing yourself off a cliff and assembling an airplane on the way down. In other words, the default is that you're dead. You have to gamble your assets very strongly in order to create something that has ongoing and persistent value. Everyone is aligned on that in the early stage. Everyone is like, "Yeah, that's what we're doing. We've all bought into the same game."

What gets complicated—and this is even before you get public—is when you have played that gamble and now have some assets. Maybe the asset is a team, maybe the asset is a market position, maybe the asset is a cash-flow business. Once you have assets, then the game is different. What's the balance between managing the asset and not decreasing value versus deploying the asset, potentially at catastrophic risk, to get something better? That balance begins to shift.

---

18 See "If, Why, and How Founders Should Hire a Professional CEO," on Reid's blog. [*http://www.reidhoffman.org/if-why-and-how-founders-should-hire-a-professional-ceo/*]

By the time you get to public companies, public investors fundamentally think your responsibility is to preserve the asset value. This is part of the reason why turnarounds in public companies, like with what Marissa and Yahoo! were doing, are super difficult. Most people won't even take that job, because actually, in fact, they would have to gamble a bunch of the assets in order to try to make it work. And yet if everyone's like, "No you don't. Just maintain and preserve the current assets as they are," that's super difficult to do while also getting to a high level of growth.

One of the things you need to consider, when you're thinking about the board, is where you are on that spectrum. Are you in the gamble, willing to put real assets on the line, possibly all of them, for a high return? Are you about asset preservation—you're trying to get as much growth as possible, but your first priority is to maintain the value of what you've got while growing it? Or is it a combination, with some real risk, together with upside?

Elad: In your experience, how can a board most effectively manage its relationship with the CEO? And what are some common pitfalls that you see?

Reid: One of the things that a lot of board members make a mistake on is—I use this way of describing kind of a red light, yellow light, green light framework between the board and the CEO. Roughly, green light is, "You're the CEO. Make the call. We're advisory." Now, we may say that on very big things—selling the company—we should talk about it before you do it. And that may shift us from green light, if we don't like the conversation. But a classic young, idiot board member will say, "Well, I'm giving you my expertise and advice. You should do X, Y, Z." But the right framework for board members is: You're the CEO. You make the call. We're advisory.

Red lights also very easy. Once you get to red light, the CEO—who, by the way, may still be in place—won't be the CEO in the future. The board knows they need a new CEO. It may be with the CEO's knowledge, or without it. Obviously, it's better if it's collaborative. But this can range from a scenario where we've got the current CEO to agree that we're looking for a successor, all the way to "Bob, meet Sue. Sue is the CEO. She starts today." It can be that entire range, depending on the circumstances of the company, of the CEO, of the relationship between the CEO and the board.

Yellow means, "I have a question about the CEO. Should we be at green light or not?" And what happens, again under inexperienced or bad board members, is they check a CEO into yellow indefinitely. They go, "Well, I'm not sure…" The important thing with yellow light is that you 1) coherently agree on it as a board and 2) coherently agree on what the exit conditions are. What is the limited amount of time that we're going to be in yellow while we consider whether we move back to green or move to red? And how

"The board is a team of people in dynamic collaboration with the CEO"

—Reid Hoffman

do we do that, so that we do not operate for a long time on yellow? Because with yellow light, you're essentially hamstringing the CEO and hamstringing the company. It's your obligation as a board to figure that out.

The next thing is, when you think of a board as a team and not just people standing in judgment, its members need to ask, "Okay, what are the things that we do to add value?" One of the things that good board members do is go into every board meeting thinking, "What's the thing that I can add?" Because a board is governance, but especially for early-stage companies, a board is also people that have serious expertise, capabilities, and networks that you couldn't hire into the company. Given that, the big question for a board member should be, "How do I bring value to the company?"

Some of it is as simple as this: I'll sit there with the company, they'll present a pattern to me—like, here are our efforts, strategy, work, operations, etc.—and I will give them feedback. I might say, "Okay, I'll introduce you to someone." That's one thing that you should certainly do. But that's kind of like saying, "Well, the way that I'm going to be an executive is I'm going to show up, and when you present stuff to me in a meeting I'll respond to it." Just as we expect more of executives than that, you also have a more active responsibility as a board member. One of the metrics to hold up as a board member is to say, "Before I go into the board meeting, what's the thing that I can bring that's most helpful?" You might even do this more frequently than just at board meetings. It might be weekly. Because part of the reason why the company has me on the board is because I'm engaged in all this other stuff. I have this depth of industry experience, I have these network connections, I have my own brain cycles. How can I show up saying, "I've thought about this, and here's something that I think is the best possible thing I can lay on the table."

"As a board member, say, 'Before I go into the board meeting, what's the thing that I can bring that's most helpful?'"

Reid Hoffman

Now, it might be as a board member you say, "I think you should build product X," or, "you should build feature Y," or, "you should execute strategy Z." Those are possibilities. But they should always be phrased as questions. For example, you might ask, "You know, I've thought really hard about the strategy that you guys have been doing, and the following thing strikes me as a risk. Do you think it's a risk or not? I thought of a way to measure it, or to mitigate it. What do you think?" If you do it that way, it's a conversation.

If the team is really, really good, you will very rarely discover something that's totally new to them. They may very well respond, "We've thought about it, and X, Y, and Z." And you say, "Oh, okay, great. I brought the best possible thing. You're already on top of it. Let me help you through it." But that cycle is still good.

On the other hand, because of your breadth of experience, your network connections, and so on, the team might say, "Oh wait, actually we hadn't thought about it that way, and that is important to think about."

Then, of course, it also gets down to priorities. For example, frequently when I bring up an idea like this in a board meeting, I'll say, "Look, I don't know. You should feel totally fine to say, 'That's interesting, but it's not on the short list right now.'" You have to be careful as a board member, because it's really easy to screw things up, in terms of the company's priorities. One of your positions has to be "do no harm."

Elad: How does this dynamic change, though, if the board has lost faith in the team, or more specifically the CEO?

Reid: Part of what happens is deciding when to make the call that the CEO is the wrong one. The CEO may make their own decision that they're the wrong CEO. But when do you make the decision that the CEO is wrong? Frequently in startups this is a catastrophically bad thing. The board's decision that the CEO is wrong essentially means, "We made a really bad investment decision."

That being said, one really important thing for startups to succeed is to have someone who has the commitment, the moral authority, the dedication, the "I gotta make it work" drive. Usually hiring an external expert is a bad play, because they lack those critical things.

Elad: You've written some great articles on CEO succession and how some founders can step aside.[19] But if you're a smaller or younger company and you come to the realization that the founder is the wrong CEO—or the founder decides "I'm the wrong CEO," often you don't have depth of bench within the organization. It's hard to recruit somebody externally to take over that role. Even if the company is growing rapidly, it may still be too early. How do you think about that dynamic and bridging that?

Reid: The key dynamic—and it's super hard—is one I learned through LinkedIn: you're actually looking for a cofounder. You're looking for a cofounder who may have a different skill set than the people who are part of the initial "family" or "tribe." But you're looking for, essentially, a cofounder.

There are various tests for cofounders. Like, "Would you do this job if we paid you half of what we're paying you? Because you're really committed to this thing?" That's not to say you should pay them half, but you want someone who sees this as the thing they want to do. If someone came along and said, "I'll pay you twice as much as you're being paid now," they'd say, "No thanks. This is the thing that I want to be doing."

People with that much commitment are also willing to take more risks. Because all startups, they go through "valley of the shadow" moments, where everyone's saying, "Oh, that's really screwed up, that's in a bad space, that's really dumb." Does this person say, "Well, hey, it wasn't my idea?" That's a professional manager. A founder goes, "No, I know I can make this work. I'm going to make it work. I'm going to take the extra risk, the extra difficulty, the sweat, the criticism. I'm going to play it through." So those are the traits that you need.

---

[19] See Reid's post on "If, Why, and How Founders Should Hire a 'Professional' CEO." [*http://www.reidhoffman.org/if-why-and-how-founders-should-hire-a-professional-ceo/*]

People frequently say, about hiring a new CEO, "Well, I'm hiring a skill set." Skill set's important—which level you're at, your ability to make it work. The reason you're hiring a new CEO is because there are new skill sets that are critically important. But if someone doesn't have the founder's mindset, they'll be fundamentally, at best, in asset management. They'll make sure that things keep running, keep going on a trajectory. But the ability to change the curve means taking a risk that a founder would take. That requires moral authority, but it also requires mental willingness—including risking hearing that, "You really screwed up, you're doing this really badly." You have to be willing to go through that in order to make it happen.

Elad: One of the things you mentioned earlier was that adding board members is adding to a team. So how do you think about board member selection? How do you approach that process and what do you look for?

Reid: It depends a little bit on stage, but there are a few key ingredients: First, you have to look at the whole board as a team. Part of how a board can be dysfunctional is that even if you have a good player, but they pull in a different way and add in a different element, then the team breaks.

At some point, you may very well go, "That person needs to be either changed or ejected." Sometimes when I'm looking at a startup and there's a problematic board member, I know that the primary role of the next board member—if the problematic board member can't be changed—is to be a catalyst. You've already addressed in one of your posts how to trade a VC off a board, but that's frequently very difficult.

Elad: It's very hard, yeah.

Reid: The path that I usually suggest is to find a board member who changes the dynamic in a very healthy way. That's usually another venture capitalist, someone with a lot of throw weight. Somebody who makes people say, "Oh, that person's smart and capable." And when they start going, "This is what we're doing," then the other board members will shift in that direction. That's how I usually solve that problem. So that's one key ingredient: You always think team dynamic.

Now, the second part of the team dynamic is that a board has to very much catalyze the CEO. I look at whether a prospective board member really extends the abilities of the CEO. Do they have a good partnership with the CEO? Roughly speaking, one of the tests I use on the CEO side is, would you want to spend an hour or two a week working with this person? You may not get an hour or two a week, but would you want to do it, trotting out the hardest problems? If that's the case, and they would add a lot to the

CEO, it kind of doesn't matter whether they have, for example, payments expertise or organizational expertise. That amplification of the CEO really, really matters.

Sometimes the CEO says, "I don't understand the banking industry and I'm doing this banking thing. I need to be spending the hour or two a week with someone who really understands the banking industry. I need that capability." Or, "I know that we're an enterprise company, so we need enterprise sales. And I don't really understand enterprise sales that well, so I need someone who helps me grow and do the enterprise sales stuff well." There will be a different set of things that will be important characteristics. But the key is that partnership with the CEO, which then spreads to the executive team.

The next thing you look for is: What are the key zones of expertise, networks, ways of thinking that add the most value into the company that you couldn't hire for? Because if you can hire it, great, hire it. Add it into the genetics of the company. But there are a bunch of people like, for example, me or Peter Chernin—you can't hire us into the company. That's not doable. In that case, the board is the way you do that.

That's the kind of thing that you look at when you're building a board: What's really adding to the company and adding to the CEO? It's not just management of the assets, it's also helping the amplification. And helping the amplification is helping the CEO, and the exec team, play the game the right way. ■

This interview has been edited and condensed for clarity.

THE ROLE OF THE CEO: MANAGING YOUR BOARD OF DIRECTORS

Managing your board effectively can help you and/or your company:

- Get strategic and operational feedback on key areas.
- Source and close candidates, particularly executive hires.
- Assess talent at the company ongoing.
- Get help with fundraises, and ensure that your board members are aligned to help you close additional capital. (This isn't always the case!)
- Be coached as CEO.
- Ensure the right person is in place as CEO.

BOARD MEETING STRUCTURE

Your board meeting structure[20] is likely to change over the course of the company's evolution, as you move from an early-stage venture struggling for product/market fit[21] to a more mature organization preparing to go public. For an early-stage company, board meetings may be primarily about reviewing a handful of fundamental metrics (e.g., "Are we running out of money?" and, "is our product working?") as well as broader strategic input, organizational advice, and hiring help for the CEO and executive team. Later-stage board meetings tend to broaden to include advanced strategy questions (e.g., M&A and other conversations).

The larger the board is the harder it will be to manage it and keep it both focused and productive. Just as scaling your team from 10 to 10,000 people changes how you communicate with and manage them, growing the board also changes the conversations and communication styles you need to use at the board level. The hard part is ensuring that meetings remain productive and useful for the company.

Remember, board meetings exist to (1) help the company and (2) provide proper corporate governance for all classes of stock.

---

[20] Mark Suster has a good post on holding better board meetings. See eladgil.com.
[*https://bothsidesofthetable.com/why-you-re-not-getting-the-most-out-of-your-board-abf9e8b891d9*]
[21] What Marc Andreessen calls "the only thing that matters." See eladgil.com.
[*https://pmarchive.com/guide_to_startups_part4.html*]

In order to make a board meeting effective, the CEO should try to do the following prior to the meeting:

1. **Send out the board deck and other materials at least 48–72 hours before the meeting.** You want people to have a chance to review it in advance.[22]

2. **[If you have three or more non-founder members only] Call board members in advance for a 30- to 60-minute 1:1 briefing.** This allows board members to give input (and, in some cases, vent) in advance of the board meeting.

3. **[If you have multiple board members only] Plan a board dinner the night before, or lunch/dinner right after.** While optional, these dinners are an opportunity for board members to form bonds with one another and potentially with you and your team in advance/after the meeting. This works best if your board members are from another geography and need to fly in—otherwise they may not have the time or interest.

BOARD MEETING AGENDA

Once you're in the meeting proper, it will likely include the following items:[23]

1. **Board business.** This should be short. Get it out of the way quickly.

2. **Big picture summary.** A short, high-level overview of the state of company.

3. **Quick review and discussion of key metrics.** You'll want to pay particular attention to those metrics that impact company strategy. These metrics should all have been in the slides sent out 48–72 hours earlier.

4. **Follow-up items from last meeting.** You can also do this section after the strategy topics. Really what you want is a large block of time to focus on strategy.

5. **Discussion of 2–3 key strategy topics important to company.** These topics and background on them should have been in the slides sent out 48–72 hours earlier.

---

22 For good examples of board decks, see eladgil.com. [*https://www.sequoiacap.com/article/preparing-a-board-deck* and *http://resources.iaventures.com/#board*]
23 Sequoia's Bryan Schreier has a useful post on preparing a board deck. See eladgil.com. [*https://www.sequoiacap.com/article/preparing-a-board-deck/*]

"The reason you're hiring a new CEO is there are new skill sets that are critically important. But if someone doesn't have the founder's mindset, they'll be fundamentally, at best, in asset management."

—Reid Hoffman

The bulk of your time should be spent on #5. Your board members should have reviewed the materials in advance. If you have a larger board, you should have called each member prior to the board meeting for a quick discussion/queue-up of the strategic topics. This allows you to avoid a long rehash of metrics and background that eat into the discussion time.

You can have various members of the executive team attend all or parts of #2–4. Navigate carefully, though: invitations to board meetings can start to become politicized and a sign of the relative importance of members of your executive staff. Be thoughtful about who to invite and why.

BOARD OBSERVERS AND RANDOM PEOPLE SHOWING UP TO BOARD MEETINGS

Some venture firms will ask more junior members of their investment teams to show up along with them at board meetings. Or, they may bring more senior partners to sit in if your company is doing well. Don't tolerate random people showing up. A board meeting is not open to whoever the venture firm wants to include. If the firm wants an additional member to attend—e.g., a junior partner who can help with follow-up for your company (and these people can occasionally be quite helpful)—negotiate parameters with your VC partner. What are the expectations on the junior person's role at the board meeting? Will the board observer have the right to speak up? What specific items will she help with?

Mark Suster has a good post on board observers.[24]

OTHER BOARD INTERACTIONS

Depending on your relationship with board members, or on their inclinations, board members can help you with a variety of items outside of meetings too. You might ask a board member to spend extra time with a member of your team or to work with a key function to help it run smoothly. For example, a board member with significant experience taking companies public or managing public companies as CFO could help coach your CFO or her team. Board members can also be valuable for 1:1 conversations with you or your executives on key strategic questions, management and organization, or other items. Board members can also help with interviewing or recruiting key executives.[25]

24 See eladgil.com. [*https://bothsidesofthetable.com/rethinking-board-observers-the-role-of-the-silent-observer-eee4ccecac7d*]
25 For more readings on board meetings, see eladgil.com. [*http://www.bothsidesofthetable.com/2013/12/09/why-youre-not-getting-the-most-out-of-your-board/*; *http://www.joangarry.com/executive-session/*; *http://venturehacks.com/archives#board-of-directors*; *https://www.sequoiacap.com/article/preparing-a-board-deck/*]

PART 1: MANAGING YOUR BOARD

PART 1: MANAGING YOUR BOARD

An interview with Naval Ravikant

Naval Ravikant is the chairman and a cofounder of AngelList. He previously cofounded Epinions (which went public as part of Shopping.com) and Vast.com. He is an active angel investor, and has invested in dozens of companies, including Twitter, Uber, Yammer, Stack Overflow, and others.

As one of Silicon Valley's most respected angel investors and entrepreneurs, a veteran of some of the Valley's biggest startup success stories, and an investor in many others, Naval has a uniquely broad perspective on startups.

In this part of my two-part interview with Naval, we spoke about the intricacies and delicate issues involved with managing boards.

Elad Gil: On the board side, is the idea to only raise from people who won't take a board seat? And how do you think about also getting rid of earlier board members as part of late-stage financing?

Naval Ravikant: Companies are this weird thing. The whole point of a company is to try to be efficient and get stuff done. And when you go through human history, you find that when you want to prevent an entity from having too much power, you defuse that power by having committees or groups. Go back to the Romans; they had the Senate, and all the senators had to agree. But when the Romans went to war, when they wanted to be efficient, they elected a dictator. And that dictator then took charge of everything and went off and fought the war—and usually ended taking over all of Rome afterward, so it kind of backfired. But the Romans were aware of that model, and the trade-offs.

In companies, you have a dictator at the top, a CEO, or the founders. Then all of a sudden it turns back into a butterfly network, and now you report to a board, a bunch of people. And inherently, the founder-dictators tend to be very risk-prone. They have a lot of vision, they have a lot of drive, they know where they want to take the thing. They like to make risky moves and bets and pivots and turns.

But boards don't like that. Boards don't like to be dragged along. It's a group of people. It's groupthink, it's committee-think. No committee ever built anything great. So related to that, no board ever built anything great. Boards can be helpful; they can be sounding boards. But you do not want the board to be running the company. And the larger the board, the more you're going to find yourself spending time just keeping them up-to-date and in sync.

I know there's this belief that venture capitalists can add a lot of value on the board. And they can—under very specific circumstances and situations. They're experts at financing, they're experts at knowing the external market, they might have deep domain expertise in one particular thing that you might encounter.

But by and large, your average VC board member is on ten boards, so they're taking ten different board meetings every month or two. On top of that, they're spending half their time looking at new companies. They're also managing their investors and LPs. And, let's face it, anyone who's been in the venture business knows it's not really a full-time job. Maybe for the best VCs it is, but your average VC does not work the hours that your average entrepreneur does. Your average VC is a retired entrepreneur; your average entrepreneur is not a retired VC. So they just don't have that much time. You're spending most of your time keeping them up to speed, and then you're hoping to get some value and wisdom out of their expertise and years and years of learning.

You don't want your board to be too large. The larger your board, the less it is going to get done. Every experienced board member will tell you that they favor private company boards of five or six people or less.

You can keep the board small in multiple ways: one is, don't give up more than one board seat per round. The most common mistake I see entrepreneurs make is this: they want to get two investors involved, they do a two-VC round, and they've got two board seats from one round. That adds up really fast. Because then when you get to series C, series D, series E, you've suddenly got a six-, seven-, eight-person board.

Second, you can actually put it in the early term sheets that the investor will leave that board seat when another board seat comes in later. First Round Capital, I think, is famous for doing this. They'll usually step out of the board when the next round takes place.

Elad: Yes, but they tend to do that since they're a seed-focused firm. How do you do that for people who are traditional series A, B, C investors?

Naval: Well, the smart ones—I've seen Fred Wilson do it—will actually step out when the company is getting closer and closer to going public. You can also try to just negotiate it early on. And you can do it in the new rounds. Let's say that you're raising $50 million in a hot growth round. You could go to your series A person and say, "Hey, this is your opportunity to get off the board and recover your time. We'll leave you with the protective provisions that you negotiated, so you're not going to lose anything. And I'll keep you on the mailing list and I'll send you the board decks, so you get the updates remotely. But you don't have to sit on that conference call every month. You don't have to do the board meetings."

"Every experienced board member will tell you that they favor private company boards of five or six people or less."

—Naval Ravikant

Elad: The primary thing I've seen people be willing to do in circumstances like that is effectively get partially bought out. Then it's an excuse to get them off. Because I feel that a lot of early-stage investors, if the company is doing really well, they want to maintain association with the company, both for their personal brand and as a vehicle to buy other things in their portfolio that aren't working as well.

Naval: That's right. It's a credit thing, so that always does make it tough. It's sad, but I see too many late-stage entrepreneurs spending literally half their time just doing board management.

The other thing you can do is space the board meetings out further. So maybe have a board meeting every three months, and then do an update call every month. And keep that call short. I'm a bit of a jerk with my companies, when I'm the entrepreneur, in that I set the expectation very, very early on that I'm not going to do a fancy PowerPoint deck. I'm going to have a sheet of paper with the big points on it and the big numbers on it, and then we're going to get together and have a conversation.

It's very important as a founder-CEO that you manage your board. Because if you don't, then whoever the next most aggressive board member is will step in and fill that vacuum. You don't want to be in that position where you're always responding to them or answering their questions. You want to guide the board and guide the company.

"I see too many late-stage entrepreneurs spending literally half their time just doing board management."

—Naval Ravikant

Elad: Have you seen any circumstances where people have used a chair for that function of coordinating with the rest of the board members? Or does that happen more with public companies?

> **Naval:** Yeah, that's more of a public thing. Generally—I'm thinking of the founder-CEO model, which is the most successful model in Silicon Valley—if there's going to be a chair it may be the other founder or a departed founder or a retired founder. But it's sort of odd to have a chair who's not also a founder.

Elad: How do you get rid of somebody who is starting to be destructive at the board level? The nightmare scenario, to your point, is that it's your first company and you do a shotgun process. You end up with somebody awful for your series A, and then your company is really working well and you're stuck with this person. What should you do?

> **Naval:** Terrible situation. It's very, very hard to navigate. Usually you end up buying them out for more than they're worth, which sucks. And usually your other board members really help you on this; this is where the other board members earn their keep. Generally the most senior person on your board, someone who is good to work with, will hopefully help you with that.

Elad: Is there anything you can do with the VC firm itself? Can you go to the firm and complain? Can you ask for a different partner?

Naval: That's a last resort. That's going nuclear. It only works if the person who is being difficult is a very junior person and you're willing to take the gamble that they've been exposed internally. But that can backfire on you just as much as not. It's almost like going to a husband and saying you don't like his wife or going to a wife and saying you don't like her husband. VC partners are married to each other in these very complex, decade-long or multi-decade-long arrangements. So I would not attempt that maneuver unless there's someone on your board who's willing to do it on your behalf, who says, "Oh yeah, I know so-and-so who runs the firm and I have a good relationship and I can give him that feedback."

Elad: And at that point, you have to go to the person running the firm. You can't go to another junior partner. You have to go to the very top.

Naval: That's right.

Elad: I guess it also depends a bit on firm structure. Because if there are multiple senior partners, then power is fragmented. And then it really becomes a weird situation.

Naval: Yeah, I've seen that situation actually kill companies. My solution to most board problems is going to be highly unacceptable to the venture community, but we don't give out permanent board seats. We would never ever give out a board seat that we could not remove. And in AngelList and my company, that's what I've done. The only board seats I've given out are ones that can be removed; there's no such thing as a permanent board seat.

Elad: It sounds like that's something you should start negotiating from your very first round.

Naval: Experienced entrepreneurs will. Otherwise it's marriage with no possibility of divorce.

The way my company is structured is that everyone can be removed, including me. Then it is actually a very consistent moral argument that I can make, which is saying, "Hey guys, you can remove me as well if I'm out of line." Nobody is safe, and that forces everybody to behave. ◼

CHAPTER 3

Recruiting, hiring, and managing talent

CHAPTER 3

Recruiting, hiring, and managing talent

One of the biggest challenges a company faces as it scales is to revamp its recruiting and employee onboarding processes. When Twitter bought my startup it had just 90 employees. By the time I left two and half years later, Twitter had grown to close to 1,500 people—93% of the employees were new.

In order to add 500 people a year you need to change the way you approach and scale your recruiting organization, you need to think deeply about employee onboarding, and you need to maintain and evolve your culture. In this chapter we cover these and other shifts required to hire and manage talent.

RECRUITING BEST PRACTICES

As you scale from hiring 10 people a year to 10 people a week, a small number of recruiting processes can go a long way in maintaining a high bar and expediting key hires.

WRITE A JOB DESCRIPTION FOR EVERY ROLE

Many companies start off recruiting via personal networks for a small number of roles—e.g., engineers and designers. As a company scales beyond individual contributors in a handful of functions, it is important for people hiring for a role to understand what is important in the person they hire. For example, if you are hiring a business development person for the first time (see "how to hire great BD people,"), what should people look for in that person and role? An engineer on the interview panel might not know the difference between a business development and a sales person. Clarifying skill set and role is important so everyone is looking for the same type of candidate.

For each role you should write a job description that explains what the role will do, and what experience and background you are looking for. You can also the list the things you are not looking for, or consider less important. This description should be circulated to people interviewing for the role with a short note explaining what the hiring manager is looking for and prioritizing. If your team subsequently raises questions about who to hire for the role, you can refer back to the original job description to correct any bad assumptions.

ASK EVERY CANDIDATE THE SAME QUESTIONS

For each candidate for a given role, ask the same or similar interview questions. This will allow you to calibrate candidates across identical questions.

ASSIGN FOCUS AREAS TO INTERVIEWERS PRIOR TO THE INTERVIEW

Often you want to interview candidates for specific aspects of their role. For example, you might interview a product manager on their product insights, past accomplishments, culture fit, etc. Rather than have every person the candidate interviews with ask the same set of questions for every area, you could have three or four interviewers each focus on a different area that you assign to them before the interview. This will allow for an in-depth view of each area, versus a shallow view of all areas.

Additionally, if you bring the person back for a second round of interviews, you can double down on areas of concern with more focused interviews.

"One of the biggest determinants of candidate conversion is how quickly you interview them and how quickly you can make an offer."

— Elad Gil

WORK PRODUCT INTERVIEWS

For some roles, the best way to assess a candidate (outside of direct prior knowledge working with them) is to have them develop a work product as part of the interview. This could happen either onsite or as a take home. For example, an engineer could do a coding exercise, or a designer could be asked to do a quick set of wire frames or workflow for a hypothetical product. A marketing person could be asked to generate a hypothetical product marketing plan. In general, it is good to avoid asking for work or output on an existing company product to avoid the perception of getting free labor out of a candidate.

CANDIDATE SCORING

As each person finishes their interview, it is good for them to enter feedback about the candidate before talking to other interviewers. This avoids people biasing each other and forces each interviewer to take a written stance on a candidate. You can also adopt a numeric ranking system (e.g., 1–5 points) or a simple "hire, no hire" scale. The key is consistency, as well as providing interviewers with a clear definition of what these outputs should mean. Consistent scoring can allow you to quickly reject or pursue candidates. In general, your scoring system prevents interviewers from having the easy out of a "neutral" option. Hence the "hire/no hire" framework would lack a "no opinion" option.

MOVE FAST

Every company I have ever worked for, or with, has realized that one of the biggest determinants of candidate conversion is how quickly you interview them and how quickly you can make an offer. Beyond conversion, a key metric to track is how long candidates spend in each step of the interview process. You should optimize for shorter times between each step and for rapidly getting offers out.

CHECK CANDIDATES' REFERENCES

Reference checks are often the clearest signal on a candidate. You should reference-check everyone. Be careful with businesspeople—they tend to provide friends in their organization as references, and in general will get glowing recommendations from their friends. I have found engineering and other functions to be more direct/honest when providing references for their friends. To compensate for this, try to broaden the scope of references you check for businesspeople to other functions to ensure clarity of their skills and areas for improvement.

DIVERSE CANDIDATES

Ensuring diversity (of gender, race or ethnic background, sexual orientation, social class and background, and more) in your employee base and interview process is the subject of numerous books and blogs. One excellent resource for this is Joelle Emerson's Paradigm Strategy website, whose focus is diverse hiring practices.[26] You can also read the interview with Joelle later on in this book.

There is a lot of detail and nuance in getting to a diverse workforce. A few key items:

1. **Ensure that you have diverse candidates for each role.** You will never have a diverse employee base if you do not ensure diverse candidates in your funnel. Building a diverse funnel means not only sourcing a broader spectrum of candidates, but also thinking through the language in your job descriptions, how employees are represented on your website, and other factors that will impact who applies.

2. **Focus on eliminating biases from your interview approach.** A number of biases exist in standard interviewing approaches. A simple example would be whether the names and gender of candidates is blinded at the resume review stage.

3. **Provide benefits that support the needs of underrepresented employees.** Paid parental leave is one simple example. Think through your broader potential employee pool and what benefits would support their ability to focus on their work at your company.

For a more in-depth resource, I recommend you read a white paper from Paradigm.[27]

---

[26] See *https://www.paradigmiq.com/blog*
[27] Link on eladgil.com. [*https://paradigmiq.app.box.com/s/bpk3v4umfbj8dkakepwvqpqt79y87tyt*]

SCALING A RECRUITING ORGANIZATION

The use of recruiters by a startup will shift dramatically over the lifetime of the company.

As a small startup (e.g., 3–10 people), using a recruiter is usually not as useful as direct founder or employee networking, using LinkedIn and other tools. In contrast, when I was at Twitter, the company grew from ~90 to ~1,500 people over a 2.5 year period. As your company scales into the hundreds and thousands of people, you will want to bring specialized recruiters, sourcers, university programs managers, etc. in-house and potentially use retained external recruiters for executive hires.

EARLY DAYS: YOUR TEAM AS RECRUITERS

Early on, the best approach to recruiting is to have people on your team actively refer in people from their network. Similarly, many founders & early employees spend as much as 30–50% of their time early on (e.g., when scaling from 3 to 15 people) on recruiting. There is no easy fix around it. You need to just grind through large numbers of people (via networking, LinkedIn, friends, etc.) to find the handful of people to join your team.

Some startups I know successfully hire someone who is a mix of office manager/social media manager/recruiting coordinator. This person will often spend a lot of time scheduling referred candidates and reaching out to passive candidates via email and LinkedIn. Once the candidate expresses interest they pass them off to a founder or hiring manager.

INITIAL SCALING: THE IN-HOUSE RECRUITER

Once a company hits a certain scale and is growing fast enough (adding 15–20 people per year or more), hiring in-house recruiters makes a lot of sense. The recruiter initially plays a few different roles that in larger stage companies will get split up including

- Sourcing.
- Running the recruiting process (scheduling, collating feedback, coordinating with hiring manager etc.).
- In some cases delivering offers (although I think often hiring managers or founders can do this).

Depending on the strength of the recruiter (and, importantly, the company branding with your candidates), the recruiter will be able to hire 1–4 engineers per month. This shifts as the company scales and adds more differentiated roles (see below).

"The importance of the hiring manager and other executives being involved in the recruiting process cannot be over-emphasized."

— Elad Gil

This means that if you are hiring fewer then 15 engineers a year, you may want to have a part-time or split-role recruiter, grow organically via company referrals, or find an alternative structure with external recruiters.

For non-engineering roles (e.g., sales) a single recruiter may be able to hire a larger number of people per month. This is driven in part by the referral-heavy nature of sales hiring as well as the fact that there are fewer high-growth companies for sales, marketing, and business development people to go to. In contrast, every startup is trying to hire engineers and designers.

Things that impact the ability of the recruiter to be effective include:

- Brand of the startup with candidates.
- Strength of the hiring manager and executive team as recruiters. If they are active and engaged, it makes recruiting run smoother and will help to source and close more candidates.
- Breadth of network of the employees at the company.

The importance of the hiring manager and other executives being involved in the recruiting process (through informal conversations, extending offers, meeting for lunch, etc.) cannot be over-emphasized, no matter how strong a recruiting org you have. The candidates will always want exposure to people in key roles in the company (Mark Zuckerberg at Facebook is famous for his "closing walks" with mid-level candidates).

HIGH-GROWTH: MULTIPLE RECRUITING ORG ROLES

When a company is growing really fast, the set of roles on the recruiting team tends to fragment and you need to start to specialize the types of people on your recruiting team.

1. **Sourcers.** Sourcers research, cold call, email, and otherwise create a path to passive candidates. In some cases they then transfer the candidates over to recruiters who will feed the candidate into a coordinated interview process. Some sourcers manage candidates up through an onsite interview, but seldom beyond.

2. **Recruiters.** Recruiters manage the process of coordination of the candidate through scheduling various interviews (phone screens, onsite, executive, etc.) and then circling with the team or hiring manager to determine whether an offer will be extended. At some companies the recruiter may extend the offer, in others the hiring manager does so.

Your first few in-house recruiters should have experience sourcing as well. This helps in a number of ways:

- The recruiter will likely be more effective in sourcing and recruiting specialized engineering roles.
- There will be fewer hand offs between people on the team (e.g., sourcer, recruiter, hiring manager, etc.) which means less friction to the candidate and fewer people fall through the cracks.

Splitting the recruiter and sourcer roles tends to work best when you are hiring large number of people of a specific type. For example, if you need to hire 50 back-end engineers, 30 front-end engineers, and 20 PMs, starting to segment recruiting roles makes a big difference.

3. **Candidate researchers.** These people may scrub LinkedIn for all the engineers at Google, prioritize them, put them into a spreadsheet, and then hand off the spreadsheet to the sourcers to actually do the outreach/pitch the candidates to interview.

   These people usually only really get added to the team as it scales from 100+ to 1,000+ people, and you are hiring large numbers of people in the same role.

4. **Recruiting marketing.** These are the folks who develop marketing materials, run ads, organize recruiting events, hackathons, website content, etc. to create an inbound pipeline of candidates. At a startup, this is usually driven by someone on the team you are recruiting for (e.g., an engineering manager for engineering candidates). Alternatively, the marketing team at the startup may be responsible for this as part of their overall marketing efforts. Only as a company scales to a few hundred people or more does the possibility of a standalone coordinating recruiting marketing role emerge.

5. **University programs.** Given the specific timing and cadence of new graduate and intern hiring, some companies will specialize sourcers and recruiters specifically for coordination and hiring of new grads. When your startup is still small, instead of hiring dedicated university programs people, you can have your existing recruiting staff pivot to cover this area for the few months when it is most relevant.

EXECUTIVE HIRES: RETAINED RECRUITER

For executive hires, a retained search using an executive recruiting firm may work well. While you will continue to mine your investors and employees for leads, specialized recruiting firms have networks tailored to fill your general counsel, CFO, or other role that may simply be outside of your founder network.

For a retained search, you may pay an external recruiter some upfront fee or retainer to find candidates for you. In general, these sorts of searches work best if you are hiring an executive for the company versus an individual contributor. One reason is that executive hires may be outside of your core network, or that executives may be more willing to talk to recruiters from a brand-name firm than to someone from a less well-known startup.

There are a number of brand-name executive recruiters your angels, VCs, or advisors can connect you to.[28]

EMPLOYEE ONBOARDING

Many companies make the mistake of spending months building a pipeline for recruiting the very best people, but then spend little time actually onboarding them to make sure they are successful.

Here are some simple ideas your office manager or head of people can try as you onboard new people.

SEND OUT A WELCOME LETTER

Send a welcome letter to the new employee—and *cc* all the teams that person will be working with closely. The letter will explain the person, their role, who they will report to, what their goals are for the quarter, as well as potentially one interesting fact about them they are willing to share. The idea is to ensure each new person has a clear role and responsibilities, and that the rest of the organization is aware of these things. The interesting fact creates an ice breaker for their coworkers to be able to start a conversation with the new hire.

---

[28] Thanks to Ardy Daie and Chris Shaw for comments and feedback on this post.

WELCOME PACKAGE

Create a checklist of items that each new person receives as they show up for their first day at the company. This should extend beyond the utilitarian items of laptop and email address. Include a book on management the company aspires to emulate, a T-shirt or hoodie, and if they have a newborn leave them a onesie. You can also have a handwritten (or signed) note welcoming the individual to the company.

BUDDY SYSTEM

High-growth companies tend to have their own jargon, internal tools, and random processes that are unique to them. Pair a new hire with a "buddy"—someone who is not in the reporting chain of command with them who can take them to lunch, introduce them to people, and importantly answer any "stupid" questions they may have. Buddies tend be paired for one to three months.

MAKE SURE THEY HAVE REAL OWNERSHIP

The biggest obstacles to happy employee onboarding tend to be (1) a bad manager/employee relationship, and (2) a lack of feeling of ownership for the area they were hired to do. The prior owner of a project may linger longer then is needed in order to get credit for the prior work done. Acknowledge their work but ramp them down as quickly as is reasonable so the new employee can find their legs. If it is a short time window (two weeks to launch) you can have the original owner launch the product or do the work. If it is a longer timeframe (two months) you should transition the project.

SET GOALS

Each manager can set 30-, 60-, and 90-day goals for new employees. This gives a sense of direction, context, and structure for the new employee. It also emphasizes what is important to get done and that individual's priorities.

OLD-TIMER SYNDROME AND EARLY EMPLOYEES

Some of the most valuable long-term employees of a high-growth company join early on. These employees often have earned the trust and admiration of the founders and CEO, and they have the cultural context and long-term mission of the company in mind, which enables them to achieve outsized things in a high-growth startup. Examples like Susan Wojciki (Google employee #16 and eventual CEO of YouTube) and Google and Chris Cox at Facebook (who joined as an engineer in 2005 and is now chief product officer) come to mind.

Unfortunately, some early employees also dramatically overstay their optimal tenure at a company as it scales. They may have gotten too rich and lost their hunger, or simply not scaled their skill set and mindset along with the company. Some cling to the past when they had lunch every day with the CEO and had input into every company decision.

EARLY EMPLOYEES THAT SCALE

Early employees that can grow and scale responsibilities within a company are invaluable. They can channel the mindset of founders/CEO (and therefore get quick buy-in for their teams), have the trust of the executive team and their peers, understand internal processes and jargon, and have a deep understanding of the company operating procedures and culture. Their "old timer" status allows them to challenge convention (or provide context on it) in ways that enable them to reshape or remove rules or old processes.

While many early employees may lack deep functional or industry expertise, the trust of the CEO allows them to hire, manage, and learn from more experienced industry executives. Early employees who are humble enough to realize they can learn from fresh blood can grow with the company and use it as a personal platform for their own learning and impact. Some early employees will stick with a breakout company for decades and their personal story arc mirrors that of the company. These employees tend to be hungry to learn from others, understand that the company, their role, and its culture will inevitably evolve, and are open to change.

A common sign that an old-timer will work out is their eventual acceptance that their role and influence at the company will shrink in the short- to medium-term as the team scales, but that it will expand with time as they continue to learn and the company continues to scale.

OLD-TIMERS THAT SHOULD MOVE ON

In contrast to the early employees that scale, there are also a set of old-timers that should probably change roles, quit, or be managed out. Often the temptation is to keep giving early employees chances or to move them to a spot that they are not hyper productive but is "less important." Usually this suggests that the fit between the employee and the company is not a good one. Often the employee will be happier to leave the company but feels obligated to stick it out due to loyalty to founders or the company.

When dealing with an early employee who is failing to grow with the company, you can take the following steps:

1. **Identify the problem and whether it is solvable. Potential issues may include:**

- **Does not evolve with the company.** Some early employees fight cultural, organizational, product, or other changes to the company. They may fight against the hiring of a sales team, the professionalization of staff, or the sun setting of an increasingly irrelevant product or strategy.

- **Cannot scale into the role they want.** Early employees are often the first or only person in their functional area. Your first marketing person may not be the right long term VP marketing, and your first engineer may not make sense as your CTO. Individuals may lack the skill set, experience, or maturity for certain roles. Given their early tenure at the company employees may nonetheless ask for roles that are beyond their capabilities. Founder CEOs will often put up with poor functional or team leads who cannot scale, but who have deep founder relationships and trust.

- **Feeling left out.** When the company was 12 people the early employee had lunch with the founders every day and had the chance to give her opinion on all major company decisions. As a company scales, most early employees no longer have as strong of a voice or influence. Some of them may start to act out by blocking new projects or inappropriately escalating to founders they still have relationships with.

- **Inappropriate exertion of power.** Some early employees or founders may have a large title as a historical artifact but little influence. The person who was CTO at 10 people may still be CTO at 1,000 people, despite not having any reports or real responsibilities. This is even stronger with cofounders, who will have strong influence at a startup whether they are still active with the company or not. Some cofounders or people with fancy titles may lobby or push parts of the company to do things they want even if they are not supposed to. Often, the other employees do not realize the cofounder or titled employee is acting out of band with the rest of the executive team.

- **Getting too rich.** Due to secondary stock sales and tender offers it is possible to partially cash out. Some employees may suddenly be liquid to the tune of tens of millions of dollars and get distracted by travel, buying houses and cars, or other issues.

"Early employees who are humble enough to realize they can learn from fresh blood can grow with the company and use it as a personal platform for their own learning and impact."

—Elad Gil

2. **Put emotion aside and understand if there is a problem.** As a founder CEO you will feel you owe the early employees for their early work and dedication. People may come to you with issues around a person that you will ignore or defer. This will create a bad environment for everyone including the early employee. It is best to understand the situation and then act quickly and decisively.

3. **Address the issues head on.** As a first step, you should discuss the issues with the early employee. Sometimes the issues are addressable and the frank conversation with the employee turns things around. If there is a fundamental mismatch between the role they have and their skills, it is best to move them to a place of good fit. This may lead to a demotion and the departure of the employee. It is okay to discuss this frankly and explain why you are making the change, and whether they will be happy or thrive with it. As an early employee they are likely a large equity holder in the business and should act with you to maximize equity value. Often, CEOs try to find early employees a place where they won't do much harm, versus a place they will excel. If you find yourself thinking this way, 99% of the time the right answer is to part ways with the early employee. You can let them go with grace and they may be relieved to be free to do something new.

CEO GROWING PAINS

An interview with Sam Altman

Sam Altman runs Y Combinator. He was cofounder and CEO of Loopt, which was funded by Y Combinator in 2005 and acquired by Green Dot in 2012. At Green Dot, he was the CTO and is now on the board of directors. Sam also founded Hydrazine Capital. He studied computer science at Stanford, and while there worked in the AI lab.

Perhaps the biggest innovation in venture investing of the past decade is Y Combinator and the early-stage revolution it engendered. Since 2005, YC has funded over a thousand startups, including Airbnb, Dropbox, Gusto, Instacart, Reddit, Stripe, Zenefits, and others.

Since Sam Altman took over as President of YC in 2014, YC has launched a growth-stage fund, expanded the type of companies YC invests in, and established a nonprofit research lab. In parallel, Sam has coached and mentored many of Silicon Valley's smartest high-growth CEOs, drawing on both his experiences as founder and CEO of Loopt (funded by YC in 2005, and later acquired by Green Dot), as well as his time working with many rapidly growing startups as an investor.

Sam and I discussed an area he has thought deeply about: the role of the CEO, and the hurdles that most often trip up leaders at high-growth startups.

Elad Gil:
You mentioned that staying focused as a CEO—how to distinguish between things that seem important but aren't and things that don't seem important but are—is top of mind for you these days. What do you see as the role of the CEO, and what are some common mistakes you're noticing?

Sam Altman:

The role of the CEO is basically to figure out and decide what the company should do and then make sure it does that. Many CEOs try to outsource those things. Sometimes they want to hire a VP of product or hire a COO and make him or her do everything. But really the CEO has to drive the company's overall direction. There are a few other things that only the CEO can do, or that the CEO at least has to be heavily involved in, like recruiting and evangelizing the company to new hires, major customers, investors, whatever. And there are some jobs where people only want to talk to the CEO; fundraising is a great example.

But really the only universal job description of CEO is making sure the company wins. And so deciding what the company is going to do and making sure the company gets that done—that's the most critical part of the job.

Elad: And that statement, if you unpack it, contains a lot of the sub-pieces you hear a lot: Make sure you don't run out of money, make sure that you're allocating resources to the right spots, make sure you're all moving in the right direction.

Sam: The hard part is that most people want to just do the first part, which is figure out what the company should do. In practice, time-wise, I think the job is 5% that and 95% making sure that it happens. And the annoying thing to many CEOs is that the way you make it happen is incredibly repetitive. It's a lot of the same conversation again and again with employees or press or customers. You just have to relentlessly say, "This is what we're doing, this is why, and this is how we're going to do it." And that part—the communication and the evangelizing of the company vision and goals—is time-wise by far the biggest part of the job.

Elad: As companies scale, I've seen people run into the fact that they end up with a lot of overhead. The bigger your company gets, the more time you end up spending on process: Figuring out your sales comp plan and how it should be structured, getting involved with certain aspects of customer support and exception handling, and all that stuff. A lot of people start to lose track of that bigger picture, of where the company should be heading. Are there key approaches to avoiding that trap, where CEOs end up on all the tactical stuff and forget to pull back out?

"You have to get really good at saying no."

— Sam Altman

Sam: Everyone wants an answer like, "Well, you should not do any of the tactical stuff," but actually a lot of it is really critical. The hard part—and this takes most first-time CEOs a while to figure out—is determining which is which. What is the tactical stuff that seems like a waste of time but is important, and what seems important but is a waste of time?

For example, I do think figuring out compensation structures is really important and something the CEO should spend time on. And it's something that most CEOs don't. You're building what the company measures and what salespeople get paid for, and that's one of those counterintuitive areas that I do think is really important.

The trick to being effective at this is that you have to get really good at saying no and just not doing things. There are a lot of things that are urgent but not important. The hard part of being a good CEO is that you have to be willing to let some things fall apart. You don't have enough time to do everything well. And in practice, what that means is that there are some urgent things that you just don't do. Getting comfortable with that takes a long time. It's hard.

Elad: What are some examples of things you think are often urgent but don't necessarily merit time if you're scaling like crazy and just trying to keep up with everything else?

Sam: I saw one kind of crazy example recently, a founder from a company that YC is an investor in that is not doing particularly well. I was talking to him about how things aren't going that well, and he said that one of the mistakes he made is that he has 74 investors. But he was really proud, because for those 74 investors, he responded to every annual audit request. They told him that he was one of the only CEOs that responded right away. He was really proud of this. And I said, "Look, this is a crazy thing. Your company is on fire. You got one not-important tactical thing done while the company is failing, and you feel great about that. All your investors, no matter what they tell you, will be far happier with a big return than you responding to their annual audit request." And he kind of got it in that moment. But it was this thing that people told him was really important, that he had to do. He felt good that he was doing that, even though he wasn't doing all these other important things—like, you know, getting users and getting revenue.

The hard part of getting users and getting revenue is that it means spending your time building stuff and talking to users—and the implication is you should do nothing else. That's not entirely true, of course, because there are things—we just mentioned employee comp structure—that are really important. But there are all these other things that seem important, like responding to investors' audit requests, that you can just not do.

Elad: It sounds like you just answered the question, but I'll re-ask: What are the things that you think people should stay focused on as a company scales?

Sam: If the CEO disconnects from the product, that's usually bad. And that is something that you see happen to varying degrees as a company scales. There are a lot of CEOs that say, "Well, I want to just go think about strategy all the time. I'm really tired of managing people." Because managing people is hard. And so a lot of CEOs have tried a structure where they bring on a COO (that's a good idea) and then stop going to the executive team meeting (that's a very bad idea).

Elad: You mentioned getting disconnected from product. How much do you think that depends on the founding team? How do you think about the broader leadership team versus the CEO as the full driver or primary owner of things?

Sam: I do think there are many examples of teams that have several strong founders, where you see these roles get divided up. And I actually think that can work really well. It's important to know who's doing what and have some amount of clarity. But I think it can work really well to have multiple people sharing the responsibilities.

Elad: How do you think the role of the CEO, and what the CEO should focus on, shifts in a downturn? Or alternatively if the company is just not doing well?

Sam: In general, the other thing that CEOs should not lose sight of is that they're building businesses. And at some point they have to deliver returns and make money. People always say that the CEO's job is not to run out of money, and what they usually mean by that is fundraising. But the other way you can do that is to make money. And so I think if the company is not doing well or if the environment is really hard, it becomes much more urgent that the CEO—who should never lose sight of the financial performance of the company and the cash flow of the company—is really looking at that all day.

Elad: When it comes to board management and communication to boards, what is the most important role of the CEO?

Sam: I think the most important thing is that boards hate surprises. And boards hate feeling like you're trying to hide bad news. You want to over-communicate with boards for sure. Certainly if you have bad news, you want to get that to them ahead of the board meeting.

As a general operating principle, I also don't think it works super well—most of the time, there are occasions when it does—to go into a board meeting and say, "Hey, I'm really struggling with this idea. What should we do?" Not only because boards don't like that. (And in general they don't; they want confident leadership.) But because in a board meeting, you usually have all these weird dynamics of different VCs trying to impress each other. You're actually just much better off to have individual conversations ahead of time when you really want open-ended brainstorming. You're likely to get better results.

Elad: Are there any other CEO distractions that you see a lot? One thing I've noticed, for example, is that a lot of founders equate press with success. So you see these CEOs chasing press, when that's really not the most important thing they should be doing in many cases. Unless it's a product like Twitter where the press is really the customer acquisition mechanism very early on.

Sam: Yeah, I think it's almost always a huge mistake. Twitter is one crazy example—as far as I can tell, Twitter's best users are still journalists. If your customers are the press, then yeah, go after the press. But most of the time press feels great and delivers nothing. There are exceptions; that's a little bit of an overstatement. And it's usually somewhat easy to get press if you're doing something interesting. But I think most founders—actually, I'm pretty confident in saying almost all founders—overweight the importance of press. So you should do it. It definitely can be helpful, and there's clear value in it. But you see far more startups make the mistake of orienting their entire company around press than making the much smaller mistake of not focusing enough on press.

Elad: Speaking at events, too—it seems like people will end up on these speaking junkets versus being in the office and focusing on the business or meeting with customers.

Sam: Yeah, a lot of founders fall in love with that. It's not that hard and you get to travel and your company pays for it. And you feel special. The point that I always try to make is that it's important to do very small amounts of that. Less is more. If you look at the most successful founders, they're not the ones that are on the circuit.

Elad: What are the biggest challenges you see as companies scale? And how does the role of the CEO need to change accordingly?

Sam: I think the biggest change people fail to make is that at some point your job becomes more about hiring people and working with them to get what you want done than doing it yourself. The number one failure to scale that we see in CEOs is the failure to make that transition. You need to be conscious as it's happening, and realize that at some point you'll get far more leverage on your time if you hire people and work with them closely than try to do everything yourself. And that's a hard transition for many CEOs to make.

Elad: How do you see people navigating that well, or what are some tips to do that effectively?

Sam: No one does it well the first time. No one is naturally good at letting go of something they care deeply about. So, I think you just have to give yourself permission to screw it up for a while. You can internalize that it's important to delegate and give people authority, but you won't do it well the first few times. Just continually try to get better at it.

Elad: Relatedly, I think CEOs often forget that the same thing is happening to members of their team who joined early, maybe just out of school, and who are managing for the first time. They need to learn that skill too. And so you see, at some point of scale, different team members bite the dust in terms of effectiveness. Then the organization limps on until they figure how to either coach that person or bring in somebody more experienced.

Sam: Yeah, this is actually a pretty systemic mistake that I think very few companies get right, which is how you evolve early employees. Obviously I think that's a really important thing to do. These people have been with you for a long time. They're probably extremely talented—if you've done well, you usually have very good early employees. A) I think it's the right thing to do for the employees, and B) I think they have institutional knowledge that no one else does. It's really worth trying to keep them.

Elad: When those early employees haven't scaled to the point where you want them to, though, what do you do? Do you try to offer them an individual contributor role? Do you offer them more of an influencer role, where they're, say, a CTO but don't have direct-line reporting? Do you get a coach for them?

Sam: I don't think there's a one-size-fits-all answer to that. What I tell people is just that I think it is really worth more effort than you would normally spend on an employee to try to figure it out.

"People always say that the CEO's job is not to run out of money, and what they usually mean by that is fundraising. But the other way you can do that is to make money."

— Sam Altman

Elad: Do you have any advice for people who are trying to scale as CEO, but are so busy that they don't have the time to properly hire the people that they need? Is literally the only thing they can do just take a big step back and not get certain things done?

Sam: I have come to that belief. It's never easy advice to give or to hear, but I haven't seen anything else work.

When you're at these breaking points, I think what happens is most CEOs find some sort of formal or informal coach, often a board member. In my case it was one of my board members. We set up a dinner once a month. I would talk to him, and he was incredibly generous with his time. He was a former, very successful, CEO. And I basically said, "Hey, things are breaking. This is not going to go well. Will you teach me how to be a CEO?" And he did. I think most founders find someone to have a similar dynamic with.

Elad: I think a lot of people too should actively look for that, or reach out to people that will have those additional experiences and are willing to put in the time. You have to be very proactive about it and figure out what do you want from that person.

Sam: One of the hard things is that, as the landscape of investing has shifted, there are fewer and fewer investors willing to really put in the time on one company. And that is really bad in this particular case.

Elad: One way we've tried to manage that at Color Genomics is by finding investors who don't have a lot of angel investments but who've built businesses from the ground up. There's a number of people like that out there, but traditionally people didn't go after them as investors. People just stick to the same pool in Silicon Valley.

Sam: Yeah, I think that's incredible and a really, really good thing to do. Founders don't realize how important that is until things break. And so they go for the big-name investor or the investor paying the highest price. And then a year or two later, everything is on fire and they really wish they had allocated their round differently. ■

This interview has been edited and condensed for clarity.

CHAPTER 4

Building the executive team

Building the executive team

HIRING EXECUTIVES

First-time founders or CEOs typically find it hard to hire the first executives to join the team. As a founder, often without deep work experience, you have pulled off the impossible and created a product or service lots of people want to use or pay for. And you did so without any fancy executive-type people from Google or Facebook, with their expensive paychecks and reliance on process.

At some point, however, you will notice that lots of things start to break down. Communication within the company gets gummed up. Various product teams start to lose coordination. You don't have time to get every important thing done in the day, and indeed you start to run out of time to think. Your hiring process falls apart, and it takes weeks for you to follow up with candidates. Your sales pipeline is largely dependent on you and a handful of inexperienced individual contributors—and suddenly follow-through crashes to a halt. You may try to promote existing employees (who also have no prior experience) to run various areas, and in most cases this fails or does not really help anything.

Suddenly you realize that you really need someone with more experience on your team.

Hiring executives for the first time can be quite tricky for a founder. However, once you hire your first seasoned exec who works out, you will be grateful for her presence. All sorts of things will magically just get done. People will get hired, deals will get closed, process will tighten up. It can be a wondrous experience. You will kick yourself for not hiring an experienced, high-capacity executive sooner.

Unfortunately, things could also go badly. The executive is a bad culture fit, or is too senior for the role and spins his wheels. Time is wasted and progress lost on a poor fit—or even worse, some of the best people on your team quit when managed by someone who's not working out.

Finding a great executive for your company can be challenging, but it's well worth the effort. And there are some steps you can take to maximize your chances of success:

HIRE FOR THE NEXT 12–18 MONTHS

If you have a 10-person engineering team, and in 12 months it will grow to 30 people, you do not need to hire an SVP from Salesforce whose job is to manage a 1,500-person team. This person will get bored with the small job offered to her and may simply spin her wheels. She is too senior for the role.

When hiring executives, look for people who have the experience and background that would make them a good fit or hire for the next 12–18 months. Anything shorter than that and they will not be able to scale sufficiently far relative to the time it takes to hire them. Anything longer and you will over-hire and end up with someone who is a bad fit for the job.

TRAITS TO LOOK FOR IN EXECUTIVES

Whatever the role, there are a few key skills and traits that you want your executives to bring to the table:

1. **Functional area expertise.**
   - Do they understand the major issues and common failure points for their functions?
   - Do people in their organizations respect their opinions and feel they can learn from them?
   - Are they right for the current scale and trajectory of your company? You can over-hire for a position, as well as under-hire, given the phase your company is in. For example, do you really need to hire Ruth Porat, Alphabet's CFO, to manage the finances of your pre-revenue 10-person team?

2. **Ability to build and manage a team in those functional areas.**
   - Can they recruit exceptional people? Can they build a recruiting culture within their teams?
   - Do they know how to motivate people in their functions? The incentives for a salesperson are different from those for a product manager.
   - Can they effectively manage people from their function? Managing designers, for example, requires different approaches than managing a customer support team.
   - Do they understand how to build out an organization with multiple layers if needed? How deep of an organization have they managed in the past, and how does that fit your current needs (again, think 12–18 months here)?

3. **Collegiality.**
   - Do they play well with other executives who are their peers?
   - Can they put a collegial, mutually supportive environment in place for the company as a whole, as well as their function?
   - Do they try to do what is right for the company even if it is not in their own best interest?
   - Do they fit your culture? Each culture is unique, and like all employees, some executives fit a culture and some do not.

4. **Strong communication skills.**
   - Are they strong at communication across the company?
   - Can they consistently get other executives, and the CEO or founders, on board with team changes, promotions, road maps, goals, etc.? (Exec-to-founder communication may be its own magical art, depending on how introverted or opinionated the founder is.)
   - Are they able to understand underlying issues and communicate them within their teams? Are they able to communicate to the board, external partners or customers, and other major stakeholders?
   - Do they have "cross-functional empathy" that allows them to work with, and communicate effectively to, other functions they work with closely?[29]

5. **Owner mentality.**
   - Do they take ownership of their functions and make sure they are running smoothly and effectively?
   - Do they own problems and solve them? Can they engage in "black box" abstraction of their functions so the CEO can engage on them, but does not need to be involved day-to-day?
   - Do they understand that, as company executives, they should think like owners?[30]

6. **Smarts and strategic thinking skills.**
   - Do they think strategically and holistically about their functions? Many people don't realize that almost every function can act strategically. It is a good exercise to ask yourself as CEO, "What does a strategic X org look like?" (where X can be HR, ops, product, etc.).
   - Do they think about how their functions can be a competitive advantage for the company? Most companies are only good at one or two things, which is often enough to be successful. But companies that can tackle more than one thing well tend to outshine everyone else (e.g., Apple with hardware design, supply chain, and marketing).[31]
   - Are they first principles thinkers? Can they apply their expertise in knowledge in the context of your company, team, and product? Or do they just try to implement exactly what they did in their last role?

"Once you hire your first seasoned exec who works out, you will be grateful for her presence. All sorts of things will magically just get done. People will get hired, deals will get closed, process will tighten up. It can be a wondrous experience."

—Elad Gil

29 Thanks to Mark Williamson for the "cross-functional empathy" point.

30 Optimally this is true of all employees. But for executives who set the tone of their entire organization, this is especially true.

31 Read the original post at eladgil.com [*http://blog.eladgil.com/2014/02/6-traits-for-hiring-executives.html*]. Thanks to Ali Rowghani for early feedback on this chapter.

DEFINE THE ROLE AND MEET WITH PEOPLE WHO DO IT WELL

Most of the time, a founder will have no idea what to look for when hiring someone to run a particular company function. What does a CFO, general counsel, or even VP of sales really do day-to-day? How can you spot someone who is exceptional at each role? What characteristics should one type of VP have versus another? For example, how does a VP of engineering differ from a VP of sales, or even a CFO?

If you want to learn more about what a great CFO or VP of engineering does, your best bet is to reach out to people who are great at these roles and ask them for advice. Your investors or mentors may be able to suggest which companies have the best people for each function. For example, if you are hiring a CFO, go and meet three or four great CFOs at companies a few years ahead of yours or larger public companies known for excellence like Google or Netflix. What would they hire for in a CFO? What traits would they look for? What interview questions, work projects, tests, reference-checking questions, or other approaches would they take to vet a candidate in this area? For your company size and 18–month growth road map, what should you look for?

In order to get in touch with great leaders in finance, sales, engineering, and more, ask your investors or advisors for introductions. Or, you can ask the founders of other companies that are a few years ahead of you to introduce you to their CFOs or VPs of product for advice and perhaps candidate suggestions.

Once you have figured out what you want in the role, write it down and share it with the team that will be interviewing candidates for that executive hire. You want everyone to have a common view of what to look for, as well as what to select against. You can also use this as an opportunity to reemphasize the cultural characteristics the candidate must embody. Clearly establishing what you are hiring for will make a huge difference as you collect your team's feedback and discuss candidates. It will also prevent poor hiring (or, alternatively, rejection of a great candidate) due to a lack of common understanding of what you are looking for.

KNOW THAT YOU WILL SCREW IT UP ONCE OR TWICE

Some companies are known to have turned over their entire first (and even second) executive team over time. Facebook, for example, let their first executive team go early on and saw quite a bit of executive turnover until Sheryl Sandberg and others came on board.

While you should establish processes to ensure that you have a high hiring success rate, you also need to recognize that you will make mistakes. And that's okay—as long as you learn from the mistakes and iterate on your hiring process. I have seen too many founders take too long to make hires out of fear of doing something wrong. As a founder you need to give yourself permission to make hiring mistakes as long as you are willing to quickly correct them. You obviously cannot make too many of them, but an occasional error is correctable and, frankly, expected.

An interview with Keith Rabois

Keith Rabois is an investment partner at Khosla Ventures. Since 2000, he has been instrumental in driving five startups from their early stages to successful IPOs, with executive roles at PayPal, LinkedIn, and Square, and as a board member with Yelp and Xoom.

At Khosla Ventures, Rabois has led investments in a broad array of startups including DoorDash, Stripe, Thoughtspot, Affirm, Even Financial, and Piazza. While working as a VC he simultaneously cofounded Opendoor, a startup in the real estate tech world.

I sat down with Keith Rabois to talk through some of the nuts and bolts of pushing a hypergrowth company to the next level: when (and why) to IPO, how to find stellar executives, and why a lot of founders need to pare down their roster of direct reports.

I think a lot of founders struggle with how to hire their first CFO, their first general counsel, even their first even VP engineering. Those may be functions they're unfamiliar with, or functions where they don't really have a network. I guess the first part of hiring is knowing what "great" is for a role or function. How can a founder who's never done it actually know what's great?

Keith Rabois:

That's a very significant challenge for people hiring outside disciplines that they've actually worked in. So a great designer tends to know how to hire a design lead. A great engineer may know how to hire a VP of engineering. But they may not even know what a CFO does, let alone what a great CFO is versus a good one versus an excellent one.

One technique I learned, actually from Brian Chesky at Airbnb, is to go find the five best people in Silicon Valley that do that role, and just have coffee with them. And just chat. In that dialogue, I think you form an ability to benchmark the differences between an A+ and a B+, so that when you meet new candidates, actual candidates, you can triangulate against the people you've met that are clearly stellar. And so you should use your board, your investors, any connections you have to get introduced to the five best people, and then spend some time.

Secondly, if you have great investors or board members, absolutely they probably have some experience in hiring some of these roles. And you want to rope them into the interview process earlier rather than later. That can be a high-leverage move.

But it is challenging. You may be able to find a friend or colleague or comparable founder who actually grew up with a different background than you that you can trust, and ask him or her to interview people. Back in the day, after I left PayPal and was doing some other startups, the biggest challenge for me, not being technical, was to hire a VPE. So when I'd get to finalists for VPE positions, I'd ask Max Levchin, who's an extremely strong technologist, to interview the one or two finalists and give me feedback. Obviously I couldn't borrow all of Max's time, and I couldn't constantly ask him to interview people. But when I'd get down to one or two choices and it was a really important hire, I'd ask him to send me feedback.

"One of the things you should always ask is, 'If this person joined my company, would you join?'"

—Keith Rabois

Elad: Outside of either board members or venture investors, how else would you go about sourcing an executive? Would you use a recruiting firm?

Keith: I would. For senior executives, executive recruiters can be very beneficial. And what I mean by that is if it's a C-level officer, or a VP or above, executive recruiters really know how to surface candidates. They don't know how to get you directors or more junior managers. But if you're actually aiming at the high end, I think an executive recruiter can be very beneficial for two reasons: One, they have a network. They know who's on the market, who's looking around for new opportunities. They also know reputations. They've probably performed reference checks on these people before. And you can avail yourself of that.

Two, they will install some process. Just the discipline of having weekly meetings can accelerate your search. So I think that's a very good idea. I highly recommend it for senior hires. It's not that expensive in the grand scheme of things. You're talking about $100k, which, if you're hiring a great CFO or VP of engineering is totally worth it.

A lot of the VC firms that you may be working with also have internal executive recruiting and talent partners that are high-end executive recruiters, or were. So you can leverage them for free. For example, we meet with senior executives at companies as they're starting to think about moving on. And we will figure out what their criteria and skills are and try to repackage them and recycle them into portfolio companies. So that can be a free way of jump-starting the process, which is not a bad place to start.

In addition, these days, use social media like Twitter. You know, if your company is doing really well, post that you're hiring a CFO. You never know who responds that you might have been afraid to approach. I see some of our companies having great success with tweets about "I've got this great opportunity." So there's a lot of room for creativity as well. But I think the basic blocking and tackling of using an executive recruiter can work.

Now, there are some disadvantages of using an executive recruiter that are worth highlighting. Their incentive is to close a deal; they get paid when you hire somebody. So they're going to want for you to hire somebody. And they may, if they're not an awesome executive recruiter, be biased toward people who are easier to close. Just classic incentive alignment. They will find people that are easier to close than your dream candidate. Your job as a CEO is to get your dream candidate, and it may take you a year to get your dream candidate sometimes. So there is a little bit of a misalignment there that's worth tracking.

However you source candidates, one key criteria for any executive is their ability to attract and become a magnet for talent. So when you're doing reference checks, you really want to understand: Does this person have a pool of amazing people that will want to join a company? Can they immediately upgrade the entire talent of the organization because they're so talented that other smart people really want to work with them?

That's something you can tell from reference checks. And you should thoroughly do reference checks on executives, without fail. There are sometimes excuses why individual contributors don't get reference-checked to death. But with executives, there's no reason ever for hiring someone without thorough reference checks.

So, when you talk to various colleagues of this person, one of the things you should always ask is, "If this person joined my company, would you join?" And yeah, people may say, "I'm retired" or "I'm a VC now," and all these reasons. But fundamentally you should hear in their voice, "Absolutely, yes." At least some of the time. It doesn't have to be a hundred percent of the time, but you want to hear that. And if you don't hear that spark, there's probably something there that's worth really probing into.

Elad: One of the things that I tell founders often is that they should give themselves permission to screw up when making an executive hire, because I think fear really stymies or prevents people from going ahead and doing it. What do you think are signs that somebody is working or not working out as an executive, and how quickly can you actually tell?

Keith: Usually for an executive, it's pretty reasonable to know in 30 days, certainly by 60. It does depend upon the complexity of the business. Some businesses are incredibly complex, like, let's say, Opendoor, where even the best executives in the world take a little bit of time to really master how everything connects. But typically executives are super savvy. The pattern recognition that they've developed over their careers enables them to cut to the chase quite quickly. And if you see them struggling early, it's often a major red flag.

Now, that said, your job as CEO or founder is to help them be successful. I think taking the obligation personally and doing everything in your power to make your new executive successful is part of your job. And some founders don't do that. They just assume, "I've hired this person and this person will get up to speed and start doing things." But I think carving out 10, 15, maybe 20 percent of your calendar to help make this new executive successful is an incredible investment actually, with very high dividends.

Because there is some expense. If you're wrong, there is definitely some pain and friction in replacing the person. That said, it's rarely fatal. Lots of companies, lots of founders, have made mistakes at the executive level, and upgraded. So for example, Mark Zuckerberg basically replaced his entire management team starting in 2007. By 2007, Facebook was a very successful platform and company. But there is literally nobody left on the executive team that was an executive in 2007.

So clearly you can constantly look to improve. You don't have to find the magical solution right away. If you aim for zero-defect hiring, it's a little bit like zero-defect decision-making: you're probably too conservative. We teach, and I subscribe to the view, that you want to pull the trigger on an initiative or an executive hire when you're about 70 percent confident that it's the right decision. Below 50 percent is kind of reckless. But if you go for 100 percent, you're waiting too long and you're probably losing candidates. Your false positive rate may be low, but your false negative rate is going to be very bad, too. And a lot of people hiring don't track their false negative rate of people they didn't get that they should have gotten.

Elad: Are there any early signs of somebody not working out?

Keith: Yeah, usually the signs are that they don't take ownership of decisions. Now that can be somewhat CEO- and founder-driven, too. Sometimes giving them license to start doing stuff requires a direct conversation. They may be a little bit too nervous of rocking the boat. So that's one, they're too passive, in effect.

The other is when people start circumnavigating around them and back to you with problems. That can be a sign of two things: It can be a sign that the executive isn't doing well. It can also be a sign that you made a political transformation, which isn't the easiest to disentangle. Obviously if you made a significant leadership change, there will be people who want to work within the old regime. And you may see some of that show up on your desk, so to speak. But often it's also a sign that the executive isn't doing well when people are still coming to you to problem-solve in areas that the executive should be managing.

Ultimately, the way I grade people is pretty subtle. You can usually look around an office, especially if it's an open office, and see who's coming to people's desks. The people who are thriving—at any level, junior to senior—tend to have people approaching their desk all the time. Because it basically means that someone is going out of their way because they believe that this person can be helpful. And so insofar as people start going to this executive frequently, even people beyond the organization that the person is managing start approaching them and working with them and meeting with them, those are really positive signals.

Another lesson that I learned from Brian Chesky—one way to think about when to upgrade executives—is that a really great executive is about six to twelve months ahead of the curve. They're already planning for and acting on things that are going to be important six to twelve months in the future. A decent executive is delivering in real time, now to one to three months in advance.

So you can start measuring your executives that way. Are they seeing around the corners of whatever they need to? Because not everything can be changed overnight. So let's say you needed fifty more engineers. You can't hire fifty engineers tomorrow. But a great VP of engineering or someone more senior may realize that the strategy requires us to have fifty more engineers, or there's no way we're going to be able to deliver on what we need to deliver. So they start recruiting a year in advance. Things like that.

Elad: They're really thinking far ahead on the curve. I guess the flip side of that, though, is the exec who's five years ahead of where the company should be.

Keith: Yeah, that doesn't work. That's why I think the six to twelve months is about right. One to three months, you can leave them in place but they're probably not ideal. Six to twelve months is a superb executive.

And it may look flawless. You actually have to know what's going on very precisely. To many people in the organization, the executive may just look flawless, because they always have an answer. That's partially because they're six to twelve months ahead in their own brain. They know what's going to break. They know what's going to take time to fix. And so by the time it starts showing up in the organization, they can say, "Aha, we'll just do this, this, and this."

It's like great software architects for companies. When they have scaling issues, they already have their silver bullets in their pocket. They've already thought through, "If we went on Oprah today and got 10X the amount of traffic concurrently, what would we do? I'd do this first. I'd throw this CDN at it, then I would do this. And I'd have this hardware over here. Servers take long lag time, so I'd have to have those." They have all that stuff in the back of their brain.

It's just like that for business problems. Under the worst possible circumstances or the best possible circumstances that I foresee in the next three to twelve months, what are the lead times associated with those various things? So I have those tools at my disposal when I need them, and I can just snap my fingers.

Elad: How many mistakes can you tolerate in executive hiring? Is it a certain number per role? Is it a certain number of executive mistakes per year?

Keith: I think it's about one. You're only going to add so many executives. Most companies are probably adding one to three in a compressed period of time. If you start having multiple mistakes, I think there may be something wrong in your process. One is perfectly normal and natural. But if you start seeing multiple, then I would think through, "What am I doing wrong?"

Elad: And by "multiple," do you mean over a certain period of time? Because every 12–18 months, many companies have to upgrade their team if they're growing very fast. And some of those execs will continue to go with that growth, but some will also break over time.

Keith: Let's say, in an eighteen-month or two-year time frame, one clear mistake. There's a difference between a mistake and someone who doesn't scale. I would separate those into two camps. So the mistake is, "Oh my god, I just need to make a change. This wasn't the right decision." That's something you only want to do about once.

The person who's not scaling to the new level of complexity of the business and the size of the team and the different kinds of problems, that's different—that's not necessarily a mistake. You would possibly have made the same decision if you had the same information you have now. Whereas the mistake, if you had the same information, you would not go back and make the same decision. So that one, you definitely want to limit to one digit if you can.

"The people who are thriving—at any level, junior to senior—tend to have people approaching their desk all the time."

—Keith Rabois

The scale and upgrade is also a function of the growth rate of the company. So the faster the company is growing, the velocity of that change has a different slope. And the executive's learning curve may be below that slope. Then you might have to make a change.

Elad: Now let's say that you've built out your executive team as a CEO. There's a huge transition when going from 20 or 50 people to hundreds as CEO, in terms of how you actually manage your own team. How do you think a CEO should think of their team overall? Who should report to the CEO, and who should not report to the CEO?

Keith: It's a great question, and I don't think there's a paradigmatic answer that applies to all companies. It depends upon what the company does and where what I call the seams in the business are.

Depending upon what types of decisions have trade-offs, you want those—the trade-off decisions—to be made very infrequently by the CEO. You don't want to have to be a tiebreaker every day, or every week even. Once a month or once a quarter, it's fine to tiebreak between different parts of the organization. But anything more frequent than that, you need to unify the functions underneath somebody. So that's one thing I would look for.

Second thing is just skills. Different executives come with different strengths and weaknesses. And sometimes, even if on paper you draw a perfect org chart, an executive doesn't have a particular skill but is awesome at other things. So you might make some compromises in your org design to reflect their strengths.

For example, I have a friend who's a leading product guy who happens to understand biz dev and partnerships really well. That's actually an unusual combination. So if he was a senior executive, I would throw partnerships and complicated negotiations with music studios or something like that under product, even though that would not be the standard design. He's just extraordinarily good at it. So there are times when you can do that.

It does require a diagnosis of your organization. Also, what are the key risks to the business? What are the most important two or three things? You want the things that are one, two, or three to report to the CEO. Fundamentally, what makes or breaks the company should probably be reporting to the CEO. Because ultimately the CEO is responsible and accountable for everything. So if you do the rank prioritization of what gets you from point A to super successful, what are the two or three key levers? You want those two or three levers pretty close to your span of control.

Elad: What do you think is the right number of reports? Obviously it's contextual and it varies by the skillset and all the rest. I'm just curious roughly what you think is a ballpark.

Keith: The traditional advice derives from High Output Management—you know, Andy Grove in 1982—which is at most seven. Or five. Five or seven. The reason why is that you want to do a certain number of 1:1s at a weekly pace, and you want to do about one a day. So that means five or seven or something like that. I think if you can get down to three to five, that's ideal. If you have to go four to seven, that's definitely possible to scale. So anywhere in those ranges can work.

Elad: I feel like a lot of the executive teams I see these days have a dozen people reporting into the CEO.

Keith: That's crazy. That's totally crazy. That being said, you may have to deal with that for a period of time as you're recruiting someone to unify some functions.

For example, there was a point in time at Square where I had somewhere between 11 and 13. And, you know, Jack was furious with me about it. My board was furious with me about it. And I was totally aware that it was not a sustainable situation. But rather than artificially unify things, I wanted to find people that would start bringing together some of those direct reports. And I eventually did. But I figured rather than make a mistake and have someone report to someone where they wouldn't be able to create value, I would deal with it on a temporary basis. But I would urgently be recruiting.

So, I think you can have periods of time—measured in months, not years—where you violate the rules. But that becomes your number-one priority: to stop violating those rules.

Elad: I think the biggest fear that founders have when consolidating their teams is flight risk. They think that if they layer somebody or somebody else comes in, employees will leave. What do you view as the best ways to mitigate that? Do you view that as a real issue, or is it okay if that person ends up leaving?

Keith: It is a definite concern, and I think it is the biggest reason a lot of founders procrastinate. The standard I was taught, which I subscribe to, is you only want to layer someone if the person above them is clearly superior.

One of the techniques if you have too many direct reports is to move somebody to report to another person that's already in the organization. The problem is, unless there's a clear separation between them, it just doesn't work. It's not fair, and it will create flight risk. But if there is a clear separation, where the performance is differentiated enough—looking at both the way you measure it and how other people perceive the two executives—then I think that can be a smart move. And then you don't have the organ-transplant issue of bringing in a new executive. So that's possible, but there has to be a significant delta in performance. If it's even a debatable delta in performance, it's not a good idea to ask somebody to report to someone else.

If you're going to hire someone externally, I think generally the way to retain people who are performing and who you really want to retain is to hire someone that they can learn from. And if that's true, a lot of well-motivated people will stay. Where they don't perceive that they can learn from the new executive, it may be better for them, psychologically or professionally, to go somewhere else and get on a steep learning curve again. So it does depend. But I don't think it's a reason to avoid hiring.

At the end of the day, if one of those 11 or 12 executives is so valuable to you, you can do a couple things. One is to put them on a mentoring path and try to teach them how to accelerate their growth so that they can handle the larger function. But it depends on the company's velocity whether that's possible. It also requires you to have a network of mentors that you can throw at this problem, and you can't do it with multiple executives at the same time. So if I had a high-potential VP of finance and I really wanted to groom him to be CFO, it's possible to do that rather than layering him behind the CFO. But it takes a lot of energy. I can't do that with my director of product, my director of engineering, and my VP of finance at the same time.

"The way to retain people who are performing and who you really want to retain is to hire someone that they can learn from."

— Keith Rabois

Elad: How should the CEO run their own team meeting?

Keith: That's a great question, because I think everybody gets frustrated by this topic at some point. One of the lessons I've learned is the executive team meeting is not necessarily just for the CEO. It's actually often more important and more valuable to the executives that participate in the meeting. They get to be on a stage with their peers. They get to understand what's going on laterally in the organization so they can make smarter and better decisions.

The meeting may not be particularly insightful to you, because you're doing 1:1s with all these executives and functional organizations. You may know everything that comes up in this meeting, and you probably should. But it's the debate or dialogue or the lateral sharing of information that makes that meeting constructive.

I think a lot of CEOs get frustrated because the meeting isn't adding value to them. But they forget that it's adding value to the three or four or five other people there. And if you can make your executives more successful with an hour of your time or two hours of your time, that's totally worth doing. It's a classic high-leverage activity.

Elad: What do you think is a great agenda?

Keith: I think limiting it to about three topics. There's information sharing, but then there's discussion and debate topics that are actionable. And I think people's attention span sort of wanes if you have too many debates at the same time.

Some organizations allocate a full day to this, and they go very deep. I'm not sure that's a great idea. It does depend upon how tightly aligned your organization needs to be to function well. I tend to think one to three hours is more than sufficient, especially if you have tools in place—metrics tools, KPIs, dashboards—so that everybody really understands the business before they've even shown up to the meeting.

In that case, I tend to prefer circulating notes the night before. They can be bullet point-style, using the three Ps—plans, progress, problems—and shared in advance, so that people's brains are chewing on what's going on. And then there's a couple discussion topics that affect the organization, or where the CEO wants broader input because he or she doesn't actually know what the right answer is.

Elad: The other thing I've noticed is that early on in the life of a company, a lot of topics exist in the one executive team meeting. And then later they start to get split out. There's a rev force and metrics meeting that runs separately, which includes a subset of the executives. Plus there's a broader team to talk about progress in the business, which may differ from some of those strategic topics in the executive team meeting.

Keith: Yeah, sometimes you separate out strategic topics that are going to be controversial, or topics that don't necessarily have right answers but are a question of trade-offs. That's different from an operating review, which is: What are our current KPIs? How well are we doing? What's the rate of progress? What are the different things we should be doing? Sometimes you'll have the first meeting run by the CEO and the second meeting run by the COO or equivalent officer. ■

This interview has been edited and condensed for clarity.

DO YOU NEED A COO?

Ten years ago, if you were the founder of a high-growth company it was reasonably likely that your investors would want to bring in "adult supervision" as CEO to run your company. This has shifted, in recent years, to a slate of COO hires, following the example set by Facebook with the successful run of Sheryl Sandberg. It is now much more likely for a breakout high-growth company to hire a COO to support the company founders, rather than a CEO to replace them.[32]

Box, Facebook, Stripe, Square, Twitter, and Yelp are all companies that chose at one time or another to hire a COO as a complement to the founders, rather than replace the CEO with a "gray-haired professional operator."[33]

WHY A COO?

Hiring a COO is not about adding a title to your org chart, but rather finding the background and experience you are looking for. Optimally, you want someone who will come in to complement, operationalize, and execute your vision as a founder. Many technical or product-focused founders want to (and should) remain focused on the product and overall market strategy. In parallel, the COO would build out and manage areas that the founders lack interest or experience in, or simply don't have the bandwidth to oversee.

The responsibilities of a COO, for example, might include:

1. **Adding executive bandwidth.** The COO can serve as a business partner for technical or product-focused founders.

2. **Scaling the company.** High-growth companies have special needs around scaling and implementing simple processes (e.g., recruiting infrastructure, corporate governance, etc.).

3. **Building out the executive team and organizational scaffold.** COOs are often responsible for executives and teams in areas founders don't understand well (e.g., finance, accounting, and sales). They can help in screening and hiring executives for product, engineering, and marketing as well.

4. **Taking on the areas founders don't have time for, are poorly suited for, or don't want to focus on.** Typically, a COO takes on responsibility for ongoing management of the "business side" (corporate development/M&A, business development, sales,

---

[32] If a company is not a true breakout, it might be hard to hire a COO of the same caliber that you could get in a CEO—i.e., there are still great executives out there holding out for a CEO role that would not be willing to do anything else.

[33] Other interesting early examples include Microsoft, where Bill Gates in the 1980s had seasoned "presidents" working for him, and Oracle, where Larry Ellison has gone through various COOs over the years. Gates, of course, only brought in venture money after Microsoft was profitable, so he had sufficient control of the company to not worry about being replaced.

HR, recruiting, etc.), while the founders continue to focus on product, design, and engineering (e.g., Mark Zuckerberg's focus on product at Facebook). There are some counterexamples of this too where the CEO wants to be sales focused and hires in a product-centric COO.

5. **Shaping the culture for the next phase of the company's life.** Sheryl Sandberg has impacted how Facebook is run across the entire organization by, for example, bringing a culture of people development and managerial excellence.

WHY NOT A COO?

All growing companies need to build out their executive teams, as well as the ability and expertise to scale. That can be done by hiring or promoting a set of people who, in sum, complement the founders and allow the company to grow rapidly and effectively. It is not necessary that one of these team members have the COO title. For example, prior to Polyvore's acquisition by Yahoo!, the company's CFO owned multiple areas beyond traditional finance.

Additionally, the COO title sets a very high bar for who you hire for the role.[34] You can't really hire above the COO later like you could with a VP, which means losing some flexibility in your future organizational evolution as the company goes from, say, 100 to 5,000 people. If the COO is out of her depth, she often won't accept a demotion to VP and will leave instead.[35]

HOW DO YOU CHOOSE A COO?

For COO, you optimally want someone strong enough to be CEO of a company, or at least someone with solid general management or key functional experience. Sheryl Sandberg interviewed for other CEO roles before accepting COO of Facebook. Similarly, Box's COO, Dan Levin, was a CEO or president of two companies and a GM at Intuit before joining Box. You want someone so excited by your company's vision and opportunity that she is willing to give up some of the perceived upside of being a general manager or CEO elsewhere to join your company.

Additional criteria to look for are:

1. **Maturity and lack of ego.** Look for a seasoned executive who is willing to suppress her own ego to partner with, and execute, a founder's vision.

---

34 Some companies will first hire someone with the "general manager" title and then convert him to COO later. This allows them to ensure that hire's fit and capabilities prior to committing to him as COO.

35 Of course, another option is to replace yourself as CEO instead. Reid Hoffman wrote a great piece about this topic; see the link on eladgil.com. [*http://www.reidhoffman.org/if-why-and-how-founders-should-hire-a-professional-ceo/*]

2. **Chemistry with founders & CEO.** If the COO cannot mind-meld with the company founders, conflicts and a bad ending to the relationship are on their way.

3. **Past experience scaling a company or organization.** Managing a 1,000-person team is very different from growing something from 20 to 1,000 people. Look for someone who has dealt with hypergrowth or rapid growth in the past if you need help scaling quickly (versus just building out functions). Claire Hughes Johnson scaled operations and business teams at Google before doing so at Stripe.

4. **Entrepreneurial mindset.** Optimally, you want someone who has both operated at scale and worked in a startup environment (or scaled something from scratch at a larger company).

5. **Functional expertise.** A COO hire should have previously run a reasonable subset of the functions you want her to own initially at your company.

6. **Ability to hire.** This person will be building out a chunk of your company's organizational skeleton. You need someone who can hire well and manage executives herself.

7. **Someone you can learn from.** As a first-time founder or manager, you want a COO who can teach you about management or other areas. Bill Gates famously said that he often hired senior executives so that he could learn from them.

8. **Process focus.** The optimal COO candidate can bring lightweight processes or best practices from other companies, and be smart about how to craft new ones for your company.

Finally, when hiring a COO, you should have a clear sense of what responsibilities you want to keep as founder (e.g., design, product, marketing, engineering) and what you are willing to truly delegate (e.g., business development, sales, corporate development, finance, HR, operations, etc.). Without that clarity, you may be setting yourself up for failure from the start. You should also remember that a COO does not necessarily need to run everything you don't. For example, at Microsoft, Gates ran product, Steve Ballmer ran sales, and Bob Herbold as COO ran finance, HR, marketing, PR, and other areas.[36]

I don't think every company needs a COO; a well-rounded executive or leadership team may allow you to do without one. However, if you do decide that you need the management chops and experience of a COO-caliber candidate, proceed with the hiring process carefully and deliberately.[37]

---

[36] See "The Secrets of Working With Bill Gates." Link on eladgil.com. [*https://www.americanexpress.com/us/small-business/openforum/articles/the-secrets-of-working-with-bill-gates/*]

[37] Thanks to Aaron Levie, Jess Lee, and Keith Rabois for reviewing and providing feedback on the original version of this post on eladgil.com. [*http://blog.eladgil.com/2013/02/should-you-hire-coo.html*]

"You want someone who will come in to complement, operationalize, and execute your vision as a founder."

—Elad Gil

HIRING A COO

An interview with Aaron Levie

Aaron Levie is Chief Executive Officer, cofounder and chairman at Box, which he launched in 2005 with CFO and cofounder Dylan Smith. He is the visionary behind the Box product and platform strategy. Aaron is sought out by many founders on topics of scaling. Aaron attended the University of Southern California from 2003 to 2005 before leaving to found Box.

I spoke with Aaron Levie about the COO question—that is, whether (and when) to add a chief operating officer to your executive roster. Five years after Aaron and Dylan founded Box, they brought on Dan Levin as COO, in 2010, so I was eager to ask him more about that transition.

Levie's a big proponent of adding to the leadership team, so I asked him to weigh in on the merits of hiring a COO and share a little bit about how the decision played out at Box.

Elad Gil:
You were the driving force behind hiring a COO for Box back in 2010. Why did you decide to do it on your end? Do founders need to reframe how they think about the COO question?

Aaron Levie:
A lot of times, at the board level, a conversation will start with, "Do we have the right CEO?" And especially for early founders, you ask yourself that question. "Am I going to be a good CEO? Am I going to be able to scale the company?" But when you ask that kind of question, you end up defining what a CEO is in unnecessarily strict terms. Whereas, actually, the most important job of a CEO is just to make sure that the company succeeds. So if there's a whole chunk of work that you're not good at, you don't personally have to be good at it to be a good CEO. You have to make sure the company is good at it to be a good CEO.

Early on, when we were scaling Box at 20 or 30 employees, we came to this question. And I asked myself, "Do I look like these other CEOs that have scaled big companies?" A lot of times it didn't feel like I was like them. I focus on a very different set of things. I don't really like all the stuff that they like to do. But I ended up realizing that it was actually just my job to make sure that we got all of the problems solved, not that I had to personally solve them all.

I end up seeing a lot of companies make this mistake—and it's obviously happening much less these days than in the '90s and early 2000s—where you shoot the founder and then bring in an experienced CEO. Imagine all the better outcomes we would have if those companies actually kept their founders focused on what they're great at, and then added counterparts to help them build the business.

Elad: So you see the COO as a counterpart to the CEO. How can leaders go about defining the role in concrete terms?

Aaron: I think COO is probably one of the most generalized jobs, but ultimately one of the most specific to the individual and to the company. Unlike CMO or head of product or whatever, where generally you know what's in their purview, COO is highly variable. If you found five companies with COOs, the job descriptions of those COOs, or the things that they were responsible for, would be different by each company. The way that Sheryl Sandberg operates at Facebook is likely different than how the COO at Yelp operates, which is different than how the COO at Box operates. So first, I would just dispel the notion that COO is one particular type of job or type of function.

I ended up bringing on a COO because I wanted somebody who had a depth of experience in scaling up companies and organizations and working in large environments, to be a sort of counterpart as we were building the business. I cofounded the company with a friend from college, and neither of us had any kind of real scale experience. So by bringing in a COO who had managed a thousand- or multi-thousand-person organization and had managed multiple hundreds of millions of dollars of revenue for a very large business, we could bring on experience in all the sorts of disciplines we were looking for.

In our particular situation, the COO that we brought on was formerly a general manager of a large division of Intuit, and a CEO prior to that. So he had a lot of experience owning all the major functions of an organization. He had a particular interest in things like talent development, organization design, and scaling up of organizations—so a very people-oriented COO.

In general, we created a structure where he really owned building up the company and really owned building up the individual organizations. And then my job was focusing on strategy and where we want to go over the long run. I stayed highly tuned toward things like the product and the product strategy.

Elad: That makes a lot of sense. It seems like many people claim that the COO role is sales and the CEO handles product and engineering. But there are so many counterexamples. So that really resonates with what you're saying: each company is different.

Aaron: Yeah, I think that my best description of why and when to get a COO is this: If you as the CEO are uniquely strong in a couple of areas, and you want to supplement or complement those areas—if you need to fill the gaps—consider a COO.

No matter what, your business needs to have a well-running set of organizations. And if you're not interested in managing those organizations, or you don't have the bandwidth, then you need some kind of counterpart to help you.

If you're a very sales-oriented founder, then you might get somebody to augment on the product side. If you're a very product-oriented founder, you might get somebody to augment on the sales side. If you're a very sales- and product-oriented founder, you might get somebody to augment you on the pure operational infrastructure side. There are so many different flavors of what this means. In most cases, it's actually just as important to understand and be clear about what the CEO does as it is to understand what the COO does.

"I ended up realizing that it was actually just my job to make sure that we got all of the problems solved, not that I had to personally solve them all."

—Aaron Levie

Aaron: I think it doesn't make sense until there's some sort of inflection from a growth standpoint. The idea is not to hand a COO random busywork from around the company. Instead, consider some key criteria: Are you scaling at a rate where your own time is now spent primarily on pure operational activities—like hiring and building up goal-setting structures and performance reviews and helping people with organizational issues and process? Is that pulling you away from things like your product strategy and product design or working with customers, for instance? You have to solve all those problems either way, and at some point in the inflection curve, it just makes more sense to get a partner to help you with the operational stuff.

In some companies, that could be when you hire your twelfth employee. In some companies, if you're growing at a steady rate, instead of instantaneously, that could be once you reach a couple hundred people. You might not need it very early on. So I think a lot of it is the rate of change of the business. Add the COO role when the rate of change is reaching some kind of escape velocity.

Elad: What background did you want in a COO? You mentioned that for other roles it's very clear—if you're hiring, say, a VP of product, you're looking for very specific experience. But what would you recommend people look for in particular in COO candidates?

Aaron: Again, you have to first ask yourself either: What are you not good at, or: Where are you spending time that you don't want to be spending time? And you have to make sure that there's a surface area that is large enough for a COO. If you're just finding yourself in a lot of legal conversations or finance conversations that you don't want to be in, then really what you need is a general counsel or an attorney, or a CFO or head of finance.

So the first thing is to actually identify the areas where you're going to want a partner in helping you scale. From there—and this is one of those things where you should go on a mountain and light some candles and really tap into your inner self—honestly answer some key questions. What are you really good at? What do you want to get better at? And what things aren't going to be a competitive advantage for you to personally get good at? Because you can't be great at everything.

Elad: What did your list look like? How did you get started with the search?

Aaron: For me, the list was a bunch of more generalizable things, like management and organization development and adding processes to the company. Those were things that I was uniquely bad at. As soon as we were at 40 or 50 people and we decided we really wanted to scale the business, we realized that it was going to require a different kind of mindset and mentality than what I had and what my cofounder had.

In our COO search, we actually meandered a little bit. We thought maybe we wanted a chief revenue officer, but then we realized that we had, again, a more generalizable issue around a lot of the operational stuff. So ultimately we came up with a job spec that was about getting somebody in here that had seen a couple thousand people, had seen a few hundred million dollars in revenue. From a job spec standpoint, it was: Has seen scale, has managed scale, has driven very large revenue targets, has been in a somewhat operationally complex, or at least multifaceted, environment—so sales, marketing, customer success, product, engineering, etc. We wanted someone who knew their way around lots of different parts of the business.

Once we found somebody with all that, and who was a great cultural fit, the next question was, can I actually get along with them? Can we divide and conquer in a very collaborative way? Being a COO at times can be a very thankless job, where you have to leave your ego aside to some extent. So you have to make sure that you have a very collaborative structure, and that each person deeply respects the other person. You have to make sure it's somebody that you do want to spend a lot of time with—because you're going to be in the trenches with that person.

When you add up all those factors, it becomes one of those things where there's a whole bunch of people you'll have big question marks around, and then there might be one or two people where you think, "Okay, this really fits." And you want to wait for the person that really fits.

Elad: How did you figure out who was the right person for you? What was your hiring and interviewing process?

Aaron: We had a very roundabout way of doing this, so I don't think that my experience is a lesson that can be replicated easily. We had an advisor that was introduced to us by a board member. Through working with that advisor, I don't know, a dozen or so times, I got the sense that there was a whole world of management and building companies out there that I had never really imagined. Because I was a very product-focused person. I thought, you just build a product and everything falls into place from there. And just the vocabulary this advisor was using and the concepts that he was imparting on me—it was like learning a completely new trade. And I realized that we really needed to get better at this kind of stuff.

And so we actually brought this advisor, Dan Levin, onto our board. Then we kicked off a search for a CRO/COO, and after three or four months of that search, we'd met a whole bunch of people. And every single time, we realized that I didn't get along as well with any of those people as I did with Dan.

I ultimately spent two or three months just trying to convince him to join. So it was probably six-plus months, or maybe nine months, from meeting him to having him join as COO. But it was hundreds of hours of interactions between me and executives and the board and him.

Elad: Are there things that you think CEOs should never give away? For example, are there certain things at all-hands meetings that only the CEO should ever talk about? Should the CEO always run board meetings?

Aaron: Again, this totally comes down to what the CEO is good at versus just what the COO is good at. I don't think there's any rule here that I've seen. Our COO runs the executive staff meeting. I think it's probably indistinguishable who runs our board meeting between me, our COO, and our CFO.

The most important thing is just to make it clear who owns what. That's a whole element of discipline around all of this: What jobs and what deci-

"You have to make sure it's somebody that you do want to spend a lot of time with—because you're going to be in the trenches with that person."

— Aaron Levie

sions do you separate between the two functions? And how do you make that clear to as many people as possible in the organization so it's not confusing?

For us, we basically said, "If you have a people-related issue, if you have an organization-related issue, if you have a process issue, you go to Dan." And in fact, from a functional reporting standpoint, most of the executive team, except for my cofounder, actually report to Dan. On the other hand, if you have a major strategic thing, or if it's product-related or if it's brand-related, then I'm going to own that and get involved in that.

So this means that at times, as an executive at Box, you have to go to one person about one thing and a different person about a different thing. But it means that, when it comes to doing your job, you are hopefully getting a non-diluted experience. Dan is far, far, far better at all the things that he is good at than I am, and I have a fairly long-term view around the strategy side that has ended up being helpful as well.

Elad: Is there anything specific that you felt was important that you did when you onboarded Dan as COO, or anything that you wish you'd done differently?

Aaron: This was a long time ago! But I'll say something kind of generic that would apply to almost any executive: you need a COO to deeply integrate into the company as quickly as possible. In the first 30 days, they should go and interview every single employee that they can get their hands on—

about what's working, what's not working, what they want to see improved, where they want to take the business. The key is to just get very, very integrated into the culture, and get to know the individuals involved, in the first 30 to 60 days.

Having some early wins is certainly helpful too. So somewhere in the 60- to 90-day time period, the new COO should implement a few things that make everybody go, "Oh wow, this is cool. This is helping. We now have this new process that makes us perform a lot better and has reduced wasted effort in the wrong areas." Having some early wins to show immediate value, and getting to know the company and the culture—that's all super important early on.

But again, this stuff breaks down because of swim lanes more than anything. The key is just to be crystal clear about what each person is going to own and ensure that you have a process for resolving things when there is conflict or overlap or a gray area. Because there will always be some gray areas—it's not like it works perfectly. But starting with as much clarity as possible is incredibly important.

Elad: Last question before we wrap up: We've been proceeding from the assumption that a founder wants to stay on as CEO. But when should founders acknowledge that they don't want to keep going, or that they shouldn't keep going?

Aaron: My thing is this: Founders can get burned out for two reasons—I mean, probably a hundred reasons, but let's just say there's two for now. One reason is that you're tired. You just aren't as passionate about the problem space anymore, and you want to go off and do something completely different or take some time off. That's scenario one, and realistically it probably happens just as much as scenario two.

But I think sometimes it can get confused with scenario two, which is when you are doing a set of things that you no longer like to do, and you have not found a way to get them off your plate. You haven't found a way to get back to focusing on the thing that you are uniquely passionate about. If I spent 90% of my time in performance-review meetings and organization meetings and compensation-decision meetings, I would be burned out and say, "This is not what I want to do."

The key is to not conflate what you are doing on a daily basis with falling out of passion with the overall mission. But a lot of times you end up doing that if you don't have any way to complement your skills.

So my recommendation to anyone who's running into that situation would be to try a COO first. See if the desire to stop has to do with dreading your day-to-day activities, or if it's actually where you are in life. ■

EXECUTIVE TITLES AND PRAGMATISM

Companies tend to have two philosophies on titles: The Google approach, which Facebook copied, was to give low titles to people as they joined. People who were VPs at Yahoo! or eBay joined Google as directors or manager: while people who were VPs at small startups may have joined as individual contributors or junior managers. The alternative approach is to give everyone big titles to partially compensate them for the risk of joining an early-stage company. Neither approach is right or wrong, and both have trade-offs; you should just choose one and apply it consistently. I personally favor the "try to keep titles low" approach for as long as possible, as I think it decreases hierarchy and prevents people from valuing a VP's opinions more than a non-VP's.

When hiring executives, you'll find that candidates may or may not be willing to capitulate on title. By joining a startup, they could be leaving millions of dollars on the table and will argue that a step up in title helps to compensate for the risk (e.g., a director from Google will want to join your startup as a VP or maybe COO, CMO, etc.).

One way to deal with this is to negotiate a vague title—e.g, "Head of Sales" versus "VP of Sales," or "General Manager" rather than "COO"—or agree to defer the title choice to a later date. You can also agree that if the person performs at the level of the title they want, then when you roll out titles for the broader team they will get that VP or COO role.

Finally, remember that it is difficult to hire someone above a person with a CXO title. That is, you can hire an SVP, EVP, or COO above a VP of Sales. But if you make someone who should have been VP of sales the COO, you are likely to have to let her go (or offer a demotion that will likely lead her to quit) if you want to hire above her one day. Similarly, a director-level title is easier to hire over than a VP-level one, although both are doable.

FIRING EXECUTIVES

It is always painful to let people go. When you fire an executive, it can be hard not only on you and the executive but also on his entire organization.[38] There are some steps you can take, though, to minimize the uncertainty and confusion that come along with these difficult decisions.

Before you let an executive go, you should make sure to have the following in place:

1. **Discuss it with your board.** Your board of directors will want to be aware of any key executive changes before you make them. It is possible one or more of your board members has worked with the executive before, or referred them to you.

---

38 See related post by Ben Horowitz. Link on eladgil.com. [*https://a16z.com/2011/08/24/preparing-to-fire-an-executive/*]

It is best to call each board member 1:1, explain to them why you want to make the change and how you plan to do it (including a potential transition plan), and if needed the details of any severance package. Once you have spoken to people 1:1 you can do a follow up board call if needed in the case that active discussion is necessary.

2. **All the paperwork for the separation agreement with the executive.** Your lawyers can prepare this for you. You should also decide on the severance you'll be offering and other details up front.

It is sometimes helpful to write out a script for the discussion. Whatever you say, it's important that you:
- Be firm. This is a done deal.
- Be professional.
- Be clear on your reasoning.

If you have been managing your employee well, this should not be a big surprise to him. That is, you should already have had a series of conversations around fit, responsibilities, alignment, etc.

3. **Transition plan.** Who will manage all of this person's reports? Make sure to clearly communicate whether this change to a new manager is a short-term one, an interim solution, or a permanent change.

4. **Communication plan.** You should have a clear view of what will be communicated when, and to whom on the team. If the person (or your company) are especially high profile you will also want to have reactive press ready to go. Alternatively, you and the person being fired may negotiate on, or agree on, a common story to be shared with the press or in a tweet. Don't be petty. Allow the executive to leave with dignity and reputation intact.

For example, a communication plan when letting go of Bob, VP of marketing, might look like the below. This is an idealized plan and you should not expect things to necessarily go so smoothly.

- Tuesday, 9am: Meet with Bob and inform him that he's being let go. Discuss how to position this with others in the company and agree on approach.

- Tuesday, 10am: Let your direct reports know that Bob has been let go. Explain concisely some background on the decision and provide clear guidelines on how your team should communicate it to their reports, exception handling, etc. Explain the transition plan—e.g., that Sarah, who runs sales, will also run marketing, and that this change is permanent. You should obviously have already discussed this with Sarah in advance.

- Tuesday, 11am: Along with Sarah, meet with the marketing team to let them know about the change.

- Tuesday, 11:30am: Email the company to let them know about the change. Explain the transition plan and the objectives for the team (if well-defined and consistent).

  If there are any concerns of impact to specific people on the marketing team, you or Sarah can meet with them to discuss, depending on the context and relationship.

- Friday weekly all-hands: Be ready to answer questions, with a well-prepped FAQ.

HOW TO HIRE GREAT BUSINESS DEVELOPMENT PEOPLE

Great business development (BD) people are hard to find. You may meet a smart, charismatic, articulate BD person who can't get anything done. Or a highly networked deal person who leaks value when he misses all the details of a deal and structures terrible terms. It can be hard to differentiate between what deals people actually accomplish versus what they take credit for in terms of a product's success.

So what should you look for in a BD person?

GREAT BUSINESS DEVELOPMENT PEOPLE

The best BD people are:

- **Smart people with lots of raw horsepower.** Smart, creative, and think well on their feet.

- **Articulate/good communicators.** Need to communicate well with both internal teams (engineers, PMs, lawyers, execs) as well as the customer or partner (which may include their legal, engineering, and deal people).

- **Creative/fearless in deal terms.** Push the envelope on what is possible and are willing to make a crazy ask of the partner or client. You never know what someone will give away until you ask.

- **Able to get shit done.** Have a history of closing multiple complex deals with creative or aggressive terms. One person who worked for me at Twitter closed three or four partnerships while he was a part-time intern working remotely during his school year.

- **Structured/can run a deal process.** Structure is underrated in deal people. You want someone great at shepherding all internal and external stakeholders through the various phases of a deal (ideation, pitching, negotiating, structuring, closing, implementing).[39] You want these people mining a list of prospects, aggressively framing a negotiation, and setting up internal prep meetings before calling external parties. Unstructured deal people create churn internally due to a lack of consensus on external gives or lack of planning for a negotiation.

- **Detail-oriented.** Reid Hoffman once told me he expected his deal people to read every word of every contract, including all the legal language. This allows them to catch all sorts of gotchas that are otherwise buried in unexpected ways and to think through the implications of what the contract says.

- **Part lawyer.** Able to pick up and grok key legal nuances, even without an overt legal background.

- **Good culture fit/put the company first.** You want your businesspeople, like all your employees, to put the company first. There are all sorts of ways businesspeople may benefit themselves rather than the company (more on this below).

- **Able to work well with others across the organization.**

- **Pragmatic and keep big picture in mind.** Figure out what is important, optimize for it (80:20 rule), and get the deal done. Don't optimize for little things that don't matter, except as a negotiation tactic. Similarly, some deals should not get done. Great deal people will take a step back and decide whether to walk away, and they won't try to force a deal to happen if it shouldn't. Some of the best "deals" are the ones that don't happen.

- **Able to understand partner and market needs.** Understand what partners really want (versus what they claim they want), as well as trends in the marketplace that may impact both their company's and as well as the partner's leverage and needs.

- **Tenacious.** Deals can take a long time and a lot of back and forth. Bad deal people give up toward the very end to "just close the deal" and may leak enormous amounts of value that they didn't need to give up.

- **Relentless.** Sometimes you need to keep knocking at a door over and over until someone finally answers.

- **Moral compass.** Like all employees, you want people who will do the right thing even if it is uncomfortable or against their self-interest to do so.

---

[39] Thanks for Marc Leibowitz for spelling out the various deal-making stages, as well as other ideas.

BAD BUSINESS DEVELOPMENT PEOPLE

Bad business development people may exhibit the following:

- **Great at selling, bad on follow-through.** Some BD people are charming, fun to talk to, and really smart. Unfortunately, they have terrible follow-through and can't seem to get anything closed. They may be full of empty excuses for why they had to give on a major term that is important to your company. The only way to screen these people out is reference checks, as they are great at selling, poor on substance. Raw charisma is drastically overrated by technical founders. Don't be fooled just because someone is friendly and charming.

- **Disorganized/unstructured.** Fly by the seat of their pants, don't send follow-ups, or communicate poorly internally. Needless meetings or internal churn often result.

- **Leak value.** Often overthink what is "fair" for the other side. Make too many assumptions about what is important to the other side and just give a lot of terms away. Or, they just want to close the deal at all costs versus thinking through what is actually good for the company they work for.

- **Don't think like an owner.** Bad deal people don't think like business owners. They treat the company's money or resources as not a big deal to use and will give away extra value in a negotiation because "it doesn't matter," "it's within 20%," or the like.

- **Don't think the details matter.** See above.

- **Outsource too much.** Bad deal people become too dependent on other company functions—for example, not understanding a legal term that comes up over and over because "that's Legal's problem." Sometimes terms important to the business are buried or hidden as legalese or "technical specs." A great deal person will ferret these out.

- **Optimize for themselves and their network versus the company.** As gatekeepers to external parties, some business development people may use this point of leverage to benefit themselves. They may build relationships at the expense of the company by being too easy on a deal so that the partner likes them. Or they may constantly network at external boondoggles and on panels to build their own reputations, rather than working.[40]

- **Display a cowboy mentality.** Some deal people go off and strike a deal, or mention terms to an external party that you can't back away from, without any internal discussion or approval. They may act defensive when questioned about this and feel they are "getting it done."

---

[40] Some external speaking or networking events may be useful to your company. But the businessperson should choose the small handful of events that really matter, and have specific goals for them, rather than just claiming "all exposure is good exposure."

- **Are emotional.** Deals have a lot of ups and downs—you need an even keel.

- **Spin things internally.** Deal people need to be able to "turn it off" when it comes to selling something internally to their boss, peers, or executive team. You need to hire people who won't BS or spin internally, even if it is sometimes their job to do it externally.

HOW TO SCREEN FOR A GREAT BUSINESS DEVELOPMENT PERSON

- **History of deals.** What deals have they themselves negotiated? How complex were the terms? What is an ask they received that no one else at the company believed they would get? What is a clever deal hack they pulled off? What impact did the deal actually have on the company?

- **References.** Deal people often have lots of friends, as their job is outwardly focused and they can be charismatic. They may give you a long list of meaningless references (e.g., friends at their current company, who actually don't know much about their work but think they are a "great person"). Get references from people who worked with them directly on deals. Back channel more information on them. Ask about the specific deals they worked on, how relentless and creative they were, and the tangible impact their deals had on the company. Did the terms end up working out or backfiring? Were there edge cases they did not think about that came back to bite? Did they champion a radical position that paid off big?

- **Follow-through.** How is their follow-through during the interview process? How structured are they? What approach do they take in negotiating compensation?

- **Culture.** What are they optimizing for? Title? Equity? Future growth? Something else? How do they fit in your culture? Businesspeople will be different from technical or product people in a number of ways, but they should still hold to your core cultural values.

A GREAT DEAL PERSON IS NOT USUALLY A GREAT PARTNER MANAGER

Don't expect the people who are great at thinking of and executing deals to be great partner managers (post-deal management). You will eventually need to find both types of people for your team.[41]

---

[41] Thanks to Marc Leibowitz, Clara Shih, and Kim Malone Scott for feedback, ideas, and comments on versions of this chapter. Read the original post at eladgil.com. [*http://blog.eladgil.com/2013/02/hiring-great-business-people-is-hard.html*]

An interview with Mariam Naficy

Mariam Naficy is the founder and CEO of Minted. She founded Minted to create a retailer that could stay fresh forever, using crowdsourcing and analytics to bring the best design to market faster than anyone. She has pioneered consumer internet models since 1998, when she cofounded the first online cosmetics retailer, Eve.com, which was sold for over $100 million. Mariam sits on the board of Yelp and Every Mother Counts. She is a Stanford Business School and Williams alumna.

Mariam Naficy knows a thing or two about scaling. Since the e-commerce site was launched in 2008, it has grown beyond custom stationery to sell limited edition art, housewares, wedding goods, and more—all created and curated by an ever-expanding global design community.

Naficy's latest venture has grown while maintaining a notably lean team, so I was eager to learn how she approached scaling, and what lessons she would share with entrepreneurs facing high-growth for the first time.

In the conversation that follows, she shares her insights into everything from how to hire GMs for new business units to if and when to tackle the technical debt that often accompanies rapid growth.

Elad Gil:
Minted has grown to include several verticals, and 200 employees, in the nine years since you founded the company. What would you advise other entrepreneurs to keep an eye on as they try to expand their companies?

Mariam Naficy:
A lot of people talk about scale as it relates to the size of the company—that is, numbers of people. But I actually think there's another dimension which really significantly affects scaling, and that's the differentiation or complexity of the business.

Reid Hoffman, for example, tends to focus on, "What happens when this company is like a village, versus a city"—you know, his whole analogy for the size of a company. I've seen companies that have a very basic model that they're not changing a lot have an easier time scaling at first. The kinds of things that I've seen really complicate scaling are when a company, for example, enters a new vertical. Michael Porter's work on this, his seminal article called, "What Is Strategy?" is a really, really good thing to take a look at.[42] It talks a lot about how there are different activity maps that underlie different businesses.

At Minted, for example, we went through this whole process for our strategy this year where we really asked ourselves the tough question, "How many businesses are we actually in?" Because the activity maps that underlie the strategic advantage in some of our businesses are actually quite different.

What I've found is that the ability to scale is complicated if you are both growing fast and developing the business through different verticals. In my space, in e-commerce, there are those who have focused on one thing, and there are those who've spread, and spread very fast, in some cases. There are e-companies like Amazon, which started in one thing, like books, then added on music and other things at a fairly fast clip, successfully.

The way that I think about scaling is: What are the core activities? For example, if I'm acquiring one customer base, then hopefully I've got an acquisition team that is able to scale and do one thing repetitively over and over again. The functional team becomes more and more experienced, which really helps with scaling. And if you're doing that, and it's not differential across all these businesses, then you've got a better scaling model, right?

Elad: So you're basically talking about repeatable versus non-repeatable scaling, in terms of certain competencies you develop for certain activities. The canonical example is a company that builds one software product. You're Google, and all you do is focus on distributing search and growing and growing and growing your search market share. But then suddenly you build Gmail, and you're like, "Do I have the same skill sets? Do I have the right people in place? Do I know how to get acquisition for Gmail instead of search?"

Mariam: And not only that, "Do I have the right innovation infrastructure?"

Elad: What have you found to be the toughest part of that then? Is it finding the right people, is it developing new skills as a company, is it finding the right customer base? How did you guys think about it?

Mariam: When you do these expansions or extensions—completely new entrepreneurship within a company—you're trying to find some overlap where some kind of core competency can be grown or monetized more. So, for example, Minted's design community is the key asset we're trying to parlay into new verticals. And hopefully, hopefully, our customer base too. Hopefully we're saying it's the same customer who's going to continue buying other things from us.

Sometimes you go down this path and you realize, that's great, but there are actually some operational things that are very, very different that are important to the success of the new business. Or some customer acquisition aspect or experiential aspect that creates a need for very different strategies and very different kinds of thinking.

Most importantly, as the entrepreneur or CEO in charge, you need to understand what the strategy should be. Meaning that—even if it is the same customer and the same designer, let's say, that's making the goods—acquiring the customer in art, for example, may be very different than acquiring the customer in stationery. Even transferring an existing customer to a new vertical might require quite a bit of entrepreneurship.

It's not as simple as saying, "I'm going to just hire somebody to just run this thing." It's about having to split your time executing your way successfully into these different businesses. So hiring people to run these verticals or to do these things becomes quite difficult, because you have to find people who are very good entrepreneurs. You need to find people who are inventive, because they're still inventing their way into early-stage businesses.

But the thing is, if you're really successful, over time—unless you've got an engine that really will not stop growing—a lot of very large, mature companies have a portfolio approach to investment, where they say, you know, "I'm going to take 15% and put it into completely exploratory things. I'll take 20% and put it into something that's past the exploratory gate, and now I'm going to try to commercialize it. And then another—the rest of it, let's say 60%, 65% of it is incremental improvement in the core."

Elad: So when do you think is the right time to expand out of a company's original product or business line? Google is a great example, where it took them, three, four, five years before they started doing Gmail. And even then it was very controversial internally. So how do you know that it's the right time, or that you have the bandwidth to be able to add a new line of business or a new vertical or to internationalize?

Mariam: Well, I think you have to look at your growth curve, your year-over-year growth rates in your core, and try to project out when you think there will be some inevitable decline in those growth rates. Then figure out how many years will it take to get the second thing that you need to layer into your growth cake ready to actually take its place. And you can model that out and try to predict that.

I know it sounds like I'm making something very complicated sound easy, but we try our best to model that out. Some companies have to do it earlier than others. It just depends on the strength and the legs of the core business, the first business, and how breakable versus non-breakable its customer acquisition model is in the beginning. How self-powered, how self-generating that is. So it's really about trying to predict the core and what's going to happen to the core.

The problem with this, of course, is that the second business typically has to get started pretty early. It could be a business that's growing 500% year over year, but if it's such a tiny part of the mix, the problem is the mix. It still blends down very low if you've got a core that's growing too slowly.

So in general, it often takes years for companies to really achieve traction with new ideas and new businesses. It does point toward doing what Google did, which was start a little earlier than you think. So that's the conclusion that I've come to so far.

I'm really glad I started the art business, because it's a very high-growth business, and it's enough of the mix right now to have a significant effect on the blended growth rate of the company. But we're going into our fourth year of the art business. We did a little baby launch in 2012, and we started Minted in 2008, to give you a sense of how many years it took before we decided to diversify. It took a while because we were concerned about the scaling problem.

The complexity or difficulty you add to your company significantly affects scaling, much more than just the number of people you hire. The number of people thing is easy compared to the other issue to me.

Elad: How did you think about the trade-offs between, for example, internationalizing more aggressively versus entering this other market?

Mariam: This sounds very simple, but in our particular case I was concerned that the photo-card market was not the same internationally, culturally, in other places as it was in the U.S. That's one issue.

The other issue was that I really wanted to make sure that Minted's core was about design, not about stationery. And so what we needed to do was in our core market, the U.S., make sure that our positioning was starting to shift to where I wanted it to get to, which was not being pigeonholed into stationery, but being thought of as just a broader design marketplace.

I knew if I went too long or too far in stationery, I would have the Zappos problem. I like them a lot, but I always know Zappos as shoes, even though they've been trying to sell accessories and other things for a very long time. I just can't get them mentally out of the shoebox, if you will. I didn't want that to happen to Minted. So I had to move a little earlier in the expansion of what the brand stood for.

And then the other thing is, I felt that the complexity of going overseas was pretty massive, actually. The trouble that it would place on the company's executives to have to split their time in a very, very taxing way, involving a lot of travel and a lot of hours, I just felt was going to really break us. It would actually be a little easier to start a different business in the U.S. than to take the other business overseas.

Elad: When you decided to start that new business, how did you think about hiring an initial team? Was it just transferring over people who were internal? Did you hire anybody external?

Mariam: From the beginning, we tried to put very little money into the test. It was very much an MVP. So I integrated it into people's existing jobs. The merchants, the people who ran the competitions, they all just started launching art challenges. And then the supply chain people started trying to figure out how to print and frame art. They clamped it onto their day jobs, to try to see whether this test would work.

And then when the test began to work, the first hire we made was a woman early in her career, right out of Stanford. And she basically was the entrepreneurial "I'll do it all" kind of person. Because we still didn't have enough scale yet to throw a huge amount of loss into this business. It's kind of crazy:

"There's another dimension which really significantly affects scaling, and that's the differentiation or complexity of the business."

—Mariam Naficy

I think we built a couple million dollars of revenue with that one great hire and by leveraging a lot of other people. Then it got to the point where it became clear that the business needed its own set of marketing initiatives and strategies, and we hired a director of marketing for art. It's a matrix organization; it's not a GM organization.

We are thinking about experimenting now with a GM organization. It's just that we were warned that we needed to be careful about a GM structure because it carries the risk of creating politics. That it would silo the brand away from the main Minted brand, and that it wouldn't hang together.

What we've found is, if you're going to think about a GM, look for a GM who leans toward naturally solving problems together, who's happy to collaborate, versus the personality who wants to really run their own island—that makes things much harder when you're running a business where there's supposed to be this integrated customer presentation, a holistic presentation of the brand and the company. It's much easier when you have people who are very collaborative at the top of those internal businesses.

It's a little bit of a personality test actually. I've had to develop interview questions to try to suss out who would be good as a GM in this kind of model. But that's one of the really, really important attributes: whether they're truly willing to make collaborative decisions about the business with the CEO and with other GMs.

What I asked this person was, "What would you want from me as your manager? What kind of interactions do you want?" You can tell from the answer whether the person really wants to have anything to do with you or thinks that you have something to add.

The person in the interview kept saying things like, "I will communicate just to make sure that you have absolutely no negative surprises." I don't want a relationship where we only communicate because you're worried about me having a negative surprise. First of all, that's not our culture, to punish people for a negative surprise. That's a big company kind of answer. So I was a little wary about the answer that I got.

"How do you communicate with your manager?" is another question. "How do you like to communicate? Formally? Informally? How frequently do you communicate with the person that you currently report to? What's the style, and how do you get in touch with this person?"

Elad: I actually think that's a really good general executive hiring question: "What would you want from me?"

Mariam: Just to understand this person's communication style is really critical. But then you can get all this other stuff out of it. "What do you want from your peers?" is another one. Either question will suggest whether the person really thinks their peers or their manager has any value to add at all, or is simply there to exist. So you can get a lot out of asking them about what they plan to seek.

The hunt for the GM is difficult. Turns out it's very hard to find good general managers because they have to be very good generalists. A lot of times they want to run their own companies, or they're already running a company. They may not start a company, but they may want to run a company. And when you have a couple divisions, you want all the GMs to be of equal caliber. Also, depending on the way the rest of the company's structured, the core competency of each GM will differ.

For example, let's say I have one GM who's very merchandising oriented, because the person came out of merchandising. And another one who's very strong at marketing, because they came out of marketing. And another one who's strong at product marketing, because they came out of PM. Creating processes that work equally well across all of them, given their different strengths and weaknesses, is actually really difficult.

I will just say that this idea of running multiple businesses has been among the most complicated parts of scaling. It's really different for each business, where you are and what your competitive landscape looks like.

Elad: One other aspect of scaling that many companies run into is technical debt. There are certain parts of engineering infrastructure that companies need to rebuild or invent over time. How did you work on the technical debt? Do you do fix-it weeks? Do you have specific projects focused on it?

Mariam: What we do is we figure out our growth road map for the year. Then we take the pay-down projects and we piggyback them along the growth road map. So we'll choose to do things in the order that the growth road map dictates.

For example, our product details page—it's the page you land on when you're looking at specific products. We had let the company launch about six different versions of this page, because a lot of different teams had worked on it. All of a sudden you have all of this repetitive, redundant code. Now we've rebuilt it to have one code base, and we can swap in different modules. So that obviously does a lot of things for us. But we did it first because that's one of the key things that was blocking the growth road map. That's one example of how to prioritize.

You also need to keep an eye on the productivity of your team. Once you see engineers starting to really slow down and be afraid to touch certain parts of the code, I think you, as a responsible person, have to create a balanced scorecard. Even if it's not directly linked to a revenue project, you can always come up with a measurable impact, hopefully, for a sound strategy. So as long as there's a metric involved, I think that we feel comfortable arranging the road map and figuring out how we can pay the tech debt down.

Prioritizing it, for us, is mostly determined by the growth road map, but then sometimes it's about productivity of people. And sometimes it's about pure happiness. If there's a tipping point where people are really unhappy about something, obviously we do take that into consideration.

The capital environment—whether capital is cheap or expensive at that time—also vastly, incredibly influences that scorecard. If capital is super cheap, you can get tons of capital to last you for a long time. And so you can think very long term. You can prioritize long-term-payoff projects. If it's very expensive, you have to start pulling your horizon in and looking for shorter-term returns, which might mean lower beta projects, things that pay off in the year that you do them. That's a very tight screen for what you might pursue. Paying it off within twelve months is a tall order, I should say. Not a lot of projects qualify.

I like to use the balanced scorecard. I do also, in general, like to prioritize revenue growth. That's probably the top one for me, but then there are other important things like brand, customer satisfaction, community satisfaction, etc. on our scorecard. But we don't like to do massive tech debt pay-down projects that have no connection to the business plan of any kind.

"It's very hard to find good general managers because they have to be very good generalists. A lot of times they want to run their own companies, or they're already running a company."

—Mariam Naficy

Elad: How do you create that culture? Because I think that sometimes there's that natural tension between engineering and the business side—engineering wants to work on projects that are either interesting or that address pieces of infrastructure. But sometimes those pieces of infrastructure, to your point, aren't really necessary.

Mariam: We try very hard to have engineering and product meet to discuss ranking and to really look at the company's goals together. Essentially at the very top level, people will leave if they don't believe in being part of a business, and they don't believe in the company's goals. They will self-select out. So hopefully in the interviewing process, we've explained, for example, that it's an e-commerce business, it's exciting for these reasons, we're building a design community and a marketplace. And one of our key metrics for success is actually size of revenue. Hopefully on the inbound, you're telling people what you value, and then people are selecting in based on that. I think the recruiting process is critical to solving that problem.

But in general, we communicate many, many, many times what the overall strategy of the company is, and the corporate goals. Finance has given classes in ROI calculations to engineers. We have a lot of finance classes, essentially, that we've organized for the engineers to understand how to commercially evaluate these things.

Elad: That's a great idea; I think more companies should do that. I'm curious how you came up with that.

Mariam: I think because I kept talking about ROI and related areas so much. Finally the PM/engineering leaders said, "I think we need to tell people what these things mean." The Head of PM actually came up with the idea of just having our VP of Finance give these classes.

The funny thing is, people seem very interested in it. A lot of the engineers come up to me after all-hands meetings and ask me questions about the stock market and stocks that they follow. Not that I'm an expert at all. But there's just a lot of interest in, you know, "Will Minted go public?" or, "I'm reading in TechCrunch that these things are happening. Why are they happening?" So there's actually a fair amount of interest among our employees.

I think we also have a language inside the company. Let's say you're logging into some Google Doc that people are using to rank projects, you're going to see all these financial terms, like "ROI" or "net present value of the revenue," because we use that language a lot. And so I think that helps. That's another thing that's just really embedded in our culture, so deeply that we don't even notice it. I'm a former investment banker, and my cofounder, Melissa, came out of the finance department at eBay. So we're both numbers-oriented.

Elad: How do you think about seniority of the team versus scaling or functional debt accruing?

Mariam: This is really important, and I think what it says is that perhaps the first place to really scale, and I mean scale to senior level, is engineering. You should never start with the cheap solution of building a whole team of young engineers. Whereas there are other functions where you can potentially get away with it.

Elad: What would be an example of a function like that?

Mariam: Things that are so easy to see on the surface that it's clear as day whether the result is good or not. So, for example, design. I think you can actually start with very young, emerging design talent, because you can see right on face value whether the work is good or not. Whereas when it comes to things which are more hidden and harder for the CEO to see clearly, you might want to hire more senior people, like in engineering—the architecture, and what's happening with the systems of the company.

"If capital is super cheap, you can get tons of capital to last you for a long time. And so you can think very long term. You can prioritize long-term-payoff projects. If it's very expensive, you have to start pulling your horizon in and looking for shorter-term returns."

—Mariam Naficy

Elad: That's a great framework for senior versus junior hires. It's okay to hire junior people for areas where it's clearly visible to the CEO if it's working. And any area where it's hard to understand things quickly and easily, then you should always have senior hires. I think you should call that the Naficy framework.

Mariam: That's how I operate. So I've hired very young people and junior people in design areas and merchandising, where I can see everything.

The only place where I think engineers might get into trouble is on the marketing/finance side. I see that a lot. There's this very important issue of getting your business model straight. And just as businesspeople have trouble figuring out who's a great engineer, I think sometimes engineers have a really hard time figuring out who's a good business person. It's just this crazy divide unfortunately. There are not that many people who really understand both the financial side and the engineering side.

I've seen engineering-oriented founders struggle a little bit trying to figure out, "Do I trust this person or not in engineering my financial structure, or my marketing/financial structure, my customer acquisition stuff?" And some of that can go really wrong, really quickly. You can go really wrong spending money on customer acquisition if you don't know what the right metrics are. So that's one of those things that you need to hire for carefully.

It doesn't necessarily mean you need a senior person, but you need a really, really good person. And that person is probably not the cheapest hire.

Elad: The one other thing I'd add to your framework is that there are certain specialist roles that are existential to your company, and that's also where you want to hire senior people. So an example, back when you still had data centers, the person who was running your data center build-out had to have done it before. Or in the case of Color Genomics, we needed somebody senior who'd run a clinical lab to run our clinical lab.

Mariam: Yeah, exactly. You guys have some serious governmental and regulatory issues that have to be contended with. I totally agree on that. Legal is another area where I really don't think people should go cheap and junior. The legal stuff can get really bad if you don't get someone experienced. I mean, I think that's probably obvious, hopefully. ■

This interview has been edited and condensed for clarity.

CHAPTER 5

Organizational structure and hypergrowth

CHAPTER 5

Organizational structure and hypergrowth

ORGANIZATIONAL STRUCTURE IS ALL ABOUT PRAGMATISM

First-time CEOs and entrepreneurs often call me to discuss how to structure their organizations. Common questions include: Should I hire a COO or not? Who should the VP marketing report to? How should I split up product and engineering? Should our international arm build out its own functions or be matrixed with U.S. headquarters?

There is often fear in the mind of the entrepreneur that there is a "right" answer to how to structure an organization—and that if she screws it up by doing the "wrong" thing, the implications could be disastrous. This is an incorrect perspective. Most of the time there is no "right" answer and org structure is really an exercise in pragmatism. That is, what is the right structure given the talent available to your company, the set of initiatives you need to pursue, and your company's 12- to 18-month time horizon?

Here are a few key takeaways and things to keep in mind about org structure:

IF YOU ARE GROWING FAST, YOU HAVE A DIFFERENT COMPANY EVERY 6–12 MONTHS

When I joined Google, it grew from around 1,500 to 15,000 people in three-and-a-half years. After my startup was acquired by Twitter, Twitter grew from about 90 to 1,500 people in less than three years. A company that grows that rapidly is literally a different company every six months. This means that every 6–12 months the company's org structure may change.

When choosing an organizational structure for your high-growth startup, focus on the next 6–12 months. Don't try to find the "long-term" solution, as in the long term your company will be completely different and have radically different needs. Eventually, your executive team will start to stabilize but the teams under them will have more frequent re-orgs as each organization ramps in size.

THERE IS NO "RIGHT" ANSWER

Often there is no one answer to how to structure your organization. Rather, it is a series of trade-offs. Two different structures may be equally "good" and "bad." Don't sweat it too much—ultimately if you make a mistake, it will be painful but you can undo it.

Communicate to the team that as your company grows quickly, things will shift around. Make it clear that it is normal for that to happen—it's a sign of your success—and that other companies that grow fast do the same thing.

SOMETIMES BANDWIDTH MATTERS MORE THAN PERFECT FIT

Executive bandwidth may be more important than a traditional reporting chain. For example, Alex Macgillivray, the talented former general counsel at Twitter, had user support, trust and safety, corporate development/M&A, and other areas reporting to him at various times, in addition to legal. Many of these departments normally would not report to a GC, but Alex was talented enough to take on more in the absence of other executives with bandwidth to own these areas. As new executives were hired or promoted, things then transferred over to them from Alex.

As CEO, you should look at your team and allocate functional areas based in part on who has the time and skill set to focus on and make that area succeed. This does not mean the chosen executive needs to manage that area forever. Remember, nothing needs to be permanent. There are also some cases that don't make sense from a tie-breaking or skill set perspective—e.g., your VP engineering should probably not run sales in addition to engineering. However, if needed, your VP engineering could potentially manage the design or product teams in the short term or, if it makes sense to do so, even longer term.

ORG STRUCTURE IS OFTEN ABOUT TIE-BREAKING

Reporting chains are ultimately about decision-making. For example, there is a natural tension between engineering and product management, so where do you want most decisions to be taken if the two groups disagree? The person who both functions report to ultimately functions as the tie-breaker between the orgs. This is a good heuristic to keep in mind when thinking about org structure.

HIRE EXECUTIVES FOR THE NEXT 12–18 MONTHS, NOT ETERNITY

As an exhausted founder/CEO, the temptation is to try to hire an executive for a role who will last for the remaining history of the company. This leads to over-hiring, or hiring someone who will likely be ineffectual at your current scale. For example, you do not need a VP engineering who has run a 10,000-person organization when you only have 20 engineers. Instead, hire someone who has led a 50- to 100-person team and can scale up your org to the right level over the next 12–18 months. Either that person will grow with the team or you will need to hire someone new in the future. Ben Horowitz has a good perspective on this in his book, The Hard Thing About Hard Things.

Of course, if the executives you hire do grow with the company, all the better; a stable management team is a big positive for a company. Even if the executive team evolves only slightly over time, though, you should realize that your org structure may still change more rapidly.

There is no perfect organizational structure for a company. A company is a living, breathing thing and will change with time—as will the organizational scaffolding on which it is built. As CEO, focus on a pragmatic solution for the next 6–12 months of the company's life, rather than the perfect long-term solution. [43]

DOING A RE-ORGANIZATION

When your company is in hypergrowth, you will be doubling the team every 6–12 months on average. At that pace you could go from 20 to ~300 people in two years and to 500 or 1,000 people in four years. You will be adding new functions rapidly (finance, HR, legal), potentially expanding internationally, while product road maps will expand and new areas will be launched or acquired into the company.

You will effectively be working at or running a different company every 6–12 months, with most of the people at the company having joined in the last 12 months. When I was at Google, it more or less 10X-ed from 1,500 or 2,000 people when I joined to >15,000 people when I left 3.5 years later. My startup was acquired when Twitter was ~90 people, and I left a full-time role with Twitter at over 1,000 employees. 90% of the people at Twitter had not been with the company just 2.5 years earlier.

As the company scales and increases in complexity you will also need to change the organizational structure of the company to reflect new executives, new functions, more employees, and changing alignment against your market and product. In other words, re-orgs will occur at the company frequently.

---

[43] Read the original post at eladgil.com. [*http://blog.eladgil.com/2015/10/organizational-structure-is-all-about.html*]

"Eventually, your executive team will start to stabilize but the teams under them will have more frequent re-orgs as each organization ramps in size."

—Elad Gil

Early on many of the re-orgs will be at the executive level and then cascade down. As you add more functional areas, there will be finer division of executive roles. If you add a CMO or other CX-level person then some of the executive roles may consolidate under that individual.

RE-ORGS AT THE COMPANY LEVEL AND THE FUNCTIONAL LEVEL

Early on, you may re-org the entire company frequently. But once you hit 500 to 1,000 people, you should expect fewer company-level re-orgs and many more interfunctional re-orgs. For example, a change within the structure of the sales team, versus changes across all teams simultaneously. Some teams such as sales are more likely to re-org frequently at that point as they scale, while others like product and engineering tend to be more stable. Part of this has to do with where head count grows and needs change most rapidly in a company as it switches from being solely product-centric, to focusing more on go-to-market. The biggest cross-company re-orgs later as the company scales will occur when changing product/engineering/go-to-market simultaneously, adding new product areas or acquisitions, if a company flips from a matrix to business unit-like organization, or flips between centralized and decentralized internationalization.

Early on, you as CEO will need to be adept at re-orgs. Later, as re-orgs shift more frequently to functional organization, you will need to make sure your leadership team knows how to approach them. Most companies and new managers screw up their first re-org or two, causing unnecessary pain in the organization. Below is a simple guide to re-orgs.

HOW TO DO A RE-ORG

1. **Decide why you need the new org structure.** Determine what the right structure is and the logic for why this is better than before. Do you need renewed focus on a specific area? Are there collaboration issues? Has the team grown dramatically and now needs additional management? Has something changed in your market that means you need to re-align functional priorities or the set of people working together? Spell out to yourself the logic of why you need to re-org first, and then think through the leadership and org structure that works best.

2. **Determine what org structure is most pragmatic.** Who on your leadership team is overloaded and who has bandwidth? Who is building out a great management layer? What areas would fit well together? Sometimes, there is no single right answer, and you need to balance managerial bandwidth with the logic of the situation.

   As you determine who needs to work on what and the proper reporting structure, remember that nothing you come up with will be 100% perfect and that is OK.

   Should you have cross-functional product and engineering organizations or verticalized product units? Should international be distributed or centralized? These sorts of questions come up all the time as companies grow, and some companies flop between structures over time (Oracle supposedly flips its international org every few years).

   Relatedly, reporting is an exercise in tie breaking—i.e., you want people who are likely to disagree to eventually report in to a single tiebreaker (this may be the CEO, or it may be someone lower down in the org).

3. **Get buy-in from the right people before implementation.** If possible, you should consult with a handful of executives whose functions would be most impacted by the change. They may have good feedback about how changing the org in your function impacts their own functional area (e.g., changing the org structure for product may impact how engineering and design are structured).

   Re-orgs should never be open conversations with the whole company (or a functional area) about what form the new organization structure should take. This only opens you up to lobbying, internal politicking, and land grabbing. It also prolongs the angst—re-orgs should happen swiftly and with as little churn as possible.

4. **Announce and implement the re-org soup-to-nuts in 24 hours.** Once you have decided what form the new organization will take, discuss it with your reports in their 1:1s. Your executives should have a clear plan for how and when to communicate the changes to their team members. If there are key people deeply affected or likely to be unhappy with the change, you or one of your reports can meet with them either right before or right after the announcement to hear them out and re-affirm the logic for the changes.

You should never drag out a re-org or pre-announce it. Try not to announce "this week we will re-organize product, and next month we will change engineering." If possible, all elements of the re-org need to be communicated and implemented simultaneously. If you pre-announce a portion of the re-org, that team will not get any work done until the re-org happens. Instead, there will be hushed conversations in conference rooms full of gossip and speculation, crazy rumor-mongering, and executive lobbying.

5. **Every person on the leadership team should be briefed on the re-org and be ready to answer questions from their team about it.** If the re-org reaches or impacts enough of the company, the executives of the company should be briefed ahead of time. Write up an internal FAQ if needed and circulate it.

6. **Remove ambiguity. Know where ~100% of people are going.** Don't do a partial re-org. When the re-org is announced, you should know where ~100% of people are going if possible. The worst possible situation for people is to not know what their future entails.

   Make a list of the people most likely to be unhappy with the change and reach out to them quickly after the announcement, or speak to them before the change if necessary. Make sure to be accessible to these people later so you can explain the reasoning first-hand.

7. **Communicate directly and clearly, and compassionately.** Don't beat around the bush when doing the re-org. Explain in clear language what is happening and why. Listen to people's feedback but be firm about the change.

   There will always be people who are unhappy with the shift in org structure. They may feel passed over for promotion or demoted, even if this is not the case. Listen carefully and see if you can meet their needs in the future. However, keep backtracking to a minimum. You are making this change for a reason, and if you start making exceptions for the squeakiest wheels you may reverse the whole reason you are making the change, as well as show people you are open to being politicked.

   Just like letting people go, a re-organization can be unpleasant. There will undoubtedly be people disappointed with their new role or diminished responsibilities. If done right however, your company will function more effectively and be aligned to win. Re-orgs have to occur for the long term success of the company.

An interview with Ruchi Sanghvi

Ruchi Sanghvi was the VP of Operations at Dropbox. Prior to joining Dropbox, Sanghvi served as the cofounder and CEO of Cove, a collaboration, coordination, and communication product for organizations and communities. Sanghvi holds the distinction of being the first female engineer at Facebook and was instrumental in implementing the first versions of key features such as News Feed. She then led product management and strategy for Facebook Platform and Facebook Connect. She was also responsible for core product areas such as privacy and user engagement. She holds bachelor's and master's degrees in electrical computer engineering from Carnegie Mellon University.

There's a particularly tricky moment in the life of a hypergrowth company, when things have started growing rapidly but the executive infrastructure is not yet in place to handle it. And in those moments, a lot of companies begin applying human Band-Aids of sorts—trusted employees who can fill in on key roles until someone more permanent is hired to build out a given function.

I sat down with Ruchi Sanghvi to discuss this phenomenon and her thoughts on how to make it work. An early employee at Facebook, and later VP of Operations at Dropbox, Ruchi has seen Band-Aids from both sides—she's worked for them and she's been one herself. (At Dropbox, people even called her the Wolf, a nod to Pulp Fiction's famous fixer.) She shared her advice for when to slap on a Band-Aid, when to rip it off, and how to get the most from it in between.

Ruchi Sanghvi:
My first experience of the Band-Aid phenomenon was at Facebook. Matt Cohler played the role there. And the idea was that for any function that didn't have a leader or manager, he would step in. Or if there were teams that needed to be built out, he would step in. And I thought it was a really interesting role, because it was obviously impactful in the short- to medium-term to help the company scale. But it wasn't a sustainable role, either for the individual or for the company.

I had a similar experience at Dropbox myself. When Dropbox acquired Cove (where I was working), it wasn't exactly clear what role I would step into. The first thing that I did was interview about 50 percent of the Dropbox team. I asked things like "What's working well? How do you think you could accelerate the company's efforts? And what are the one or two priorities you think need to be addressed immediately?"

It didn't matter who you talked to on the Dropbox team, whether it was engineers, product people, sales people, it all boiled down to one thing: We don't have enough resources to build product, to scale, to sell the product, to market the product, etc.

I had the title of VP of Operations, but the first thing I actually ended up doing was managing the recruiting team. I directly managed the team, set goals, and figured out how we would achieve those goals. And while we had a target to hit, it was just as important to build systems to integrate new hires into the company. These systems helped to increase productivity and strengthen the culture already present.

After recruiting, I focused on marketing. We needed to build out the team and eventually hire a leader. In the same way I ended up managing communications, a third of product, and growth & internationalization.

When a company is in hypergrowth, you want to leverage the momentum and growth. It's okay to slap on these Band-Aids when a company is in that phase. But the key thing to keep in mind is that you need to be able to hire quickly so those Band-Aids are replaced by people who can actually grow solutions that will scale.

Elad: What you're describing is a little bit like what we saw at Twitter. The Band-Aid role was filled between me and Ali Rowghani. The CEO would delegate something to one of us, then we would step in, build out a function, help hire an executive. Then move on to the next function.

You mentioned that prioritization is one key to being successful in that kind of role, and really prioritizing hiring the executives to eventually run teams. What else do you think is key to the success of the gap-filler role? What sort of relationship does that person need to have with the CEO, and with other executives? How should they function in the org, and how should they be empowered?

Ruchi: It's probably easier to work our way backwards. The person who is playing the gap-filler role is in a unique position where they are tasked with scaling the team and making decisions to help move the team forward. But at the same, you don't want to push it too far in any one direction because you want to hire the right executive who can come in and bring their people, set the trajectory, and take over. It's a delicate balance, where you're not setting big goals and taking the team full steam ahead but you are waiting for the right executive to come on board to do that.

To be successful, you need to have the trust and respect of the CEO and executive team. You can't manage these teams and run the hiring process yourself. In order to scale, you need the other executives to step in and/or loan you people from their teams. It's just as important to set expectations about how the team fits in with the company's overall goals and priorities. And lastly, it's important for the other executives to recognize the contributions the gap-filler is making.

The second thing—and these are mistakes that I know I made at Dropbox, and other people may have seen other places as well—is that when looking for the permanent replacement/executive, you need to focus on the present and what you need in the next two years. Otherwise you end up chasing unicorns, people who can get their hands dirty, build a team and manage a team of 100 five years from now. Sadly, unicorns just don't exit.

As a gap-filler you need to be able to convince the CEO and other executives that it's okay to hire different types of people with different experience levels at different points in time. That's pretty critical, because as a gap-filler, you end up sourcing candidates, setting up the interview slate, moderating the debriefs, and making a case for the types of candidates that you're bringing in.

Ruchi: When companies are in startup mode they don't prioritize orgs like communications, people operations, marketing, etc. As a result you tend to Band-Aid or gap-fill these functions that aren't core in the early days. As a gap-filler, if you're doing a reasonable job at the function, the company doesn't find it necessary to move fast on hiring the permanent executive or building the right foundations for the teams. They aren't prioritizing the search and willing to spend longer than usual to find the right person.

The biggest failure mode, is not setting the right expectations. Not just with the CEO but also with people who the executive will end up managing. The gap-filler is able to operate because of trust they've built up in the organization, the organizational lines for the new execute will not be the same and aren't clear. To avoid a mismatch in expectation on both sides it's important to answer questions like: What is the role definition and extent of their responsibility? What kind of experience do they need? Will they report into the CEO?

Elad: To your point, almost definitionally, the fact that this role wasn't filled with an exec suggests that for a period of time, it perhaps rightly wasn't the single most important thing on the company's road map. You're trying to get to product/market fit, you're trying to get distribution. And then suddenly the company starts working, and the company itself becomes more of the product. Then you have an organization that doesn't know how to value the role, or how to search for the person who could fill it even if they do value it. So it sounds like being that bridge really is helpful.

How can the CEO be most helpful? What sort of characteristics should they look for in that person? And what are the two or three key things they can do to support them in their work?

Ruchi: The person needs to be deeply respected within the company and have cred, with both early employees and the current executive team. Without that credibility and trust, it's difficult to collaborate with different teams in different capacities and be culturally accepted and not rejected.

In terms of support, the only places I've seen this operate successfully is when the person is part of the executive team and reports into the CEO or COO. It allows them to surface resource constraints, ask for support, highlight successes, etc. They can influence hiring decisions and also expedite hiring decisions.

"When a company is in hypergrowth, you want to leverage the momentum and growth. It's okay to slap on Band-Aids when a company is in that phase."

— Ruchi Sanghvi

Elad: So, just for example, reporting to the CEO, having regular 1:1s with them, all that kind of stuff.

Ruchi: Exactly—or reporting into the founder.

I would also add that don't be afraid to have someone play the role of the Wolf. It's inevitable, and it is better for the CEO to delegate this than take it on themselves, because it's not the most leveraged use of their time.

Elad: How do you know when you no longer need this role? Or when should you no longer need the role? Is it a certain critical mass of executives? Is it a certain size of company? When is it too late to have somebody in this kind of capacity?

Ruchi: If someone is playing this role for more than two or two-and-a-half years, it's already been way too long. If the gap-filler is doing a reasonable job of Band-Aiding then it's usually difficult to replace them. That's when it's suboptimal, because all you're doing is locally maximizing and not globally maximizing.

Elad: When you say that two- or two-and-a-half years is too long, is that because by that point you should have built out a functional executive team across all the different areas? What's the driver for that time frame in your mind?

Ruchi: By two- to two-and-a-half years, you should have a functional executive team built out in all areas. You need to build out these functions to support your product development, your business, and hiring and scaling your company.

Elad: So for this Band-Aid person, what are the functions that you've found them filling in for most frequently at the different companies you've seen?

Ruchi: Recruiting, HR, comms, marketing. Sometimes customer support and occasionally product. The VP of product is really difficult to hire for, since it's usually filled by the CEO themselves. So it usually takes longer to be able to find the right person for the role.

Elad: And then, as companies start opening up international or other things, do you think executives in their own functions should hire somebody who's effectively playing this role for that function? Or do you think it's really only at the top level that it's needed?

Ruchi: I believe it's only needed at the top level. When you open up international offices, the main reason is to expand sales. And then over time, to become more cost-effective, you'll want to build out customer support and other functions. To scale operationally, I believe you need a different set of resources.

Elad: And do you think every company will need this role? Or do you think it really depends on the experience of the executive team?

Ruchi: I think every company that hits—I hate using these words—but every company that hits exponential growth needs this. While it looks like rapidly scaling companies have everything figured out, internally it's chaos because they are growing so fast. And it's difficult to plan for chaos which is why I think every company will need this role.

Elad: I think you're touching on a key point, which a lot of people don't understand: As companies really start scaling rapidly, from an external perception everybody thinks that things must be going great because it's growing so fast. But typically, internally it's chaos. Or slightly organized chaos.

So how should employees, middle managers, individual contributors, director-level people be viewing their roles at that moment? And how should they be navigating them, given that there's so much change and so much churn?

Ruchi: When companies rapidly start scaling, I've observed the following things:

First, everyone's workload increases 2–5X. People are scrambling to plug the holes and end up doing a lot of different things.

Second, you start hiring quickly. You think that's going to solve things but your workload only increases. Because you are doing more not less with more people. You are taking on projects you could not get to.

Third, as you onboard new people to fill out the organization and the org reaches some sort of equilibrium, your role and its scope suddenly becomes narrow. And I think this phase is really difficult for early employees especially, who acceded during the exponential growth phase.

The people who deal with that—the people who deal with the role definition becoming narrower and more focused and are able to faithfully transition through that—are the ones that grow with the company.

Elad: In other words, they succeed while other early employees will be more likely to churn out because they're not dealing with it well?

Ruchi: Exactly. They're not scaling the way the company needs them to scale.

Elad: One piece of advice I give employees at these types of companies is don't sweat it too much. Because every six months, if your company's doubling, it's a different company. So if your peer is suddenly your manager, it's possible in a year you'll suddenly be their manager's manager. So as long as you just keep your head down and do good work, things tend to work out. Because it's growing so fast that if you joined early you tend to be in pretty good shape.

Ruchi: I completely agree with that. Every six months, the company will grow and look completely different. Whatever systems and processes you're putting in place, you have to be mentally prepared to change them. And all that time you invested in coming up with the perfect process, well, you are going to have to do it again.

Elad: Are there any specific, simple processes or other things that you think are often lacking that people should put in place, from a project elements perspective, an HR/recruiting perspective, etc.? Or is that its own giant hairball to unwind?

Ruchi: I think it's its own giant discussion. In the beginning, be cautious about putting too much process in place. But when it is needed, don't be afraid to implement it.

At Facebook, early on, we hired a bunch of "adults" and I was definitely one of those kids that was thinking, "We don't need to be managed." I pushed back against all forms of process. And then at Dropbox I ended up being the adult who was brought in to implement process. Now I appreciate both sides of the narrative.

So don't overdo it when you don't need it. But when you need it, don't be afraid to implement it. And then anticipate it's going to change, and don't get frustrated.

Elad: If you were to go back in time and give yourself advice while you were still at Facebook—you were a very early employee, very influential in the organization—what piece of advice would you give yourself?

Ruchi: As the company grows and the organization scales, your role within the organization will change. It will become a lot narrower and more focused and this frustrates most early employees. But that doesn't mean you're having less impact, you are probably having a larger impact in a more focused area. So, you're right, if you're just heads down and do a really good job and you can scale through that, you'll end up scaling gracefully along with the company.

Don't look for the perfect person for the job for the next 10 years, the unicorn. The company is changing so quickly that you only know what you need now. So, look for people who are perfect for the next three years.

Elad: Any last thoughts you want to add about the Band-Aid?

Ruchi: As with all Band-Aids, you've eventually got to just rip it off. People get comfortable with Band-Aids and if the person is doing the job well it actually deters from hiring a permanent replacement. If you have someone subbing for roles like head of product or VP of communications for more than a year, the only way to force yourself and the team to make trade-offs and decisions to hire a permanent replacement would be to just rip off the Band-Aid. In other words, remove the gap-filler, the Wolf—however you want to refer to them—from the role so you're forced to build out the organization the right way.

I imagine that you had the same experience at Twitter.

Elad: Yes, Twitter was similar. To your point, I think the key is really building out the executive branch so that you fill out those roles. Because ultimately, without key leaders in place you're just never going to be able to scale the organization. I always view it as the organizational scaffolding on which you build the rest of the team. And building up scaffolding early is often something that founders miss. Then things start scaling and everything starts breaking.

If they had the experience to think 6, 12 months ahead, or even 18 months ahead, they'd start hiring with the idea that it's going to take three to six months to find a good executive. That person will then take a couple months to build out their team. Their team will then take a couple months to ramp. So in some sense, you really need a year runway to be able to start building out the organization you need for the future. So it does take a bit of time.

It's always interesting to see people play these roles. Matt Cohler did it at Facebook, you did it at Dropbox, and I did it at Twitter, and I think we probably have some overlapping experiences.

Ruchi: I think people call the role the Wolf. Have you seen the movie?

Elad: That's funny. Yeah, from Pulp Fiction.

Ruchi: People used to call me the Wolf at Dropbox.

Elad: We always called it the fixer or the gap-filler. But the Wolf sounds more bad-ass, so I think we should just adopt it. That should be the name of this interview, "Bringing in the Wolf."

Ruchi: I had mentioned this, but usually the person comes from within the organization. It's pretty hard to hire someone for this role. If you actually find someone you trust enough, then you should make them your COO.

Elad: You need somebody who has the organization's trust and credibility, and has a strong relationship to the CEO and/or founders. And so you need somebody who's either been there very early or alternatively somebody who's acquired that the CEO or the founders knew from before. Because otherwise it's basically impossible to do.

Ruchi: Exactly.

This interview has been edited and condensed for clarity.

"When companies are in startup mode they don't prioritize orgs like communications, people operations, and marketing. As a result you tend to Band-Aid or gap-fill these functions that aren't core in the early days."

—Ruchi Sanghvi

COMPANY CULTURE AND ITS EVOLUTION

As your company scales, your culture will change with it. You will be hiring a broader set of functions, bona fide executives who can function at scale, and probably people with less risk tolerance and more process tolerance. At the same time your company will grow ten- to a hundred-fold in size which means communications, processes, and adherence to various internal controls for an IPO or other reasons will need to increase. It is inevitable your culture will change alongside everything else.

As the founder or CEO you will be responsible for determining which parts of the culture you need to keep, what to morph, and what to drop altogether. You will need to communicate to veteran employees that these cultural changes are needed just as you need to keep iterating on your products and team. Your biggest levers for shaping culture have to do with who you hire, the behaviors you emphasize and reward, and the people you let go.

NEVER, EVER COMPROMISE: HIRING FOR CULTURE

While your company should be focused on diversity of background, ethnicity, gender, class, and other attributes in employees, it should also look for cohesion in purpose, intent, and baseline culture. Your culture acts as an unwritten set of rules and values that drive behavior and cohesion across the company. Your company culture is the foundation on which everything you do rests.

Cohesive cultures are more resilient and can withstand shocks (fierce competition in the market, bad press cycles, a product failure, or other issues). They can also be extremely motivational and draw out the best in people (e.g., engineers at Palantir who used to sleep under their desks in the belief that they were helping national security, or the emergence of Google's "don't be evil" doctrine).

BAD CULTURE LEADS TO PAIN

Most companies do a poor job of pursuing a common culture or are willing to sacrifice it when they hire in order to "get someone effective" or "fill a need." This typically backfires in a big way over the short- to medium term. Every single founder I know who has compromised on culture when hiring has regretted it due to the disruptions it has caused their company: having to fire bad actors, creating a crappy work environment, good people quitting, trust eroding between coworkers, product moving in the wrong direction, misaligned incentives emerging in the organization, etc.

HOW TO BUILD A STRONG CULTURE[44]

1. **Have strong hiring filters in place.** Explicitly filter for people with common values. You need to be careful that this does not act as a mechanism to inadvertently filter out diverse populations. You can have both a common sense of purpose and a diverse employee base at the same time. See later sections and the interview with Joelle Emerson for more information.

2. **Constantly emphasize values day-to-day.** Repeat them until you are blue in the face. The second you are really sick of saying the same thing over and over, you will find people have started repeating it back to you.

3. **Reward people based on performance as well as culture.** People should be rewarded (with promotions, financially, etc.) for both productivity and for living the company's values.

4. **Get rid of bad culture fits quickly.** Fire bad culture fits even faster than you fire low performers.[45]

This chapter focuses on #1 above: the hiring filters you can use to optimize for core values and culture.

---

[44] Related links on eladgil.com.
  [*http://www.au.af.mil/au/awc/awcgate/ndu/strat-ldr-dm/pt4ch15.html and https://en.wikipedia.org/wiki/Value_(ethics)*]
[45] See "when and how to fire employees" on eladgil.com.
  [*http://blog.eladgil.com/2010/06/startups-when-how-to-fire-employee-at.html*]

"Every single founder I know who has compromised on culture when hiring has regretted it due to the disruptions it has caused their company."

—Elad Gil

HIRING FOR CULTURE & VALUES

A high-growth company is fragile, and having people pull in different directions, or wasting time in pointless philosophical arguments, can be lethal. Early on, you want to hire people with common values and goals, who are all pulling in the same direction. This does not mean you want clones or want to create groupthink, but you do want people who will work well together toward shared goals.

1. **Determine the sort of values and culture you are optimizing for.** Ask yourself the following questions, and get input from the broader employee base:

   - What are the cornerstones of your company's culture? What sort of values do you want people you hire to have?
   - What are you willing to compromise on? What are you not? (note: if you are willing to compromise on it, it is not important to you.)
   - How do you plan to screen for these values in your interviews? What questions do you plan to ask at each stage to surface candidates' values? For example, if you are selecting for people who will dive in proactively to solve problems they identified outside of their own responsibilities, ask about past examples where they have done so in other jobs.
   - How do your values, interview questions, and filters ensure you can attract and hire diverse candidates?

2. **Look out for red flags.** Each company has its own values and therefore its own red flags. Some common ones may include:

- **People whose sole motivation is financial.** While you want employees to be richly rewarded for their work, you also want people who care about the company's mission or the impact it is having. Overly mercenary people will always leave for the highest bidder, or make poor short-term decisions for financial gain.

- **Arrogance.** There is a fine line between self-confidence and arrogance. When I interview people for engineering roles, the smartest people write down the question and work through it. The people who think they were the smartest try to do it in their heads and get it wrong.

- **People who will likely create a bad environment for the rest of the team.** That might be because they have low energy or a negative outlook, are needlessly argumentative, focused on philosophy over pragmatism, or other issues.

If people seem technically great but were a bad fit culturally, you should reject them as a candidate.

3. **Optimize for the long term.** Every founder has that moment of temptation: there is a big hole you want to fill. You have been looking for the right candidate for too long and can't find her. Or, even worse, you finally find someone great for the role, but he seems borderline or outright bad culturally.

The right strategy is to not hire the person. "If there is a doubt, there is no doubt" unfortunately proves itself to be true over and over again.

YOU CAN'T DELEGATE CULTURE

An interview with Patrick Collison

Patrick Collison is the cofounder and CEO of Stripe, an online payments company and emerging core part of the internet's infrastructure. Patrick cofounded Stripe with his brother John Collison in 2010 after personally experiencing the difficulty developers face when implementing a way to accept payments online for content and goods. Patrick is no stranger to the startup world having previously cofounded and sold Auctomatic, an auction and marketplace management system, which he started in 2007 at the age of 18. Just a year later, the company was acquired by Canada's Live Current Media for $5 million.

Founded in 2010, Stripe was an immediate hit among developers for its straightforward, API-based approach to getting an online business up and running. Cofounders John and Patrick Collison had seen that the internet's online payment infrastructure was broken, so they fixed it. Eight years later, they've parlayed their early cult status into a $9 billon valuation and an impressive roster of clients big and small.

Perhaps unsurprisingly, Patrick, Stripe's CEO, has a clear-minded approach to his company's human infrastructure, which now includes over 1,000 people, and offices around the world. I sat down with him to talk about culture building, the importance of explicit communication, and the lessons he's learned from Stripe's eight years of rapid growth.

Elad Gil:
Stripe has done an amazing job both in terms of scaling and in terms of attracting people with common values and a shared interest in building infrastructure for the internet economy. I'd like to hear some of your thoughts on how to build a culture, and how to let it evolve.

To start, how do you see culture evolving as an organization scales, and what you think is important early versus later in that evolution?

Patrick Collison:
When it comes to culture, I think the main mistakes that companies make are being too precious about it, being too apologetic about it, and not treating it as dynamic and subject to revision.

Generally speaking, and certainly if a company is working well to some degree—if you're making progress in building the product you want to build and the service you want to create, and if the organization is growing and customers are adopting—there are empirically some things about your culture that are working well. And I often see companies making a mistake by being too abashed about simply being specific about those.

For example, you might believe firmly in the importance of working hard. Or you might believe firmly in the importance of minute attention to detail to the degree that you're willing to redo something five times over. What often happens is that companies allude to these things, but in overly oblique fashions. They'll say, "We believe in the importance of commitment," but won't be concrete enough to say that, well, we want people who really want to pour their hearts into this for several years, and we expect this to be the singular focus of your working life.

Similarly, on the attention-to-detail front, it's easy to describe things in overly milquetoast terms without being really explicit, like: "If you work with us, you're going to have to be okay with your work being repeatedly designated as inadequate, and okay with it being redone several times over." These aren't things that everyone is looking for. And you're going to have to be okay with some people having that conversation with you and deciding that it's not for them.

If you aren't having these explicit conversations about what your culture is, the downsides are threefold: You don't have the right people joining you, and you're being unfair to those who do join you, in the sense that they end up being surprised by this emergent friction and tension in work styles. Thirdly, and I think this may be the non-obvious one, people's disposition with regard to the company is actually a function of what they feel like they signed up for. If they feel like they signed up for an all-encompassing project, they'll be much more willing to treat it that way than if they discovered it by surprise later on. And so you can actually change the outcome simply by being explicit at the outset.

Elad: And by outset, you mean during the interview process? Or during the onboarding?

Patrick: Before offer acceptance. I think it can still work during onboarding, but ideally before acceptance.

The other failure mode, then, once you've succeeded in being explicit enough about your culture, is becoming overly wedded to it. And this is the tension: you need to be explicit about what you are, but also willing to revisit it. One of the most difficult exercises in judgment that has to be applied by the leaders of a startup is continually balancing this tension. Where are outcomes undesirable or insufficient because of deficiencies in the degree to which people are following the culture, and where are they deficient because of what the culture itself is? Is it the implementation or is it the spec?

The degrees of freedom involved here are so great, and the data you actually have is so sparse, and the commingling and interference effects are so strong, it's very hard to separate all these concerns. So it does just come down to being a very challenging judgment call.

One common misjudgment you see is companies or organizations that benefited from really lightweight or indeed nonexistent management structures either falsely diagnosing early success to that trait or correctly diagnosing early success to that trait but being unwilling to appreciate the extent to which it's no longer the right thing for the organization when it's 40 or 70 people, rather than just seven.

Elad: You're pointing out a really important cultural failure mode, where it's very hard for people to revise early culture, or you have an old-timer cohort that gets stuck on it. What are some of the tactics that you've used to deal with cultural revision?

Patrick: The first-order thing is simply being clear that you do not want to preserve culture; you want to collectively steer the right evolution of the culture. And that might sound like a fine distinction, but people will talk about early culture a lot. They'll get misty-eyed about the halcyon days of yore. And you really have to push against it: "In so many ways we were derpy back then. We didn't know what the hell we were doing. And even if it worked, there were undoubtedly so many things that took longer than they should have or were more painful than they should have been."

It's really easy to learn the wrong lessons from early success. I really think you need to be explicit about that, that the challenge is not in preserving the culture but in having it evolve the right way. And I would highlight some of the early things you inevitably did that were just kind of stupid.

The second thing is, when doing things that involve change to the culture—maybe hiring a senior external leader or creating a new function in the company—embrace and be explicit about the fact that it is going to change the culture. So, for example, you're hiring a new head of sales, and people are concerned that that's going to shift the culture, rather than saying, "Well, we've taken all these measures to avoid that happening, and we're going to be hyper attentive to anything that looks like a shift," be honest. Part of the point of hiring this person is to change the culture. If this person has no effect on the culture, they've probably failed. You're hiring a senior sales leader because you want the company to sell more, and you want the company to become a culture that is better at selling things.

I think deep down people know that intellectually, but it's often messaged the wrong way. So in Stripe's case, when we hired our COO—she was previously a senior leader in Google's sales organization—people were worried that she would change the culture.[46] We had to be explicit and clear about the fact that she would. That was the job. And I think the changes she has helped bring have been very healthy and beneficial for the company.

Elad: How do you deal with naysayers? Because even if you're very good at selecting people up front, especially if a company is very good about discussing culture or progress, there's going to be people who will push back or bring their own very strong perspectives.

Patrick: Again it's a delicate balancing act, in the sense that people are going to disagree with you or raise problems for different reasons. Often when people raise problems with you, they'll be real problems, legitimate ones, ones you'll ideally fix. They're raising a problem out of good motivations and it really behooves you to listen to them closely and do whatever you can to help resolve it. You often have to emphasize to people that that's typically not going to be a quick process, and that's part of what you have to get okay with as a startup. But generally speaking, you should lend them a very sympathetic ear.

---

46 Claire Hughes Johnson. See her interview in this book.

Sometimes, though, people are going to disagree with things or raise objections or indeed be naysayers for reasons that you simply disagree with. They think the company should work X way, and maybe it used to work X way, but you have now made the decision that it ought to work Y way. In those cases, to have a healthy and effective relationship, it's necessary to be explicit with that person that they need to decide either that Y is a thing they can be okay with and can enthusiastically sign up for or that this may not be a happy and fulfilling environment for them over the long term.

This can be a painful conversation, because these people are often naysayers because they're deeply invested in what the company is. But sometimes that becomes an investment in what the company was. Most people are quite good at staying with that evolution, which is a difficult exercise and an unnatural exercise in some ways. But not everyone is. And that doesn't mean they're bad people. It doesn't mean they won't be fabulous contributors to a broad swathe of organizations. It may just mean that they're no longer the right person for the particular organization that you are at that point and will be going forward.

Again, the mistake that I see companies make all the time is simply not being honest about those conversations. It drags on for a year or two on both sides, and then in the end people are dissatisfied, they're not doing well at their job, and they depart on bad terms.

I would just try to front-load those conversations. Keep things non-acrimonious, and sort of non-emotional, where it's, "Look, we're going to do Y. Can you set aside your perhaps underlying desire for X and sign up for it? Or not? We're not going to judge you if you don't want to do that."

Elad: At every company that I've seen scale aggressively, a subset of the early employee base will turn over. And that should be considered natural and actually good for that employee base. Many folks just don't want to work in a larger organization, or they may be looking for something very specific, and if the company no longer serves that purpose they're going to be happier somewhere else.

Patrick: Yeah. It's like, say, an organization that doesn't fire anyone. It's possible that they're so staggeringly good at hiring that that's in fact the right thing to do. But of course that's statistically extraordinarily unlikely, and they would have made an interviewing breakthrough that nobody else in the world has.

Similarly, if every early employee is still with the company five years in, it's possible that you hired such an amazingly adaptable array of people that that is in fact the right thing for the organization. But again, statistically speaking, that would be unlikely. Again, the more people you have that are in fact truly adaptable and can stick with it, the better. But you should really question the degree to which you think that's in fact everyone.

Elad: How do you think about reinforcing or reminding employees about an organization's cultural values? Do you incorporate it as part of performance reviews, incorporating it into weekly all-hands?

Patrick: I think the macro thing to bear in mind with a lot of culture stuff is that a rapidly scaling human organization is an unnatural thing. The vast majority of human organizations that we have experience with, be it the school, the family, the university, the local community, the church, whatever, these are not organizations that scale really rapidly. And so the cues and the lessons and the habits you might learn from them are not necessarily going to be sufficient for the kind of human organization you're building, which is perhaps doubling—or even more—in size, year over year.

As a consequence of that, you'll often hear people talk about things like using explicit cultural values in performance reviews or in weekly all-hands. And you think, "Well, most of the other human organizations I see don't do that," and so it seems sort of contrived or whatever. But the difference is that you actually have a much more difficult challenge, which is to maintain a high degree of cohesion despite the really rapid evolution in the group of constituent participants.

So I'm a big fan of all the things you just mentioned. I think most companies start to explicitly encode and articulate their principles or values too late. I would try to produce a provisional revision literally when you're just a handful of people. Then continue to update it on an ongoing basis, because assuredly there will be things you realize or come to appreciate are wrong over the course of the company.

But I would start with something right from the outset. And I would absolutely weave it into your product development, your collective communications with each other, your decision-making in general. For example, when you're choosing the right series A investors, say, I think it would be ideal if the principles by which you ran the organization and the culture internally could help guide you to the right kind of investor for the company.

Elad: How do you think about things like a culture czar, or appointing somebody who's the owner of culture?

Patrick: I think it's generally a bad idea for a couple of reasons, if by culture czar you mean someone who is not the CEO. Firstly, the people who you'll be tempted to appoint as that individual are typically people who have a great degree of personal, emotional investment in what the company is. And that needs to change. Again, it may be the case that you're improbably lucky, and that person can navigate all the progressions and advancement that the culture will require. But more likely, they won't. And the fervor of the attachment that they've developed to what the company presently is will actually stand in the way of the evolution that the culture ought to undergo.

The second reason I think it's a bad idea is because the CEO ultimately does not have that many jobs, but I think culture is among them. And it ought not be delegated. Briefly speaking, I think there are five top responsibilities of a CEO: being the steward of and final arbiter of the senior management; being the chief strategist; being the primary external face for the company, at least in the early days; almost certainly being the chief product officer, although that can change when you're bigger; and then taking responsibility and accountability for culture. And culture is so fundamental to what the company is that it's truly problematic to delegate.

Elad: Do you think there's a natural ceiling on growth because of the work it takes to onboard people to company culture? In other words, when do you know that you're growing too fast? Is it when you're tripling instead of doubling? Is it a certain number of people joining? Do you think there's a natural law like that, or is each company different?

Patrick: I think it's primarily a function of the experience and cohesion of your management team. So if you started out with 30 experienced managers and leaders who are all clear together on the strategy, I actually think you could scale astonishingly rapidly. Now, developing that sort of cohesion and selecting those people and hiring them and everything else—I don't know of a company that in fact did start out with 30 of them.

But I would think about it primarily in terms of leadership bandwidth. And you can even apply this within specific areas of the company. If you have a really good sales leader or HR leader, and maybe the organization is only two or three people today but you can just see that it's working and the person is on the same page and integrated and so forth, then I think you could scale from two or three to 30 very quickly and it would probably go well. Whereas, on the flip side, if you happen to be a five-person HR organization and it's working pretty well but you lack the right leader for it, then even just going to 10 people could be very challenging.

"You do not want to preserve culture; you want to collectively steer the right evolution of the culture."

—Patrick Collison

In practice, when organizations scale at more than 2X year over year—they don't always fail, but it's particularly challenging. You need a strong case for why you are unique and why you will not encounter the default outcome of true chaos. Such examples exist, but they're rare. The mega-cap company over the last 20 years that's done the best job of scaling from a cultural standpoint is Facebook. And they were really careful about not growing more than around 60% a year, and being very deliberate about that. That could merely be correlation or coincidence, but I don't think it is.

Elad: How do you think about culture in the context of an international office or distributed team?

Patrick: Stripe now has on the order of 10 international offices of various sizes. And I think the key things are to have the right site lead and initial seed crystals. It's not just about the lead; it's about the two, three, four people around whom the culture of the office is going to form.

Elad: Do you try to send people who were previously working at Stripe headquarters, or do you just try to hire people locally who have the right characteristics?

Patrick: I think you want to have the seed crystals be people who either spend a whole bunch of time at headquarters first or, to your point, have worked at headquarters for a while and want to go live or work elsewhere. For a long time, you also want all employees at the new office to start out in headquarters for at least weeks and potentially months.

So, for example, in our Dublin office, which is now 70 people, almost everyone started out for the first couple of weeks, at least, in our headquarters in San Francisco.

Patrick: Almost everyone interviewed in headquarters. And obviously that's going to change at some point. But the long-term value for them for just having built connections in headquarters and seen more of it is really hard to overstate.

The other point—and this seems superficially minor, but I think it's actually a big deal—is to think about the mechanics of communication. So have a really good videoconferencing setup, and rooms wired for it. Make it really easy to record a meeting, broadcast a meeting, have remote participants, and so forth.

Secondly, think about the timing of your key meetings. It often seems a bit unfortunate, I think, from a cultural perspective to move your all-hands from 5pm on Friday, when everyone's having a beer, to Friday morning or Thursday morning or something that's friendlier to Europe or Asia. But if you're actually serious about these other offices, I think it's necessary.

Thirdly, once you get big enough—which I suspect is not a huge number of people, maybe 100 to 200 people—think about internal communications as a function unto itself. Again, I think a lot of people are resistant to it because it seems somewhat corporate. But if you actually think that people understanding what's going on at the company and what the top priorities are is important, it would seem a little bit strange to leave it to happenstance and to leave it as everyone's 1% job in the back of their mind. Having somebody who's taking overall ownership and responsibility for broad-based clarity of communication—people are generally surprised by how valuable it is once they eventually start doing it a little bit later than they should have.

Elad: Have you looked to any models for building your culture? Do you study other organizations that you think have done this work effectively?

Patrick: I think people should select carefully the companies they seek to emulate and learn lessons from. It's very easy to choose those that are contemporaries of yours or happen to be top of mind and salient. But generally speaking, if they're contemporaries—and certainly if they're of a remotely similar size—they're likely to be insufficiently proven. We're based in San Francisco, and there's a whole host of companies here that are very prominent and easy to emulate even subconsciously but are not good examples.

So I spend a lot of my time talking to people and trying to read things about the greats of the earlier days of the Valley—the Intels and, though of course not in the Valley, Microsofts, the early days of Google, the years when Steve Jobs returned to Apple. Because we have full context of what came afterward and what the outcomes actually were.

For the contemporaries, here and now, the jury's still out. My personal opinion is that some of these companies—by no means all, but some of them—are in the process of making either major cultural or organizational errors that are going to substantially impede them from becoming that which is, or was, their potential. So be careful and deliberate in choosing your role models.

Elad: Yes, product/market fit is very different from being strong culturally and adaptable. It's easy to confuse that if you see something working really well, even if the organization is terrible.

Patrick: That's a really good way to put it. Most great products with strong initial traction fail to endure or become any kind of durable organization. Which just underscores the difficulty of that transformation. Most people who try fail, so make sure that you're modeling yourself after something that is definitively a success.

"I think people should select carefully the companies they seek to emulate and learn lessons from."

—Patrick Collison

Elad: As you look across the Valley now, it seems like there have been some shifts that have created almost a culture of entitlement. People get enormous benefits, then start to complain about things that may not be that important, like the number of times they can get a free haircut on campus. How do you manage that? As people get bigger and bigger benefits, how do you make sure they don't feel that they deserve everything?

Patrick: I think that this is simply a challenge that we collectively have in the U.S. and in the Bay Area in this era of history. Such wealth has been created by our predecessors that we're short-term benefiting from that it's easy for that to have spillover effects in the culture and to distract from focus or lead to a loss of determination.

And again, if you just study and read a little about the early days, and ideally talk to people who were around, you see that at the first semiconductor companies and the early software companies and, up to Seattle, early Amazon and Microsoft, there was nothing to be entitled about. People thought that software companies were inconsequential add-ons to the hardware. They were dismissed, they were subject to brutal release cycles, companies were going out of business left, right, and center, there was a lot of concern over competition from Asia. It was a tough market to grow up in. Of course the survivors have done well. But while people are attuned to how successful a cradle for technology Silicon Valley is, they pay less attention to, and are I think less aware of, how densely populated a graveyard it is.

And so while I think that selective pressure was good for the surviving companies, it really kind of screws with our intuitive sense for what's required to actually build one of these. You have some early success or you raise series A or gain some early traction, and it's easy, even subconsciously, to start lining up the plots in your head: "Well, Facebook raised its series A in 2005, and went on to be worth $15 billion in 2008 or 2009 or whatever it was," and so on. And I think the effects of that, in blunt terms, are really pernicious. In many ways it's harder to create an organization with the kind of focused, determined, disciplined, non-complacent mindset that you need today than it was 20 or 30 years ago. That's just a structural headwind that we all face.

There are many natural benefits and tailwinds that Silicon Valley enjoys, but I think this is one of the challenges we face. And if Silicon Valley is supplanted by another region, or even just more broadly by a general diffusion, I think this is one of the top contenders as to why that would be the case. It's because we had too much wealth, we had too much early success, and it caused us to lose our hunger and our edge.

People who've spent any time with the great software companies in China—JD, Tencent, Alibaba, and now the next generation of startups—will tell you in no uncertain terms that there is a lack of entitlement, a lack of complacency, and a real determination to succeed that is at least not uniformly present here in Silicon Valley. And so I really think it's something that should be top of mind for everyone. ■

This interview has been edited and condensed for clarity.

DIVERSITY HIRING

A common culture does not mean "people who look and act exactly like me." Building a cohesive team means hiring people who have a common sense of purpose and mission, and a shared outlook on what is important within the confines and context of a company.

There has been a call within Silicon Valley to increase the ethnic and gender diversity of companies. A few tools or approaches you can use to prioritize diversity hiring include:

1. **Recruiting**
   - Make sure to source and pursue diverse candidates for a role.
   - Work with your executive and recruiting teams to think through how biases may emerge in your hiring processes.[47]
   - Some recruiting companies you could use include Jopwell and Triplebyte.
   - If using a recruiting firm, specify the importance of gender and race.
   - If you do college recruiting, make sure to recruit on campuses with more diversity in their student bodies.
   - When interviewing women, include women on their interview and hiring panels. Ditto for people of color.

2. **Role models**
   - Think about diversity broadly. Did you include women and underrepresented minorities as investors? How diverse is your board and executive team?
   - Can you provide programs to mentor women and underrepresented minorities?
   - Do you provide press or speaking opportunities for women and underrepresented minorities? This may help attract other candidates to your company.

3. **Benefits**
   - Think about the benefits you offer. Do you have a maternity policy that supports working mothers? Do you have pumping rooms or other infrastructure for new parents? Are these rooms actually reserved and available for new mothers?

---

[47] Biases may not only impact hiring diverse ethnicities and genders, but also even prevent you from effective hiring of other sorts. For example, I have seen back-end-heavy engineering teams who can't hire a great front-end engineer because their interview questions and styles are geared against this other type of engineering hire.

The hardest part of diversity hiring for startups is that startups tend to source key people out of large incumbents (e.g., Google, Facebook, etc.). These companies act as "feeders" to startups who are looking for experienced hires or executives who have operated at scale. Since these large companies lack a lot of diverse employees (particularly in engineering, product, and design), diversity hiring becomes more difficult for downstream startups. As a startup, you will need to look at less common sources for talent, and in today's environment where diversity is an increasing focus for many companies, it may be more competitive and may take longer to hire candidates with diverse backgrounds.[48]

---

[48] There has been some debate in the past about whether diversity hiring has a "pipeline" issue or an inherent bias issue. This complex issue is not an "either/or," but rather a "both." Unfortunately, the reality is that there are two types of problems: (1) companies need to change their practices to ensure that they are seeking diverse candidates and embracing/supporting diverse employees, and (2) the industry at large, particularly larger companies that employ the hundreds of thousands of qualified candidates that startups want to poach from, has a diversity problem itself.

DIVERSITY IS NOT A NICE-TO-HAVE

An interview with Joelle Emerson

Joelle Emerson is the founder and CEO of Paradigm, which partners with leaders of innovative companies to consult and advise on diversity and inclusion strategies. She has written extensively about diversity, inclusion, and unconscious bias, and her work has been featured in The Wall Street Journal, The New Yorker, Fortune, Fast Company, Business Insider, and several other outlets.

Before founding Paradigm Joelle was a women's rights employment lawyer. As a Skadden Fellow at Equal Rights Advocates, she represented women in gender discrimination and sexual harassment litigation, and she advocated for local, state, and federal policies to ensure equal pay and other workplace protections for women. Joelle is a graduate of Stanford Law School.

Joelle Emerson is at the heart of the conversation on diversity, advising rapidly growing giants like Slack and Airbnb on how to develop the strategies and mindsets that will equip them to recruit and retain diverse teams. Using a research-heavy, data-driven approach, her firm is demonstrating why varied perspectives make companies stronger and training startups to effectively source them.

I had the opportunity to speak with her about why a culture of inclusivity actually yields better products, and how growing tech startups can leverage the lessons of the companies that went before them.

Elad Gil:
Let's start with the basics: Why is diversity important, and how can companies start thinking about it early?

Joelle Emerson:
There are a lot of reasons why diversity matters, and it's important for every company that's going to invest in this—invest time, invest resources, invest energy—to have a reason that's specific to them.

The first reason is that there is a lot of research showing diverse teams are stronger when it comes to analytical thinking and complex problem-solving—basically the things that contribute to innovation. There's also research that shows a correlational relationship between companies that have diversity and positive financial outcomes. I tend to find that people aren't as persuaded by the latter (because it's hard to know what's the cause, what's the effect, is there some third factor), but they are interested in the wealth of research that shows a causal relationship between adding diversity to teams and those teams' ability to solve hard problems.

When it comes to small companies that are thinking about hard problems, they're interested in building the team that helps them do that best. And we know that when you bring together people from different backgrounds—and this has been studied in terms of gender, in terms of ethnicity, even, as surprising as it sometimes seems, in terms of political affiliation—when you bring together those different perspectives, you can create a team that's better able to innovate.

Then there's a second category of reasons why this matters for some companies, which is that if you're building for a diverse customer/user base, it's helpful to have perspectives on your team that can help you design and build products or services for those users.

One example of this I really like is the story of when YouTube launched a mobile product in 2012 that allowed people to upload videos from their cell phones. They saw that about 10% of videos were being uploaded upside down, and they ultimately found out that that's because left-handed people hold their cell phones differently. There were no left-handed people among the product or design team that worked on that product. I think we're just better able to design for a broader group of people when we have people with different perspectives designing products.

The third reason is that the talent pool is generally very narrow. Companies are just generally struggling to find good talent to build their companies. People understand that, "Okay, it's hard to find people, and if I rely only on my own network and I don't think about building a company that attracts people from different backgrounds that's limiting me logistically from hiring more people." I work with a couple of companies that are actually primarily motivated by that, by creating a company that is the most attractive to the widest set of people so they can get the best talent in.

And then the fourth reason, which it's important not to ignore, is that a lot of companies actually think this is the right thing to do, to include all kinds of communities in the design and development of technology and in creating the products that are going to define what our world looks like over the next 10, 20, however many years. They think it's problematic that groups are being left out of that creation of technology.

Those are the four reasons I see fundamentally motivating the companies we work with. And I think they're all good reasons. To start, you should know which one resonates with you so that you can design your strategy to be responsive to what you really care about.

Elad: What do you think are the biggest obstacles to companies actually being able to source and hire a diverse set of people for their teams?

Joelle: It's helpful to break it down into the two parts you articulated, source and hire.

On the sourcing side, one big obstacle is that people's networks are really homogenous, especially along racial and ethnic lines and along educational-background lines. Our networks are filled with mostly people who are similar to us, and when you're at a fairly early stage you rely heavily on your networks to build your company. Companies that want to benefit from the value of diversity need to be willing to invest some time in going outside of their own networks.

I acknowledge that doing that is an investment of time. So any company has to decide how big of a priority it is for them to benefit from diversity. And they have to decide how early they want to do that, because we know that when you wait to start bringing in people from different backgrounds, it just gets exponentially harder to get that first, that second person in. Because who wants to join a company where 50 people look one way and you look a different way? It's much easier when it's five people or 10 people, 15 people.

A second barrier on the sourcing side is unconscious bias, and maybe sometimes conscious bias—that is, certain beliefs about who's going to be a good fit for a role. With unconscious bias, our brains naturally take cognitive shortcuts and engage in pattern matching. So people think of who they've seen in a role like this in the past, and that can color who they then go look for.

Then there's what I call the culture of brilliance—which I think is a really unhealthy part of the tech community—this belief in innate talents, innate abilities, the myth of "the natural," looking for people who just "have it," rock stars, any of these sort of words or traits. We know that when we think about abilities, talents, and intelligence as fixed, innate traits, stereotypes are much more likely to guide our decision-making than when we have more of a growth mindset and we think about talent and abilities as malleable—as things people can develop. Those are two really big barriers I see come into play on the sourcing side.

On the hiring side, once candidates get in the door, early-stage companies generally have pretty terrible processes for making hiring decisions. Usually they're really subjective, ad-hoc, and different from candidate to candidate or interviewer to interviewer. We know that the more structure you have in place to guide hiring decisions, the more accurate those decisions will be and the less barriers like unconscious bias are going to creep in and influence outcomes.

For example, when companies hire for "culture fit"—even big companies, but especially companies that are 20 people, 30 people—I hear people define "fit" differently, and articulate different approaches as to how they assess for it. Some people are looking for "Who do I want to get stuck in an airport with for 12 hours?" And these are just really, really poor methods of assessing people's abilities or assessing who's going to be a good fit in the role. So I think one critical solution there is just creating some structure in the process. Be clear about what it is that you're looking for, use job-relevant work samples, actually see how people do work, and then design interviews that are objective and structured to produce relevant information.

Elad: At Color we actually went through an exercise defining what we mean by "culture fit," specifically to get rid of biases—not just from a diversity perspective, but because we wanted to make sure that everybody was aligned in terms of what we really meant by that. It was about emphasizing things like excellence and pragmatism and those sorts of traits in terms of what we were looking for, although those are particularly hard to grok sometimes.

Joelle: That's great. And I hope that the Valley in general moves away from the term "culture fit." The word "fit" almost primes us to think about "who is like people we already have on the team," beyond the specific traits we've articulated.

"You usually only need one or two key hires to make a really big difference."

— Joelle Emerson

I really like when companies think about it more in terms of values alignment or work-style alignment, people that are going to do work the way that work gets done in our organization. We've also worked with companies that call this "culture add." "Who's going to bring what we most need?" rather than "Who fits in with what we already have?" The approach to assessing for this matters more than what it's called, but words do matter, and the way that we talk about these things can have an impact as well.

Elad: One other obstacle I've seen on the sourcing side is that—for my company and a lot of the companies I'm involved with—startups tend to source out of larger, more successful tech companies. And since those larger tech companies themselves seem to have a reasonably homogenous teams, that in and of itself limits who you end up recruiting. Because you start off with the numbers against you. How do you think about overcoming those obstacles? Or where should startups look alternatively? How do you start thinking about broadening the set of networks, to your point earlier?

Joelle: When you are looking at bigger companies within those networks that you're sourcing from, make diversity intentional. Intentionally look for people that would add diversity. Different companies define diversity differently, it could be in terms of age, educational profile, ethnicity, gender. For example, we know some companies that spend 90–100% of their outbound recruiting, their active sourcing efforts, focused only on candidates from underrepresented backgrounds. They know that their inbound is not diverse, and so the only way to move the needle is in their active efforts.

Elad: What are some examples of companies that do that?

Joelle: The one company that I know that's talked about it publically is Gusto. They committed I think 100% of their outbound sourcing to identifying candidates from underrepresented backgrounds.

Elad: One of the points that you raised that I thought was really key is around being at a state where you as a company can invest in people. Many companies want to do it, but even things like hiring more junior people tend to take a lot of bandwidth from the team when the company is still on the smaller end of 50 or even 100 people. So it seems really hard to invest in people until you really reach critical mass as a company.

Joelle: I agree that doing that is really hard when you're early. As someone who has a five-person company, I know that is really hard. But even before you do that, you can achieve easier wins, like focusing your outbound sourcing on people who are from underrepresented groups, for example, or posting job descriptions on job boards and with organizations that have demographically diverse representation.

When you're really early, yes, it's hard. But the other nice thing is you usually only need one or two key hires to make a really big difference. The numbers needed to dramatically move the needle aren't that big. So it's an investment in getting a couple of those hires in the door.

I know there are candidates from underrepresented backgrounds that can meet early-stage companies' qualifications if those companies spend the time finding them. And the return on investment, as companies benefit from those employees' networks as they grow, will be so worthwhile. And then as you grow, then yes, all the things you said about thinking about growing people and having a wider sense of what you're looking for and that sort of thing, those things come into play.

Elad: You're making a great point. Because if you're really growing off of your network early on, then you should be consciously asking yourself who you want in your network early on, so you can grow off of that. Really thinking about it as a foundation early is important.

How do you think about diversity at the board level, which I think is a whole different ball game in some sense?

Joelle: It is a different ball game, and we actually don't spend a ton of time working on this, mostly because early-stage companies we work with are like, "We're not adding anyone to our board, period. We don't want a big board. We want it to be us—founders—and a couple of key investors. We just don't want to add anyone, at all." Okay, well, that's a conscious decision you can make. If you don't have any investors who are from underrepresented groups, and your board members are only you and investors, that's tough.

But as you grow, and you think about adding people with specific areas of expertise, thinking about diversity is incredibly important, and I think the only way to really do it at the board level is just do it. To actually just say, "We believe it's critical that the people issuing guidance to our company represent different perspectives."

There's a lot of research—again this is correlational research—that shows positive financial impact, and less of the types of damaging decisions companies can make financially, when you have women, in particular, on your board. So I think you just have to say, "We're going to do this, if we're adding a board seat. This is what our board looks like now, so for this seat we need someone that brings these talents and skills and that would add diversity, and that's what we're going to consider."

Again, it's usually a matter of adding one person, so you have to take time. The hard thing with companies that are growing quickly is a lot of this stuff just takes a little bit more time. I think the benefit is worth it. But there are more men that have served on boards, so if you're trying to fill a board seat quickly it's just going to be much easier to find a man than a woman. But if you want the best person and you want to create the best board, you just have to commit to it and not waver as people send other candidates your way.

Elad: Jack Dorsey actually spent a lot of time on this, both for Square and now for Twitter. So I know that if you can prioritize it then you can accomplish it. To your earlier point, it strikes me that where it starts is on the investor side. Because if you don't have any investors from underrepresented groups, then effectively you're not going to build those relationships early on. Often what I've found is that the first independent board member will often be an investor or other advisor or friend of the company who's already somehow involved, either formally or informally.

Joelle: Yeah, I agree. And there's so much responsibility on the shoulders—or there should be responsibility on the shoulders—of the venture capital industry in general to do better. I think tech companies have taken this much, much more seriously—or have begun to take it much more seriously—this kind of thoughtfulness around diversity and inclusion than VCs have. And that's really, really hard, because it's the VCs who help you build your network. They're sending you candidates, they're sending you recommendations for board seats, and if they don't have networks that are diverse it's going to make it much harder for you. So I'm hoping that as tech companies start to ask for this more, VCs respond. That's what we're beginning to see: tech companies are asking their investors to help them with this. And then we're hearing from their investors saying, "How do we help them with this?" So that's good, and I hope that that trend continues.

Elad: What are the best approaches that you've seen, for people to either get rid of unconscious bias from the job application and interview process?

Joelle: Structured interviewing is the one thing that I think is completely critical to doing that effectively, to actually hiring the best people and increasing diversity. I think of this as a four-step process.

Step one is articulating the relevant qualifications for every role, technical and non-technical (if there are non-technical qualifications).

Step two is designing specific questions to assess for each qualification. It's important not just to be clear about what matters, but be clear about how you're going to determine whether someone meets that qualification, and that everyone is aligned on what questions to ask for each competency.

Step three is limiting the domains that each interviewer assesses. You shouldn't have to go in and try to decide, "Should we hire this person?" as an interviewer. You should decide, "Does this person meet what we need on these two things?" Because what we know is when cognitive load is heavy, that's when people are most likely to take shortcuts. And when you're trying to assess people along five different lines, that's just really hard to do, for any person, especially in a 30-minute, hour-long interview.

Then step four, and this one's really critical, is creating rubrics to help interviewers evaluate answers to the questions that they're asking, or to grade work samples that they're getting. A rubric can be as simple as: A great answer will hit on these three things, a medium answer will hit on maybe two of those things, a bad answer will not talk about any of these, or maybe it'll hit on one. These kinds of things really help anchor people in what they're looking for in interviews, and they limit the common biases that we know affect hiring decisions, like confirmation bias, where you answer a couple of questions really well and I'm primed to look for all the things you do well the rest of the interview. Or I'm really impressed by your resume, so I'm primed to really think you're going to be great and pay attention to the things you do well. When you're anchored around the rubric, you're much better able to focus on the answer and figure out if the answers each person is giving are actually good. So that's one thing that I think is just critical.

And then if you're growing, think about how your job descriptions look: How are you attracting people? How are you talking about your company, and where are you posting jobs? Are you writing job descriptions that are likely to attract a narrow slice of people because you're using, for example, gendered language? Or are you talking in terms of innate abilities like brilliance?

Research shows, in particular, that women are less likely to apply for jobs that are described in terms of a fixed mindset, like brilliance, rather than a growth mindset, like learning and growth. And then where are you posting your jobs? Are you posting them on sites and in places where people from different groups are most likely to look?

Elad: There's bringing people in the door or hiring people, and then there's integrating them, mentoring them, creating an environment where a variety of people can thrive. Have you seen companies fail on that front? And if so, how can they avoid that?

Joelle: Most companies really struggle with that, even the ones that are doing hiring decently well. It's hard. But thinking about how to create a culture where everyone can feel like they belong is really critical, and not just a nice-to-have.

There's a lot of research that shows that when people question whether they belong, their work performance suffers, their engagement goes down, they're more likely to leave—all of these bad things happen. What companies typically do is build a culture that works well for the dominant group, but doesn't work well for people that may not be like the people already there.

There's a lot of research on a topic called "ambient belonging." That is, what are the little signals that we're getting from the world around us that tell us whether we belong or not? This can be really small things like the posters on your wall, or the types of social events you host. Are all your networking events or social team events happy hours after work? Well, if so, that sends a pretty strong message to people who may have obligations outside of work or who may not drink. Or do you also have events and activities that include people who might come from different backgrounds or who might not be able to do the things that you're doing? Is your office designed in a way that feels like a place anyone could feel comfortable?

I will say this: I go into tech company offices each week, and about 30% of the time I think, "Wow, I would not fit in here," before I speak to anyone. Just by the way the office is designed, the things I see on the wall, alcohol all over the place, ping-pong tables. Sometimes I look at tech company websites, and I see that the images they use to show their benefits are pictures of men. They say that they have gym benefits, and the "gym" icon is a man's arm lifting weights. Those things send a message to people. And it's easy to miss if you're from the group that is represented, but it's pretty powerful. So starting to think about how to build a culture where people can do their best work is crucial.

The other thing we see companies really struggle with is new managers, or inexperienced managers. A lot of people in early-stage companies haven't managed other people before, or don't have a lot of experience doing that. So they're just not great at doing basic manager things, like giving feedback. And giving good feedback, feedback about the process—what went wrong, what went well, how can you do better.

Early-stage companies say, "Well, we can't really develop manager training. We don't have the capacity for that. How do we do this?" One thing that you can do that's really easy is use a vendor and provide coaching. Require managers to have a certain amount of one-on-one coaching per month, or whatever might make sense. Just so that you feel like every manager on your team, even though you can't provide it yet, is getting some guidance and some direction on how to give feedback.

You can also create sample tools or templates that show people what good feedback looks like. Sometimes little things like that are so overlooked, and they're really helpful.

You can show what bad feedback looks like. For example: "You're a good communicator. You did a good job on that project." In contrast, here's good feedback: "You communicated well by keeping people up-to-date on the status of your project and being helpful to your coworkers as you worked through challenges."

Show people what it actually looks like to give process-oriented feedback that helps people grow and develop. I think coaching and using external vendors, external coaches, can be super helpful, and you can do that at any stage of your company.

Elad: Outside of people outright quitting, are there any warning signs or ways to gauge that you're creating an environment that is going to drive out certain people over time, or not help people meet their full potential at your company?

Joelle: When you're bigger—I'd say once you're 50 people—you can start using surveys. And I think surveys are really helpful, and they actually can be very predictive. There's research that shows—some things you don't really need research for—but there's research that shows that one of the best ways to predict whether an employee is going to leave is if they say they're going to leave when you ask them in an engagement survey whether they plan to be there in a year. So you can actually start to gauge how people feel about your organization by asking them.

As you get bigger, you can survey along demographic lines too, and then cut results by different groups. You need a certain n-count to do this and keep it anonymous, but once you have that you can start to see, "Oh, do women consistently feel differently about things like the quality of their managers than men?" "Do African-American engineers in our organization feel differently about advancement opportunities than white engineers?"

You have to be a certain size to be able to do that. But before you're that size, you can still create regular opportunities for employees to communicate with senior leadership about how they feel about the company. You can have regular brown-bag lunches that are specifically designed to talk about culture and how people feel. You can have monthly, or even quarterly, events where the leaders of the org get together with people to just ask about how they're feeling. You can also hold office hours, where once a month you set aside two hours and you say, "This is specifically designed with a focus on building an inclusive culture, so please come talk to me if you think there are things we could be doing better." These are things that are pretty easy to do even at a really small stage.

One other thing companies need to think about—even if they're not going to do this early—is how they are going to start measuring and rewarding performance. I think companies typically wait too long to put processes in place for this. Usually it's because they've had a terrible experience with performance review processes in the past, because most of them suck. But what we know is that if you don't have any process in place, it's really hard to make outcomes fair, because people just defer to biases. People's brains are really bad at relying on data to make decisions.

So actually thinking, "Okay, we're going to start that process at 50 people. And before we have that process, we're going to have some rigor in our leveling decisions or promotion decisions or comp decisions in this way. We're going to ask these three questions." Having even a light amount of structure, and then plans for when you're going to roll out more, is really helpful. It's important to outcomes not only that organizations be fair, but that people perceive them to be fair. When there's no process that guides outcomes, people question that a lot. So just having some clarity around how decisions are being made, and how they're going to be made as you grow, is really important. ◼

This interview has been edited and condensed for clarity.

"One other thing companies need to think about is how they are going to start measuring and rewarding performance."

—Joelle Emerson

MANAGING IN A DOWNTURN

Like all industries, the technology sector is cyclical.[19] The availability of capital during up periods allows companies to grow rapidly (in some cases with poor unit economics when growth is chased as a primary focus). During the down periods companies need to fundamentally change their behavior in a cash scarce environment (growth is often, but not always, sacrificed for profitability).

I have lived through the downturns in two cycles: the end of the bubble in 2001-2002 and then the financial crisis in 2008 (which ultimately impacted tech in only a minor way and was not anything like 2001). Given that these cycles occur in 5- to 15-year increments, a new flock of entrepreneurs is ascendant at any given tech cycle and people tend to make the same mistakes with each cycle when times turn sour.

If you are an early stage company (e.g., 5 people with $2M in the bank) the primary thing you should do is seek product/market fit. Beyond not spending irresponsibly, there is not much else you should change in how you operate in a downturn. Some of the greatest companies in tech were founded or funded during downturns (HP and Cisco being two of them).[50] Google and Amazon really hit their stride as the entire technology industry collapsed around them post-2001.

If you are a mid- to later-stage company (e.g., 40 people to hundreds of people) you should think through the company's finances and plan ahead.

During a technology cycle downturn you should do the following:

1. **Focus on cash.** Running out of money is typically how a later-stage company goes out of business. Check your cash position—how long will it last based on projections? During downturns you may want to pad things up to three years in case capital freezes up for a year or two. Ways to increase runway include:
   - Raise money. Aim to have three years or more of cash in the bank. If you have to, raise a round at a low valuation and don't over optimize.
   - Watch expenses. Don't spend money unless it is really necessary. If you need to scale up sales, definitely do so. Keep doing whatever is needed to make your company successful—but be cheap about how you approach it. Think hard about pound-foolish/pennywise trade-offs. For example, don't cut snacks in the office and then spend lavishly on first class flights for the sales team.
   - Increase profitability. How can you make existing sales higher-margin or revenue-accretive? If your current sales are unit margin negative, how do you fix that? Quit focusing on growth if you are losing money with every sale—this just means you are accelerating your burn.[51]

---

[19] Business cycles: See Wikipedia for an introduction. Link on eladgil.com. [*https://en.wikipedia.org/wiki/Business_cycle*]

[50] See Aaron Harris, "Don't Focus on the NASDAQ." Link on eladgil.com. [*http://www.aaronkharris.com/dont-focus-on-the-nasdaq*]

[51] Two counter examples to this would include:
  a. You are a consumer, network effect driven business and will largely be valued on user growth rather than monetization in your current stage of company (note, this does not last forever, but should last for the first few years of a consumer company).
  b. You have a huge pile of cash, and you can destroy your competitors by causing them to spend even more money and go out of business.

- Fire bad customers or markets. A number of your customers may be unprofitable to serve. Remove them as customers to decrease burn.
- Hiring plan. Figure out your hiring needs for the next 6–12 months. What does the company really, truly need? If you cannot raise money or increase profitable sales you may need to decrease the size of your team. If you continue to hire, soon truly great talent will start looking around for a new job. You may be able to reset your hiring bar even higher.
- Real estate: the silent killer. While you can decrease staff or other expenses, real estate is tough to unwind in a downturn. In boom times you can sublet space at a profit, but when things go bad suddenly there are a ton of people locked in to high-priced real estate. This means you cannot sublet your space, because everyone else is trying to do the same thing and the whole market is upended. If the company you are subletting to goes under, you may suddenly lose an important cash stream. Don't sign any big multi-million dollar real estate deals or build out a huge new space unless you have ongoing access to capital or are profitable.

2. **Be open with your team.** Even if you are in great shape, your team may still worry that your company may end up in trouble.
   - Ignore the noise, and tell your team to do the same. There will be a lot of noise in press and blogs about how the whole world is falling apart. This is a normal press cycle—just as it was impossible to fail six months earlier and everyone had a $10 billion valuation, in a downturn even great successes will be questioned as failures for a 6–12 month period.
   - Explain your financials. You can also work your team through financials, cash flows, and sales plan as another way to show them that everything is okay and your company is a stable oasis amidst all the noise.

3. **Think about how to take advantage of it.** Downturns can present opportunities for startups. Your competitors may run out of cash and not be able to replenish reserves: Should you start a price war with them? You can hire amazing people if others are cutting headcount: Who should you go after or revisit as a recruit? You can learn to impose greater financial discipline and recapture your frugal startup roots (if you have been spending too much).

At a high level, watch your cash, be open with your team, and don't panic.

CHAPTER 6

Marketing
and PR

CHAPTER 6

Marketing and PR

MARKETING, PR, COMMUNICATIONS, GROWTH, AND YOUR BRAND

High-growth companies' perception of marketing and public relations has shifted over the last 20 years. Product management used to be considered a subset of marketing at many companies in the 1980s and 1990s, while growth marketing did not exist. Public relations used to be about writing press releases.

Things have changed, but the one thing that hasn't: all marketing and PR efforts ultimately contribute to building the company's brand, public perception, and customer acquisition.

Below is a breakdown of various marketing and public relations functions. In general, you need to hire different employees for each function if you are to fully engage in the area.

GROWTH MARKETING

Growth marketing is analytically driven marketing and includes all quantitative areas of marketing. This includes online advertising, email marketing (where conversion can be tightly measured), SEO/content marketing, viral marketing, and funnel optimization. Growth marketing includes demand generation or lead generation, but also encompasses converting leads to customers once they've landed on your website.

Growth marketing focuses on moving a handful of key metrics (e.g., signups, logins, conversions) in an ROI-focused manner. Many growth tactics were famously pioneered at Facebook, but were really a response to a macro shift in ROI-based advertising (starting with Google), email marketing campaigns, and the more general rise of the internet as a marketing channel.

Social media marketing (Twitter, Facebook, Instagram, Snapchat) tends to fall under growth marketing or communications/PR in most technology organizations.

PRODUCT MARKETING

Product marketing (sometimes just "marketing" without a prefix word) is the canonical, old-school technology marketing discipline. This includes things like customer testimonials, feature requests, user testing and interviews, competitor analysis, collateral generation, and case studies. In the olden days (1970s and 1980s), product marketing and product management tended to be two sides of the same discipline, but this diverged over time.

BRAND MARKETING

Brand marketing is focused on the squishier side of marketing: brand awareness and perception, logos, and other design elements. It is the Nike swoosh—but more than that, it's about causing widespread association of Nike with not only the swoosh, but the attributes of athleticism and perseverance in popular culture.

All marketing efforts ultimately contribute to the company brand.

PR AND COMMUNICATIONS

Public relations is focused on story development (your company's narrative), press (proactive, reactive, contributed content), events (speaking engagements and also networking opportunities to some extent), as well as product-focused activity such as reviews and awards programs.

Media relations can benefit all areas of a company: Beyond simply telling the product story, PR can help with culture storytelling as well as executive profiles. Additionally, PR campaigns of late have included influencer relations, though this is also a function that's sometimes handled by a marketing team. PR teams are also usually the first point of contact in a crisis. Think of PR as the ongoing telling of the company story to the press and broader world.

HIRING MARKETING AND PR TEAMS

As you can imagine, there are large differences between most hires for a growth marketing role (quantitative, numbers driven) and PR (media relations, focus on the pitch, relationship building, telling a story). For example, for a growth marketing role you will likely look for a numbers-driven quantitative marketer. In contrast, a communications hire will focus on storytelling, positioning, and process management.

MARKETING ORGANIZATION STRUCTURE

Like all organization decisions, there's no right answer about which executive the marketing team should report into. Making the decision is an exercise in pragmatism. In enterprise or sales-heavy companies, marketing may report into sales, product, the COO, or directly to the CEO. Marketing may be matrixed across different lines of business, or directly into each business unit. Sometimes product marketing will report into product management while PR and branding will report into another organization.

A recent trend has been to combine regulatory affairs or lobbying with PR and communications. regulatory affairs is also often found under your legal team, proving again that organizational structure is an exercise in pragmatism.

Given the code driven aspects of growth marketing, some parts of the growth marketing team may consist of engineers reporting into an engineering group versus a marketing org.

Eventually, as your company scales you might find it advantageous to have PR and branding report to a single person who may (or may not) also own product marketing and growth marketing.

TO PR OR NOT PR

Some companies have famously gone without any sort of marketing except for Growth Marketing. Wish reached an $8 billion valuation with little brand marketing or PR. The company invested very little in targeting the mainstream press, and focused instead on building momentum via growth and distribution tactics.

The takeaway is not that you should forgo a PR team (Twitter is a counter example that grew in part due to PR). Rather, each company should tailor its marketing efforts to its user base, product, and best growth vectors. In general, a high PR profile helps accelerate recruiting, deal making and partnerships, and fundraising.

BUILDING A MARKETING AND COMMUNICATIONS ORG THAT CAN
WEATHER THE STORM

An interview with Shannon Stubo Brayton

Shannon Stubo Brayton is currently the CMO at LinkedIn. Previously, she was Senior Director of Corporate Communications at OpenTable, Inc. She joined the company when it was private and helped lead the communications efforts for the company's IPO in May 2009.

Prior to joining OpenTable in September 2008, Stubo spent nearly seven years at eBay Inc. where she was most recently its Vice President of Corporate Communications. Before that, she spent several years at Yahoo!, on both the public relations and corporate communications sides. Prior to joining Yahoo! in 1998, Stubo spent four years at Intuit Inc. in a variety of roles.

For over two decades, Shannon Stubo Brayton has crafted narratives for some of the largest and fastest-growing companies in tech, tackling everything from crisis management to product marketing. So when I was looking for someone who could give even the most technical founders a rundown on how to spin up a marketing and comms org, it's no surprise that all recommendations led to Shannon.

Shannon sat down with me to share what she's learned about building agile, efficient teams—and filling them with leaders who are equipped to thrive through all the shifts and re-orgs of hypergrowth.

Elad Gil:

I'm sure you've seen a real evolution in best practices during your time as a marketing/comms leader in tech. You run an organization responsible for product marketing, branding, PR/communications, and other areas. What has been the most significant shift the role of the CMO and of a marketing organization at technology companies in recent years?

Shannon Stubo Brayton:

One thing that has really evolved over the last ten years is the importance of internal communications. I spent seven years at eBay beginning in 2001, and internal communications was essentially how do we write emails about org changes and executive departures. It was a very different vibe than now. Internal communications and really getting your employees to be your best brand ambassadors was never in the forefront. People considered internal comms as an afterthought.

Once you get to a company size of 100 people, it's one of the first hires you should think about making. A good rule of thumb is one internal comms person for every hundred people.

It's important to make sure the brand message resonates internally with the same thing you're saying externally. It's taken on a very different flavor than "We need to help write an email about this exec who's leaving to spend more time with their family."

Elad: What do you think are the main components of internal comms? It really starts to tie in some HR and culture-related things as well, right?

Shannon: Absolutely. And I think it starts even earlier now, including recruiting and employee onboarding. During the recruiting process, the internal comms team should already be involved in what that experience looks and feels like—everything from the emails you get from the hiring manager or the recruiter to what kind of paperwork you get before you come in. You want candidates to experience a consistent brand from the very beginning, whether you hire them or not.

It's super important that employees have a great experience from week one and that includes everything, from making sure the laptop actually works to making sure they are invited to the right meetings. All the little things really do add up at this stage. Internal comms is playing a much bigger role in employee engagement and satisfaction than it ever has.

No offense to young male founders, but that special-touches thing is not something that is always their sweet spot. An experienced internal comms person will help make that a reality.

"One thing that has really evolved over the last ten years is the importance of internal communications."

— Shannon Stubo Brayton

Elad: How would you think about those activities when it comes to HR versus comms? Do you think it matters where the person sits? Is it a collaboration?

I'm asking because one of the most common things first-time founders ask me about is how to set up an org. Who should be doing what? How do I create clarity? Because everybody has every role early on. So I'm curious how you think about that organizational setup?

Shannon: Before social media, I would say a lot of internal comms functions reported to HR because it was really just an extension of HR, right? I need an email about the benefits policy or the 401k or whatever.

The evolution is that internal comms is now helping people figure out what do I say online about my company? What do I say about my experience? How do I respond to negativity that I read about me or my founder? Because of social media, everything is a communications vehicle now. And so you need a comms expert helping steer you through that, which is why I recommend internal comms being part of a broader communications team. At LinkedIn, internal comms is part of the broader marketing and communications function, as opposed to an individual team.

Where you put them also really depends on the output you need. A company like IBM is probably not thinking as much about the employee experience from day one because of their size and their scale. At LinkedIn, because of what we're doing and trying to recruit people—and the competition is so intense for the top people—we want that experience to be the best from the very beginning and that really comes down to how we communicate. How do you experience my company as a brand?

Elad: A lot of people struggle with figuring out who the right leader is to drive marketing broadly for their company, which, to your point, may include internal marketing and communications, traditional PR and communications, product marketing, branding, etc. What do you think people should be looking for in a CMO, and how should they go about that search?

Shannon: For most of the 23 years I've been doing this, the lines between PR and marketing were so unbelievably clear. PR people talked to reporters and marketing people bought ads—that was the split. It was "stay out of my business, I'm buying these print ads" and "stay out of my business, I'm talking to People magazine."

It's so different now, and what I've talked about quite a bit in some podcasts recently is that a CMO has to be such an agile, versatile player. You have to be good at a hundred different things and your CMO could come from a number of different backgrounds. I'm a CMO, but I'm an expert in comms. I'm not a demand gen expert. I'm not a brand expert. I'm not a product marketing expert. There are lots of CMOs who are and have that piece of expertise.

The number one thing you need in a CMO is somebody who is an excellent leader. Because you're never going to be an expert in the hundred things you now need to be good at, and I'm not being hyperbolic. To be a successful marketing leader, you have to have a little bit of knowledge of a hundred different skills. Everything from copywriting to creative to research to NPS.

Leadership is super important. Decision-making: super, super important. And then knowing how to tell your company's story. That narrative is incredibly critical because whatever you're experiencing and creating on the ad side or on the demand gen side or the customer side or the events side, it also needs to dovetail with how you're talking about the company to reporters or on Twitter or wherever you're sharing your story.

Elad: In a very enterprise-focused company, would you look for somebody with a product marketing background versus a comms or growth marketing background? Or do you think it's just a matter of finding a great person from any background who can then generalize?

Shannon: I think it's more the latter than the former, and I think it's awesome to have an area of expertise, but what area of expertise you should be amazing at really depends on the company. For us, it worked that I had comms expertise, but at a company like Salesforce, a demand gen expertise is going to be incredibly important. For a DoorDash, it's going to be product marketing expertise. It depends on your company.

Ultimately, you really just need to be an agile player with a whole bunch of knowledge—or a little bit of knowledge about a whole bunch of things. Have an area where you really consider yourself an expert and then focus on learning the other areas. That's what I've tried to do over the last three years.

Elad: How can a founder who has never worked in marketing identify people who would be good for this role? Are there specific things that you look for? Is there a process you would follow? Is there an exercise that you would do? What do you view as a good process, and then what do you view as positive or negative signals?

Shannon: Number one, I think you've got to have chemistry with that person, especially if it's a CMO or a comms leader. Those people end up having to be pretty honest with the CEO about what's working and what's not, what they're doing well and what they're not doing well. That's the nature of the job and so that chemistry has to be there from the beginning. You don't have to love each other right away, but you at least have to have some connection or a shared set of values. In my experience, that's something you can tell within the first hour of spending time with someone.

You also really want to understand how people approach their jobs. If you are hiring a general counsel, you'll never be able to say very specifically, "Hey, I need to understand your legal prowess in this very specific area. What would you do in this case?" Instead it's, "If I had this problem, how would you go about approaching it?" Then make sure that your approaches are somewhat close. Because if they're super disparate, that's going to be a really hard gap to close when you're in the trenches, in the job, in the middle of a problem, which we all are nearly every day.

Elad: What are the most common mistakes you see high-growth companies make on the marketing, communications, or branding side?

Shannon: The biggest mistake I've seen is falling in love with a super creative person who has zero operational expertise or interest in management and putting them in a CMO role. It's really easy to get some flashy person out of New York or wherever and bring them to the Valley, and say, "Here's your huge marketing team to manage and your budget."

I don't think that founders really double down on figuring out, "Can this person manage this team? Can they eventually scale? Can they learn demand gen? Can they learn product marketing? Can they understand communications? Do they know how to administer an NPS survey?" There's a lot of "I fell in love with you because you did that amazing campaign at company X." You know, Pepsi, Apple, Nike—all the brands that people go after. It's often really hard for them to make that switch to management.

Elad: How do you think marketing should optimally work with other parts of the organization? So obviously product marketing and product management overlap, or sales and marketing overlap. Are there any specific best practices you point to there, or specific ways that you as a leader tend to work with other functional executives? Or how do you think about coordination cross-company?

Shannon: At big consumer companies and retailers, marketing is the king of the castle. They're the general manager. If you work at a General Mills and you're a marketer, you run the whole shebang. Then you move out here and you're like, "Oh, I'm in charge of this tiny little pixel? Really? I have to listen to product and engineering?"

In the Valley, marketing people have fought hard to get a seat at the table. A lot of times, you'll get that person who relocates. They come out and they think that they're going to be running a business line and actually they're just there to enable the sales team. It's up to the marketer to make sure that the value that marketing provides is really clear up front. Make sure that you're constantly adding strategic input to this team, as opposed to investing a ton of money in that one creative hire. That's really important and hard to do.

Elad: How do you think about structuring your marketing org? There's so many different types of marketing that companies can engage in across growth marketing, different channel marketing, comms, etc. Do you try and cluster things under specific leads for broader areas? Do you think those are good standalone units that should then report in?

The reason I'm asking the question is in a high-growth company, you'll end up with maybe one person working on the PR/communications side, and then you'll have one person who starts helping out with marketing. And the way that that org grows is typically very organic and often a little bit sloppy until you bring a leader in to make any sense of it. I'm curious what you view as some best practices there.

Shannon: I always tell my teams this too: If you were to start with a blank slate, what would that team look like? Don't optimize for one person. It's very easy at times to say, "Well, we have to have Stephanie in that job because she just relocated. So let's figure out what she can do, even if she's not the right person." But you need to think about what makes the most sense for the company structurally, and then figure out if you've got the right people. And if not, there are people that need to move out and there are people that need to be hired.

In a marketing function organized by line of business, what you definitely do not want to do is create big, full teams without any horizontal shared resources. That was a little bit of what happened at LinkedIn. We had big teams that were supporting individual business lines, but there were redundant functions. There was no horizontal function that you could go to and say, "Here's my campaign. Please help me." It was all done vertically. What we ended up with was a huge team, but not a lot of best practice sharing. People had the same job in different business lines and didn't know each other.

In marketing, it's a best practice to have shared services. You need a structure where every business line works with this one team to help support their campaigns—like an ops function or a creative function. Something that's not 100% vertical, but that really is shared among all the business line leaders. I think that's a great way to set things up from the beginning.

And not everyone wants to do that, because they may have to give up dollars or share control of the final creative, but you've got to build that trust. You've got to make sure that you know there's a centralized group that is going to make you successful and get you to where you need to be.

Elad: So when you integrate those functions into a single team that's supporting everybody, you're going to share messaging, you're going to share approaches, you're going to share resources, you're going to share tools, whatever it is. You end up with one org instead of multiple orgs.

Shannon: That's exactly right. And what you avoid is getting too bloated and having too many people, and the massive redundancy that comes from that. On top of it, if you're not all using the same support, you don't build trust in the same way. Those are the benefits of doing what we ended up doing, longer term, but we didn't get there from the very beginning.

Elad: And that's a great point. A lot of the effort of a high-growth company goes to changing the org structure as you scale. You have a different company every 6–12 months, and you need to adopt different functions and different processes. And then a year later you do it again. And for the average employee, that's very discombobulating. I think most people find that a very disconcerting experience the first time they go through it, and then the second time they think, "Oh, this is expected." That's why for high-growth situations I like to hire people who've been through it before, because they know that it's normal.

Shannon: And I will tell you, it becomes really obvious when you run into someone who was great for a period of time but is having a hard time scaling. Those signs of somebody who's really hitting their ceiling, they quickly become very obvious. The tendency is to trust them and hope it's going to get better and try to coach them, but usually the person is not happy. If you get them to admit that they're struggling with the scale, you end up in a much better spot.

Elad: What do you view as the main signs that somebody isn't scaling?

Shannon: Exhaustion. Tardiness. Showing up at meetings completely late and discombobulated. I always tell people, "If you are having a hard time scaling, the best thing to do is to try to be on time so that you're hiding it a little bit." You don't want it to be this completely obvious thing. I think when people aren't scaling, they micromanage in an incredible way because they feel like that's the only thing they can really control. They can also get really tactical, really quickly. It becomes, "Well, I can cross that off my list," as opposed to, "I'm going to tackle this big, chunky strategic issue."

Those are the things to look for, so when you start to get signals from the team—"This person is micromanaging me. They seem really tired. They're constantly late. They're hard to reach."—those are usually signs that the person is over their skis.

Elad: And how often do you think people who are in that situation can course correct and be coached?

Shannon: I have infrequently seen it improve rapidly enough to be successful.

Elad: So in the majority of cases, it usually is a sign that it's the wrong role, wrong person, at that time?

Shannon: Yes, at that time and it's not a knock on that person. It doesn't mean they're not smart. This just might be somebody who thrives better in a smaller company and that's perfectly okay. That should also be the message: You didn't fail. This just isn't the right job for you or it's not the right company.

Elad: I think that's one thing a lot of founders struggle with, because often those people who are having trouble scaling are people that they hired early or that they've depended on for a long time. Now they're in a situation where they want to do right by that person. But doing right by that person is everyone acknowledging that it's not the right situation. And to your point, I think emphasizing that it's not a failure but rather an evolution of the organization and an evolution of that person's role is really important. Because founders sometimes fight really hard to keep people in spots where they're just not going to be great, or happy.

Shannon: Absolutely. And a lot of times people don't raise the issue—founders especially—because they don't want to have the awkward conversation and it's just easier to ignore it. But if you really do notice the signs and you get the person to open up about what they're experiencing, you oftentimes find that they're not happy either. It may just be best for everybody to have it come to an end.

"The biggest mistake I've seen is falling in love with a super creative person who has zero operational expertise or interest in management and putting them in a CMO role."

—Shannon Stubo Brayton

Elad: From a functional perspective, the thing I see founders struggling with most is how they should be investing in different areas of marketing. When should they start actually doing more brand-centric marketing? How should they be thinking about customer acquisition? Does PR actually ever work for customer acquisition and, if so, under what circumstances?

A lot of people I know who are running companies that are suddenly starting to work, they really struggle with some pretty basic ideas around how they should be marketing their product. So I'm curious about your macro perspective. Is there a framework that somebody should be using to determine where to invest dollars against the marketing team?

Shannon: It's such a hard one, because it really depends on what you are selling and what you are trying to do.

"If you were to start with a blank slate, what would that team look like?"

—Shannon Stubo Brayton

Elad: Maybe we could use two examples, an enterprise company versus a consumer products company.

Shannon: For consumer products, I would 100% say product marketing is the place you should invest the most heavily. You're essentially trying to build a road map. You're trying to understand how people use the product, if they like it, if they don't. I wouldn't invest in the brand at the outset, because you've got to make sure you actually have a market fit and that the product is being built in a way that people are using.

On the B2B side, I would say 100% demand gen. You've got to have customers. It's the same sort of proposition, which is that you have to have customers who like and use your product before you say, "Here's our brand."

So those are the places that I would start. And then over time, you start to figure out, I need some PR here. I need some brand. Some people make the mistake of doing just PR in lieu of brand, because they say, "Well, that's sort of a branding thing." But the landscape has changed dramatically. A big story in TechCrunch doesn't do anything for anybody anymore, whereas five years ago, it was a big deal. A company was sort of made or broken based on what TechCrunch thought about it. ◼

This interview has been edited and condensed for clarity.

PR BASICS

In the early days your company will be too small and have too little timely news to merit a full-time PR person. As the company grows, you will hire one or more PR people in house, and will often augment the in-house work with an agency.

Here are some simple basics to get you started on PR.

GET MEDIA TRAINED

Your internal PR team or your agency should start things off by media training you and any other members of your team who will be officially representing the company and/ or speaking to press. Media training will include definition of key terms (What does "off the record" mean versus "on background?"), what you can expect during different types of interviews (broadcast, in-person, phone, video, etc.), as well as practice sessions primarily focused on answering tough questions. You should practice the storyline for your company and be able to answer questions about your products, your competitors, and yourself concisely. In general, you and your cofounders will be encouraged to have a founding narrative about the company and a personal explanation for why you are working on your company. Media training will also focus on things like how to answer a question other than the one you were asked (if needed).

ITERATE ON THE COMPANY PITCH

Practice, practice, practice. Imagine that you are an actor in a play. Read through your narrative and practice your storyline. Your PR team or executive team can help you practice objection handling, fielding tough questions, and delivering the core company story. Repeat it until you have a crisp story memorized. At the same time, remember that authenticity is key. Reporters will know if you're reading from a script and it'll come across as less genuine, which can sometimes be a credibility killer. If you are on the phone with press, it is okay to have a written document in front of you to remind you of key talking points.

"ON BACKGROUND" VERSUS "OFF THE RECORD" VERSUS "ON THE RECORD"

When talking to press, you should specify the nature of the conversation and get agreement from the reporter on the terms. This is typically something your PR person will work out in advance with the reporter, and also reconfirm at the start of the call. If there is not agreement, you should assume everything you say is on the record. The general breakouts are:

- **"Off the record"**—this usually means the journalist may not write about the conversations or quote you. You can ask in the middle of the conversation to say something off the record, and if the journalist agrees, then say whatever it is you wanted to share.

- **"On background"**—this usually means the journalist may write something like "sources say that Google is moving into flying cars" without directly quoting you as the source.

- **"On the record"**—If you are not "off the record" and not "on background" then you are "on the record," which means you can be quoted specifically and directly attributed for the comments or quote.

CORRECTING FACTUAL ERRORS

In order to maintain independence and journalistic integrity, reporters are not always willing to run a story by you before it's published. If the press has made an error in fact (versus opinion) it is okay to reach out to the journalist when the story runs to correct the factual error. Factual error means things like "they misunderstood a scientific fact" or "they got the name of the product wrong." Factual error does not mean "they hate my product" or "they didn't understand its value."

Given how hard people work on their companies, CEOs may get emotional or upset about press coverage. Realize that most of the press coverage will be forgotten in the future, and most companies have had a bad story or two (or ten) at some point or another.

PRESS AGENDAS

Most people in the press are hard-working, ethical people trying to do the right thing. Occasionally you will also run across someone who has an agenda. No matter what you tell them, they will write the story the way they want it to fit a predefined narrative and they will massage facts.

It is a good idea to read a journalist's previous stories before speaking with them. If they have a long history of writing thoughtless attack pieces, you should decide how much you want to engage or talk with them.

One upside of working with a PR person internally or an agency externally is that they have great insight into how reporters work, how they're generally perceived in the industry, and what you can expect when meeting with them.

HIRING GREAT PR PEOPLE

The PR community is a small one. There are only a few dozen truly great PR people in technology at any given time. They all tend to cluster at a handful of companies and all know each other. The best way to find a great PR person is to ask other PR people, agencies, and journalists who they respect the most and who does the best work, and then go after those people. Sometimes, you can also hire a great partner-level person out of a PR agency.

PRESS RELATIONSHIP BUILDING

In the early days, it will take an investment of time to build relationships with key members of the press. This may include reaching out with articles unrelated to your company that may interest the journalist, or meeting for coffee to discuss the industry without other agendas. It is important to invest in these relationships and avoid transactional behavior. This will increase the likelihood your company will get covered.

As your company scales, building these relationships will continue to be important. However, as CEO you should be judicious with your time. Figure out what other members of your executive team you want to be spokespersons, and start to have them take the lead on some of the press relationships.

ENGAGE PR EARLY

It often takes 4-10 weeks for a company to coordinate a big PR launch—more if you are just onboarding a new PR agency or your existing agency isn't up to speed on the new product yet. Don't wait for the week before the launch to let your PR team or agency know what is coming. Just like design, product communications should be part of the product launch timing from early in the process rather than being an afterthought. Some companies like Amazon go through the exercise of writing the product "headline" at the stage of product conception. For example, when writing a design document, you might think through what the press story on the product will be when it launches. This helps to shape crisp thinking about what you are building and why.

PRESS DOES NOT EQUAL SUCCESS

While getting positive press coverage will get you a lot of attention from friends and family (and maybe some famous people), it is not a reflection of company success. Profitable, scalable revenue is a much more important metric. For most companies, PR is also not a way to get recurring distribution. Don't confuse press coverage with traction and remember to focus on the core metrics of the company. And do not think that a good press cycle can cover up a bad business decision.

PR AND CRISIS MANAGEMENT

Every company will have a bad press cycle. In general, companies tend to get built up in the press, and then torn down by the press. However, there are singular events the press will rally behind where the company has screwed up or made a mistake. During these times of crisis management, the company needs to act swiftly and wisely to protect its brand and customer base. Crisis management tends to have the following steps:

1. **Analyze the problem**

   What went wrong? How will this impact the company, its customers, or other stakeholders? How is this likely to be portrayed by the press and by competitors? What are different things you could/should do about the situation?

2. **Acknowledge the problem**

   In general, once you are in a negative press cycle, it will run its natural course. Rather than fight the press cycle itself, try to expedite its coming to its natural resolution as quickly as possible. A negative press cycle is like falling into a river and getting swept up in the current. You can swim with the current and come to a riverbank quickly, or try to swim against the current, exhaust yourself, and get swept down anyways. If you made a mistake, acknowledge it, lay out a plan of action, and take action. Do not lie.

3. **Take action**

   Do the things you said you were going to do. If you can do them quickly, expedite action so you can get through the crisis quickly.

HOW TO BUILD THE PR TEAM YOU REALLY NEED

An interview with Erin Fors

Erin Fors is cofounder and President of Cutline Communications. Erin has nearly two decades of experience in PR, with an emphasis on industry-impacting launches and media strategy. She's worked closely with giants like Google, WhatsApp, and Yahoo!, as well as startups like Instacart, Yik Yak, Polyvore, and more. She launched Android and Chrome for Google and single-handedly responded to hundreds of press inquiries pre-launch, establishing a reputation for being able to simultaneously charm reporters while offering no comment. In all of her experience, Erin's dedication and drive have had an undeniable impact on her clients and the technology industry.

Prior to cofounding Cutline, Erin worked for a range of small and large public relations agencies including Merritt Group, A&R Partners (now A&R Edelman), NCG Porter Novelli, UpStart Communications, and Fleishman-Hillard. Erin has been recognized by both Business Insider and PR Week as an innovator and leader in the PR industry.

I sat down with Erin to chat about how founders can find and deploy the best PR pros, when they should start, and why any successful communications strategy has to start with a good story.

Elad Gil:

A lot of founders ping me with questions around PR and communications, government affairs, crisis management—a bunch of things that all tie together. How should founders and CEOs be thinking about PR, and about partnering with external PR folks?

Erin Fors:

Founders first need to understand what communications and PR can accomplish for the company—and also what communications and PR cannot accomplish. Those are two things that we sometimes struggle with explaining to founders the most. And my sense is that's because they are getting conflicting advice.

You may have board members or advisers saying, "You need to get a PR firm or person." And then you read TechCrunch or you follow reporters on Twitter and they're saying, "PR is stupid. Don't work with PR firms." PR people and reporters have this long-standing tension: Reporters think they don't need us, and we're being pushed by our clients, particularly on the agency side, to go and get coverage. It can be a vicious cycle.

To me, the importance of PR and communications more broadly is that it gives the company a voice and helps create credibility, or build on their credibility. PR gives the company a way to communicate their purpose. It also helps humanize the company. And given where we are now as a society and what's going on in the world, that's really important. I've also seen good PR programs help tremendously with recruiting and morale.

Elad: You mentioned three things: One is controlling the external narrative and how people perceive the company and potentially its founders or executives. Second is around recruiting, and third is around morale. What do you view as the relative priorities of those things? How much time do you think high-growth companies should be spending on comms and PR, and does it differ by type of company? And how much of the founder's time should be going to it?

Erin: It does vary by company. Take a company like Pinterest, which is a place (whether through the app or their website) where people go to feel good. It's an incredible platform for the world right now. PR for Pinterest is way different than for another company, like Airbnb or Stripe.

For Pinterest, it's about getting users. It's engagement. It's figuring out how to get current users even more engaged, how to grow your users, and how to scale with all this content that's coming onto the platform. If you have a consumer tech company where the regulatory or privacy or security concerns are really low, do you need a giant agency or multiple specialty agencies and a big internal PR team? I think you could argue that having a small, focused internal team (or person, depending on the size of the company) with some level of agency support—for example, an agency focused on just media campaigns or launches—could work well and we see that a lot with clients.

With a company like Airbnb, they have a lot of regulatory and privacy and security issues, because they're a platform for people who rent out their homes. So for a company like Airbnb, their comms focus, at different parts of the company's evolution, is likely more on the regulatory side.

For a company like Stripe, where you get into payments and security, you need more than just an internal team and some level of agency support. You need a stronger, more solid crisis plan. Depending on the focus of the company, you might need regulatory and Capitol Hill communications plans.

It definitely varies by company. But, generally speaking, most higher-growth companies have an internal PR team and also PR agency support.

When it comes to founder support, it's critical that both founders and the broader executive team buys into the overall PR strategy, but they should trust their internal team(s) to execute the day-to-day.

Elad: Where do you see the ball get dropped, if anywhere, as companies scale up?

Erin: Ironically, I think it's lack of communication. I think a company's intent is always to do the right thing for customers, clients, or users of the platform. But there is a fear of admitting that you've done something wrong or that something isn't working when you need to change course or make a correction.

This could be any type of change or correction. Maybe you're an enterprise company and you're changing the pricing model, but you don't communicate that clearly to customers. Or you try to sneak in changes to the product, hoping nobody will notice. Or you try to bury something in a terms of service or privacy policy. I've seen this fear of backlash and/or a negative press cycle when potentially bad things are happening—but it's always best to be straightforward and ride it out.

You can generally recover from those things, but from a PR perspective, it's extremely frustrating. Because you could be a media darling and have one misstep where you communicate something really poorly, and it really sets you back in terms of the public perception of your company. It can be really hard to rebuild that trust. That's why authentic communication, never lying, and transparency—to the extent that you can be transparent—are so important.

I really do think that if companies would just embrace when things break or have to change, they would be much better off. It's true across industries. You have airlines, for example, that have issues with the way they handle passengers, and they don't handle it right. They don't just say, "This was wrong, and we don't tolerate this." They're either quiet, or they put out totally artificial, canned responses, and then there's this backpedaling that ensues.

Oftentimes, this isn't something that's driven by the PR team. It's driven by a founder who doesn't want to put their own personal credibility on the line, like, "I screwed up and I need to fix this." More often than not, PR will say, "We have to be honest. We have to say that this is what happened."

Elad: So, if you're the CEO running a company, what's a warning signal that you should quit pushing back on something that the PR team is saying? Is there any rule of thumb? Because, to some extent, especially if you have a founder-CEO, they succeeded in part because they didn't listen to a lot of people. The most successful companies often select for behavior where a founder just has to be bullheaded or has to ignore experts, because otherwise the founder would never have gotten to where they are. How can you tell when it's time to listen?

Erin: As an agency partner we often have clients who want to do something we don't agree with. In those situations, we make our case for why that shouldn't happen or why they should do it differently. But ultimately they decide to do it their way, and there's backlash or something happens or it doesn't go the way they thought it would. And then it's like, "Oh, okay, I should have listened to you. You were right." The same is true with founders. People need to fail in order to learn, in life in general and definitely in business.

I do think that it is really important when a company hires its first internal PR person that that person is in complete lockstep with the founder. Because it is all about trust. Generally companies that don't have that trust between founders and PR people are the ones that struggle with having a good PR program or comms campaigns.

Elad: How do you select for that? Do you think there's a specific style of interview or interview process that would most surface whether the person that you're interviewing is right for you for an in-house hire?

Erin: I always say PR is more art than science. A lot of it boils down to chemistry and cultural fit and experience. You could give a PR candidate different scenarios to walk through and see if your thinking aligns when it comes to how they would handle certain situations.

I think sometimes founders aren't as involved with the hiring of PR people. It's left up to marketing or to some other function of the company to make the decision. But I've been the most successful working with founders or leadership teams when they are on the same page about what PR can and cannot do and when there's really respect for PR as a discipline.

Honestly, not every company needs PR. There are some instances where maybe the company's goal is really user acquisition, full stop. That's something PR can certainly help with, but that's really more a direct function of marketing. There's more that marketing can do than PR can do. PR is really about, again, helping a company communicate their purpose, generating awareness, helping build profiles of the company, the product, the leadership.

The most successful founder/CEO and PR team relationships that I've seen are based in trust. Shannon Stubo Brayton is an excellent example. Jeff Weiner and Shannon are completely on the same page, and he fully respects and trusts her. And she has a seat at the table—that is critical. She's built this huge team, and everything they've done is incredible. And she's grown so much, too. I mean, she started out as a PR person, and she's now the CMO of LinkedIn, which is extraordinary. The leadership team at LinkedIn fully respects her, and that starts with Jeff.

Elad: Say you're trying to bring on a Shannon-style person. What do you think are the signals that somebody's a great PR person? Is it prior work that they've done, is it the organization that they come out of, is it references? How can somebody who's never hired for the role hire somebody great?

Erin: It's experience for sure to some extent, but given what we do I'd also put a lot of weight on references and people skills. And I think it's back-channel references frankly. I don't put a ton of weight in the interviewing process. At Cutline, we're very particular about who we hire, and we'll always back-channel. The Silicon Valley network, in particular the PR world, is kind of small. And relationships in the PR industry are key.

Founders should ask their board and advisors. They should ask any reporter connections they know. Start with the people that PR people generally engage with. What are the names that rise to the surface? You can even ask agency people and other PR people. Who do they respect? There's a very small list of people that I would rattle off.

"PR gives the company a way to communicate their purpose. It also helps humanize the company."

—Erin Fors

Erin: If we're talking about hypergrowth companies, it's a little different. We have a lot of conversations with early-stage startups, and I think they're often just told to hire an agency or to hire PR. And I don't know that they really know what goes into that.

For us, we look at it in different stages. So early-stage startups, they don't actually even need a person in house. They really need a freelancer or a consultant who can help guide them, and who can easily scale up and down to support different moments in time such as funding announcements or product launches. You don't need PR all the time. We work with many companies that don't have in-house PR people yet, because of where they are as a company.

But the approach is somewhat the same here as it is for hiring an in-house person. I would ask reporters for the list of PR people they respect and/or admire and look at their agencies. I would ask VCs and advisors for recommendations on agencies. And then I think that it's really important for the founder or somebody from the leadership team to be part of that discussion, too. It comes down to understanding the business and being passionate about the company and/or the product. Do they use the product, if they can? Are they excited about it? How do they talk about it?

If you're interviewing someone—whether someone for an in-house role or an agency—you can also look at how they share on social and how they talk about things publicly. What is their brand voice? You can easily determine that through Twitter, social, their website, blogs. And just see if the cultures align.

When an agency and a client really align on culture and have a shared sense of purpose, it's like magic. The results just kind of roll in. When you have an agency and a client that aren't really partners and whose cultures clash, it is virtually impossible to get results. And that's not good for the client or the agency team.

I think making sure that there is a shared sense of purpose is crucial. This probably should go without saying, but it's also critical that when a company is hiring an agency they meet, as part of the process, the actual team they'll be working with. Be explicit about that requirement. Because a lot of agencies have new-business teams, where they send in the best of the best to win the business. It's like bait-and-switch. They'll change up the team after. Make sure that the team is smart and that they're all engaged in the meeting, and that they're asking questions about the business, about the personalities of the team, about the industry.

Elad: I know common process is to also ask for some written proposal or some pitch in terms of what the agency would try to do in a given scenario. If you were on the other side of the table and you were choosing who to work with, do you think that work product is valuable?

Erin: I do. When the ask is too specific, I think it's kind of hard for agencies and it's unfair to some degree. We should have some understanding of the industry that the client is in, and it's our job to go really deep once we land the business. But I think, as part of the RFP process, clients should stick to broad asks: "We want to reach consumers in the tech space. How would you engage women between the age of 18 and 34?" Keep the exercise to something that's not too specific but not too broad.

And then the other thing that I would evaluate on if I was on the other side—and I actually was once and had to pick an agency—is whether agencies challenge you. I think that an agency that questions and pushes back instead of just delivering what you've asked them for should be weighted higher, even if the ideas don't align. That shows someone who's really looking out for the best interests of the company and what's right for you. That's someone who isn't afraid to stand up and say, "You know what, you asked for X but from a PR perspective we have some other ideas there. Based on where you are and what we know, there's more value to do it a different way."

I just think challenging—and discussion and debate—is a lost art. But it's so important.

Erin: Yes, I do. I don't think a founder or CEO should be—and I've seen this before—hyper-focused on how much coverage they get, how many pieces of coverage. The focus really should be on quality. Especially now, because reporters change jobs and their beats change quickly. There's a constant change and shuffling in the media industry as it figures out how to adapt to content consumption and figure out what the right mix is between writing, video, print, online, and more. My advice would be to focus on quality and really understand what PR can and cannot do.

I also think that there's this tendency to ask, "Why aren't we in TechCrunch?" or "Why aren't we in X blog?" or whatever. That kind of nit-picky stuff can really be demoralizing, because it's actually hard. It's hard sometimes to get into TechCrunch. And this is where trust comes into play, and making sure that your internal person, or agency, is someone who you really trust and respect.

I have seen founders who go off the deep end worrying about, "Why am I not in TechCrunch? How many stories am I going to get?" And yes, those things are important to a certain extent. But to me, founders should spend their time on making better products and scaling the business in other areas, especially if they have a PR person they can trust.

Erin: That's true. I think if the founder has something good to say and can contribute to trend conversations in a meaningful way, then yes, they should be out there talking. But not everyone has something to say. And reporters are only going to call on you every so often.

This also goes back to relationships. Some of the most successful founders I've worked with have strong relationships with reporters who call them directly. And that's good. That isn't a bad thing. Sometimes founders get this idea in their head, like, "Well, if this reporter is calling me, or you're asking me to talk to this reporter, then why am I paying you? What is your value?" But that's just not the right way to look at it. Reporters do want to have personal connections with founders and sometimes circumvent the PR person. But then it's our job to help prep, whether it's background on the reporter or figuring out what the right story angles are. So there's value on both sides.

Elad: I think the other big mistake I've seen people make is they do a launch, they get a big spike in traffic due to the PR and acquire a bunch of users, and then that goes away. They have to do the hard work of developing a channel. But they think that PR could be a way to keep that going, but that doesn't work for most companies.

Erin: That's exactly right. And that is a challenge all the time. It's also a pretty big investment for smaller companies. We work with a lot of clients to come up with those evergreen story ideas that we can pitch between big news moments. The key here is patience: It takes time to develop those angles and then to land them. Reporters are crunched for time and there are only so many stories they'll write on any given day. That's where marketing and other disciplines within the broader advertising/PR/marketing umbrella come into play. There's also social media. For companies who don't have a lot of news to work with, there are a lot of storytelling opportunities you can create—but you can also use those moments in between larger press cycles to engage with your customers where they are: on Facebook, Snap, Instagram, Twitter.

Elad: Are there any final lessons you would impart to a founder approaching PR for the first time?

Erin: I do think the biggest thing is to understand and to be clear about what your goals are for PR. To understand what PR can and can't do. PR cannot come in and fix a bad business decision. And in order to do our jobs, there has to be a story, there has to be a product or company culture or something to work with. ■

This interview has been edited and condensed for clarity.

"I really do think that if companies would just embrace when things break or have to change, they would be much better off. It's true across industries."

—Erin Fors

CHAPTER 7

Product management

CHAPTER 7

Product management

PRODUCT MANAGEMENT OVERVIEW

Great product management organizations help a company set product vision and road maps, establish goals and strategy, and drive execution on each product throughout its lifecycle.[52]

Bad product management organizations, in contrast, largely function as project management groups, running schedules and tidying up documents for engineers.

To build a great product organization you need to first understand the role of the product manager. Secondly, you need to hire individuals with the right skill sets, including a strong VP of product. Finally, establish a simple set of processes to enable the product organization and help the company scale its product development.

WHAT DO PRODUCT MANAGERS DO?

At a high level, a product manager (PM) is the single cross-functional owner directly responsible for the success of a product. Some pundits call PMs the "general manager of the product" or "CEO of the product." In reality, a product manager is the directly responsible individual for a product—they have all the responsibility for the product's success but often lack the direct line reporting of the other functions.

---

52 Ben Horowitz has a classic post on this topic.
See eladgil.com. [*https://a16z.com/2012/06/15/good-product-managerbad-product-manager/*]

Product managers are responsible for:

1. Product strategy and vision. What is the goal of the product? Who is the customer? What are the primary features and use cases? How do we define success and what metrics can we use to track the product? What are the competitive dynamics and how should we position the product against competitors? How will the product differentiate? What are some key distribution channels? What is the business model for the product? How should we price the product? The product manager will work with many other functions (design, marketing, sales, engineering, data science, etc.) to answer the questions above, but should ultimately be in charge of asking and answering these questions.

The product strategy and vision should also reflect the voice of the customer. The product manager should be on top of incorporating user input and feedback into the product lifecycle.

2. Product prioritization & problem solving. Product managers "own" the product road map and are responsible for ensuring it has the right set of trade-offs. Tactical aspects of this include: writing and receiving feedback on PRDs (product requirement documents), organizing/directing product road mapping sessions, working with all the functions mentioned above, and making trade-offs on features versus impact and work needed. Crisp product requirement documents can make a world of difference in driving concise agreement on, and execution of, the product. PRDs should clearly articulate primary features and product needs.

These responsibilities require a PM to be data- and customer-driven. Defining the right metrics, getting agreement on them, and then tracking them enables more alignment on product priorities. The more technical the product manager, the more likely they are able to analyze the data needed to make crucial trade-offs. In parallel, the product manager should strive to understand customer needs and then make trade-offs versus relative to engineering cost or business impact.

Product managers will also spend time problem-solving aspects of the product or its development. For example, how could the product be tweaked or changed to avoid a legal or regulatory issue? How could features be modified to address a competitive or pricing concern from sales?

Note: product managers will not work on this alone. Building a product, and solving related problems is a team effort. PMs will coordinate with engineering (technical constraints and feature ideas), design, data science, marketing, sales, support, legal (regulatory issues), and other functions. However, the ultimate role of product management is making or suggesting trade-offs between the pristine, platonic ideal of beauty that the design team wants, the technical pizzazz engineering desires, the "just give me some shit I can sell" of sales, and the "this may be risky" of legal (these examples are all purposefully exaggerated).

3. Execution: timelines, resources, and removal of obstacles. As part of driving the success of a product, product managers should work closely with engineering to set and hit goals on time. Often the biggest ways a product manager can help the team hit goals includes (a) lobbying for resources or attention from engineering, design, and other functions, (b) removing or prioritizing features and providing a clear road map for execution, (c) asking "stupid" questions to see if it is possible for each function to reduce timelines or remove unneeded features or work, and (d) pushing back on extraneous requests, whether those are internal (design, sales, etc.) or external (customers, partners).

Many people associate product execution as something that ends when you launch a product. In reality there is ongoing product maintenance, feature iteration, and eventually the sunsetting or killing of a product. Deprecating a product can be an art in its own right as you transition customers off, deal with pricing changes, or other issues that may cause customer backlash.

It is important to note that product managers are not project managers—i.e. a PM's primary job is not just running a schedule.

4. Communication and coordination (overlays all of the above). Product managers should organize and communicate team status, progress, obstacles, and functional sequencing to the rest of the organization. This may include driving (or co-driving with engineering) weekly team status meetings, product reviews with the leadership team, and communicating launch or other timelines across the organization.

Often the hardest part of the communication is communicating the "why" behind the product road map, prioritization, and sequencing. Part of this will be creating a framework that establishes why some things are prioritized higher than others—and it's important that all other functions buy into this framework.

Ultimately, product management will collaborate closely with, and at times have a natural (collaborative) tension with, engineering, design, and sales. Engineering will feel that since they are building everything, they should have the power to make product decisions. Design will think product management is redundant with design (these are very different functions,) and sales will wonder why product can't ship faster and why the PM is always trying to keep sales people away from engineers (it is so engineers can focus on building the product without spending all their time on one-off sales requests).

Product managers should also function as the "buffer" or shield that protects engineers and designers from other internal and external parties. Sales and marketing people will always want to meet engineers directly to lobby for their favorite features, while customers will want to have a conversation directly with engineering. Product management should be a smart buffer for these interactions and consolidate all input and questions into a weekly internal team meeting, or the PM can act as the primary point of contact for sales. This will prevent sales, marketing, and other organizations from draining too much engineering and design time. That said, sometimes the best way to convince an engineer of a customer need is to put her in front of a customer. Hearing customer feedback first-hand can often change minds or shape a great brainstorm or problem-solving session.

DO YOU HAVE THE RIGHT PEOPLE?

You can tell a good PM from a bad PM based on how much time they spend on each of the above. If a PM's time is spent solely on checklists and project management, they either *(i)* have a weak engineering management counterpart they are covering for, *(ii)* are not empowered to do their job by company management, *(iii)* do not understand their job, or *(iv)* are not respected by their peers and cannot do more important work. Optimally, most product management time should be going towards defining the product, prioritizing trade-offs, spending time with customers, and working with various functions on launch, feature iteration, and communication.[53] The hardest part may be to separate whether the right person is in the right role versus whether your company is empowering that person properly.

CHARACTERISTICS OF GREAT PRODUCT MANAGERS

When hiring product managers, you should select for the following skills:

1. **Product taste.** Product taste means having the insights and intuition to understand customer needs for a product in a given area. What product features will wow a customer or meet their core needs? If the PM is joining you from another industry they may not know the specific needs of your customers. However, they should have the skill set and tool kit to quickly learn about your customers and their needs.

2. **Ability to prioritize.** What is the value of a proposed product feature versus the engineering work needed to accomplish it? What is more important—a new product for the sales team or a feature for customers? Should pricing be optimized for consumers or small business owners? What is the 80% product that should be launched immediately and what singular customer problem does it solve?

3. **Ability to execute.** A big part of product management is convincing and cajoling teams and different resources to get the product to launch, and then to maintain the product and support the customer base. Product managers will partner with engineering, design, legal, customer support, and other functions to execute on the product road map.

---

[53] Ben Horowitz has a good post on this, although it is focused on 1990s enterprise-PMs. See link on eladgil.com. [*https://a16z. com/2012/06/15/good-product-managerbad-product-manager/*]

4. **Strategic sensibilities.** How is the industry landscape evolving? How can the product be positioned to make an end run around the competition? Intel's famous pricing strategy in the 1970s is a good example of a bold strategic move. At the time Intel understood there was a strong reduction in their own costs as they scaled unit sales. Dropping unit sales would lead to increased demand and volume, causing a virtuous cycle. Intel smartly decided to launch a new silicon product at cost below their COGs in order to scale market share faster. In response, their customers bought in volumes they had not projected until two years out, causing a massively lower cost structure for them and therefore profitability. In other words, their low pricing became self-fulfilling and sustainable through massive volumes years ahead of projections.

5. **Top 10% communication skills.** Much of the job of a product manager boils down to understanding and then communicating trade-offs to a diverse group of coworkers and external parties.

6. **Metrics and data-driven approach.** You build what you measure. Part of the role of a product manager is to work with engineering and the data science team to define the set of metrics the product team should track. Setting the right metrics can be hard, and even the right metrics can sometimes drive the wrong behavior.

THE FOUR TYPES OF PRODUCT MANAGERS

The product manager you hire depends on the type of product your company is working on. Often companies need a mix of the below. Some people can function as more than one type of PM, while other individuals are hard wired to only do one of the below well.

1. Business product manager

These product managers are strongest at synthesizing external customer requests into an internal product road map. Business PMs tend to thrive at enterprise software companies, or working on the partner-facing portions of consumer applications. They can work well with sales and present well to customers, yet are still technical enough to work with engineering and design to trade off road map versus engineering effort needed. They will have keener insights into product pricing, customer segmentation, and customer needs.

2. Technical product manager

Technical PMs are often (but not always) deeply technical people who can work with engineering on areas like infrastructure, search quality, machine learning, or other inward-facing work. Technical PMs can often work on a wide variety of products across enterprise and consumer as long as they can pick up the necessary business skills and have good user intuition to make the right trade-offs in the product.

3. Design product manager

Most commonly found working on consumer applications, design-centric product managers are more user experience-centric. Some companies will convert a designer to be the product manager for a consumer product. While designers are often incredibly talented at user experience and visual design, they may not be trained in making the trade-offs needed to run a business (e.g., advertising models, pricing, etc.) or may want a product to be pixel perfect (which means it will take longer to ship the product). In general, it is good to retrain design people who become product managers to focus more on pragmatic trade-offs between beauty and marketing. Design PMs spend the most time with internal engineering and design teams and tend to spend less time on outward facing or business-centric tasks.

4. Growth product manager

Growth PMs tend to be quantitative, analytical, numbers-driven, and in the best cases wildly creative and aggressive. The focus of the growth PM is to *(i)* determine the critical levers needed to drive product adoption and use, and then *(ii)* to manipulate those levers. For example, the growth team at Facebook added tens of millions of incremental users via email loops, funnel optimization, and large scale multivariate testing of sign up, conversion, and other flows. Growth PMs tend to work closely with engineering, marketing, UX, and in some cases partnership or deal teams. Sometimes growth marketing will play the role of growth product management and this role will report into marketing.

In general, the more technical and back-end heavy your product, the fewer product managers you will have. A database company is likely to have a much lower product manager to engineer ratio than a consumer internet company. When I was at Google, the search infrastructure team had a few-to-none product managers while the mobile team, which was more UI-centric and business-centric, had many (despite a much smaller engineering organization).

NOT A PRODUCT MANAGER: PROJECT MANAGERS

Do not hire project managers as product managers. While project managers may be great at organizing and driving a schedule, they often lack the ability to prioritize features or ask the larger strategic questions. In general, project managers are not needed in high functioning software organizations, where a mix of the engineering manager and product manager will take on project management. Project managers may become useful for hardware products, external partner implementations, or vendor-specific hardware integrations.

ASSOCIATE PRODUCT MANAGERS (APM'S)/ROTATIONAL PRODUCT MANAGERS (RPM'S)

Google and Facebook have developed extensive programs for more junior product managers joining these companies straight out of undergraduate programs. The Google program consists of two 12-month rotations, while the Facebook program is three six-month rotations. For each rotation, an APM/RPM works with a different product organization (e.g., ads, a consumer product, timeline, or search). APM/RPM programs are meant to grow an internal crop of future product leaders for each company. As your company scales to 1,000 or more people, it might be worth considering an APM-like program. Don't do this until you have a solid internal senior product management organization in place.

INTERVIEWING PMS

When interviewing product managers, it is important to keep in mind the role you are hiring her for (see the previous section "The four types of product managers"), as well as the generic capabilities sought out in all product managers (see "Characteristics of Great Product Managers") and all hires (culture fit, etc.).

Key areas to push product managers during interviews are:

1. **Product insights.** What products do you use daily? How would you change X product? How would you design X product for a specific set of users? What features would you add? What would you drop/discontinue? If you were starting a company from scratch, what product would you start with, and why? For example, how would you design a mobile phone for children?

2. **Contributions to past successful products.** When I worked at Google, I overlapped with some of the strongest product people I ever met. I also overlapped with a number of terrible product managers who happened to be at the right place at the right time. When interviewing a product manager from a successful product, it is important to dig into their specific contributions. For example: What role did you play in the product definition and launch? Who came up with which product features? Who drove the idea to price the product X way? Etc.

3. **Prioritization.** Focus your questions around prioritization on the frameworks the candidate uses for making trade-offs, rather than the trade-offs themselves. You can initiate these questions by providing a scenario or case study to work from. For example: What is a real world example where your company had multiple potential product paths to invest in but could not do all of them? How would the PM approach this decision-making choice? What factors would fold into it? What data could be used? What is an example of a product feature that the executive team requested that you pushed back on or had removed?

4. **Communication and team conflicts.** Was the PM able to sell a vision or product to their last company's leadership team? What disagreements or conflicts did the PM have with engineering or design? How were these disagreements resolved? How does the PM actively build relationships with other parts of the organization? What communication approaches does the PM use? What is important to communicate, and when? What is an example where a miscommunication caused an issue for a product? How was this resolved and what changed from a process perspective after? In general there is a natural tension between product, design, and engineering. Conflicts may arise naturally in a fast-paced environment. The key is how to build relationships to surmount disagreements and how to resolve conflicts if they do occur.

5. **Metrics and data.** What metrics did the PM track for their last product? How did they choose these metrics? What bad behavior could these metrics have driven and how would you avoid this behavior? What metrics would the PM track for your company's product? Why are those the right metrics? How often and in what context should metrics be reviewed? How do you evaluate if a product launch has been successful?

REFERENCE-CHECK ALL YOUR PRODUCT HIRES

For all hires, reference-checking is incredibly important. For product managers, it's even more important. With an engineering candidate, an interview can reveal if she is technically competent. For a product manager there is no easily testable metric of competence. Instead, past work is the strongest single indicator of whether someone may be successful again in the future. Informal backchannel, pursued appropriately, can be especially enlightening.

The best product managers have a history of launching products or features that would otherwise have gotten stuck, successfully negotiating with engineering and design to make trade-offs that contributed to the success of the product, and creating a big strategic viewpoint that drives business success.

> "Crisp product requirement documents can make a world of difference in driving concise agreement on, and execution of, the product. PRDs should clearly articulate primary features and product needs."
>
> —Elad Gil

PRODUCT, DESIGN, AND ENGINEERING: HOW THEY FIT TOGETHER

Product, design, and engineering may have the perception of overlapping roles. In reality, each function has highly distinct responsibilities.

Design: Design the optimal visual and user experience for the product.
Engineering: Build the product. Suggest how the technical road map can drive product and vice versa.
Product: Set the product vision and road map and ensure the company builds a product that the user needs. Make trade-offs and prioritize between design, engineering, and business concerns.

While design is often focused on the optimal design for a product, and engineering on the technical side, product's role is to make trade-offs and prioritize based on inputs from design, engineering, legal, customer support, and sales/marketing/customers versus the broader business needs, competitive environment, and company strategy.

Ambiguity arises largely due to designers thinking, "I own the design, why is product telling me what to tweak?", engineers thinking, "I own the technical aspects of the product, why is product asking me to stop working on feature X?", and product sometimes stepping on either function's toes.

In reality, product management should be viewed as the function in the middle that needs to make holistic trade-offs on all aspects of the product and represents the voice of the user (while making the proper business trade-offs). This role obviously requires a lot of trust from design and engineering, which is why a bad product manager can ruin perception of the role in an organization.

HIRING A STRONG VP PRODUCT

In many startups the CEO may initially play the role VP product. At some point the organization and processes need to be professionalized and a VP product will need to be hired in. Many CEOs at this point are tempted to hire a "process person" to drive product management as the CEO feels she understands product and just needs someone to execute her vision. This is often a mistake as the company scales and more is delegated to the VP layer over time. Instead, CEOs should look for a VP product who both understands product management processes as well as has a complementary or similar vision for the product and its road map.

The role of a VP product is to:

1. **Drive product strategy, road-mapping, and execution across the organization.** Obviously, this is done with the guidance of the CEO who is the final authority.
   - **Set product vision and road map.** Work with the CEO and other key executives to ensure a robust product vision and road map is set and adhered to.
   - **Think strategically and articulate that strategy.** The VP product should be able to lay out a compelling product strategy that includes a strong understanding of *(i)* who your customers really are, *(ii)* what it means to win in your market, *(iii)* how to differentiate as a product and company, and *(iv)* how to build compelling and remarkable products for your customers.
   - **Make cross-functional, strategic trade-offs.** Product management is about product strategy and prioritization. A great product leader should be able to work with the founders on company strategy and own the product road map. This does not mean the founder/CEO should not ultimately make decisions in this area. Rather, the founder/CEO should be able to delegate strategic product planning and prioritization to the VP product and then bless/modify the outcome of that process.

2. **Create and empower a professional product management discipline.**
   - **Recruit experienced product managers who have overseen multiple stages of the lifecycle of high use products.** If your company is in high-growth mode, you want to hire experienced product managers who have shipped products at scale and then managed them through their lifecycle.
   - **Represent product management at the executive level.** Work well with peers. Product is the central spoke in communicating with, integrating feedback from, and pushing back on design, engineering, sales, marketing,

operations, customer support, and other functions. This means product managers need to build deep relationships in each organization and be able to work with many different functions and personality types effectively.

- **Empower PMs in their organization to work effectively and get things done.** Help PMs on her team navigate internal politics and stakeholders. The VP product should also clearly define, and get cross-company buy-in on, the roles and responsibilities of PMs and the adoption of simple product processes.
- **Build programs to train and support new PMs.** Ensure that your company has proper mentoring and training to support new PMs as you make university hire and internal conversions.

3. **Set cross-company product management processes.**
    - **Develop processes needed to run product development efficiently, prioritize product decisions, and launch products.** This includes experience with a multi-functional launch calendar, writing simple product requirement documents (PRDs), and navigating cross-functional input and trade-offs for products. Ensure adoption of these processes by the broader company.

EMPOWERING THE VP PRODUCT

As with all executive hires, as CEO you need to spend time onboarding and empowering the VP product. This may include:

- **Delegate aspects of product strategy and planning to the VP product.** Delegation does not mean abdication. Rather, the VP product should work with cross-functional teams to generate a product road map and prioritization that is then blessed/modified by the CEO.
- **Empower and support the VP product.** The VP product may implement a set of basic new processes that did not exist before at your company. They may turn over or re-organize a subset of their team just as any new executive would. They may also carve out a stronger role for product management than has existed traditionally at your company. This may cause tension with other influential teams at the company. The VP product will need the CEO's support to make these changes.
- **Be patient.** You have been thinking and working on this company for years. It takes some time to transfer all the knowledge. It will take three months for your VP product to come up to speed on the company, product, key people, processes, etc. It will take another three months for them to start to be valuable. This is true of any senior hire, especially as your organization gets larger. That said, any senior hire should start to get some quick, low-hanging-fruit wins in the first few weeks or months and take some pressure off of the CEO. Strong onboarding is critical to any executive hire's success.

Once a CEO has seen a "great" product organization and VP product in action, product management tends to become one of the most valued functions in a company.

PRODUCT MANAGEMENT PROCESSES

For each functional area in a company, a small number of processes can go a long way (for example, doing code reviews in any engineering organization). For product management, the key processes to consider as you scale include:

1. PRD templates and product road maps
The starting point of building a product is getting agreement and clarity on what to build. While engineering owns writing the technical design documentation for how a product will be technically architected and work, product management should own writing up the set of requirements for the product itself. Who are you building this product for? What use cases does the product meet? What does it solve for and explicitly not solve for? What are the main features and what does the product do? What are the main product dependencies? A PRD may include wireframes that roughly sketch out the product user journey.

2. Product reviews
As your organization scales, so too will the number of teams and products. Many companies have a weekly product review meeting. This is attended by a common set of key executives to review progress on a given product and provide feedback on strategy, direction or launch readiness. A set of product teams will come in and present to these executives about their product development or road map.

Some companies will have projects come in as they get staffed for a baseline discussion on primary objectives, use cases, and road maps. Other companies will only focus the meeting on check-ins for major products already underway.

Product reviews are typically a mechanism to resolve uncertainty in direction or trade-offs for a given product area, or to provide cross-functional input to drive product direction or course correction. Product reviews may also be used to check in on post-launch metrics or success of the product or check in on user feedback or adoption.

The teams attending the product review usually include the product manager (who is responsible for organizing and driving the review), the design lead, the tech lead and key engineers, and then other members of the core team needed for a fruitful discussion (this may include sales, BD, support staff, legal, or other stakeholders).

3. Launch process and calendar

Some companies bundle the launch process or calendar into the product review meeting. As you scale and the number of projects skyrockets, having a stand-alone forum to discuss upcoming launches becomes useful. Many companies will have an internal web page where each product is listed with a launch date. Next to each project, each functional area can give a binary "ready to launch" or not, and add questions or issues from their function. For example, product and engineering may all think the product is ready to launch but legal may still be "not ready" due to an unresolved legal question. The launch meeting allows the executive team and functional leads to weigh in on whether a product should go out the door or if there are unresolved items.

4. Retrospectives

After each product launch a healthy practice is to get the main cross-functional members of the team who worked on it together. The purpose is to discuss what went well and should be emulated for other launches, and what went poorly. For both, you can discuss what contributed to the success or failure mode and how to deal with it for future projects.

Retrospectives serve two purposes—(1) to codify and understand what best practices are for product development and launch and (2) to allow some of the praise, as well as pressure and disagreements to vent in the open. By having a forum for non-emotional conversations around what went poorly, different teams have the opportunity to learn what to do better next time, but also to address questions or things that did not work head on.

PRODUCT MANAGEMENT CONVERSION AND TRAINING

When I was at Twitter, a number of the early product managers had been converted to product from other functions (design, sales, business operations, engineering, partner services, etc.). While a number of these individuals ended up having a thriving career in product management, others flailed poorly and had to leave the role once the organization was upgraded.

Before considering the conversion of a non-PM into a PM role, you should optimally have (1) an interview or trial process to check if someone should convert, (2) core product management processes in place so the new PM will have guardrails on how to function, (3) a VP product in place to manage the individual and ensure they are trained, and (4) some seasoned senior PMs in place to mentor and support the development of the new PM. Just as your company provides some onboarding and mentorship to junior or new sales people or engineers, the same is useful for product.

"For all hires, reference-checking is incredibly important."

—Elad Gil

At many high-growth startups, there is a common pattern for early product team evolution. This pattern is most common at startups where the founders did not have work experience at a major technology company before starting their own:

- The CEO or one of the founders is playing the role of product manager. As the company balloons they delegate to other employees already in place to take on product management. This may lead to the conversion of designers, business operations, marketers, engineers, or others into early product managers.
- With a lack of product management process and infrastructure in place and no senior PMs around, these individuals are left to fend for themselves. Some may default to playing a project management role versus a product role. For example, their time may get spent on execution and checklists versus setting product vision and road maps or troubleshooting cross-functional issues. This may lead to ongoing discounting of the role in product in the organization until a more experienced organization is built.
- A VP product is hired, restarts the product team, sets processes, and the company integrates product management in as its own discipline. It may take a year or more to recruit and empower senior PMs and to reshape organizational processes to scale the function and its impact internally.

Google is a good example of a company that experienced this pattern. Among the first product managers at Google were conversions such as Marissa Mayer (a former engineer), Susan Wojcicki (marketing), Georges Harik (engineer), and Salar Kamander (general operations). These four were complemented by some senior product management hires and Jonathan Rosenberg, an experienced VP product who came in and established a number of processes. Rosenberg also implemented a hiring and training program for new grads (the famous Google APM program). Rosenberg was a necessary component to bring stability and best practices to Google product development.

PRODUCT TO DISTRIBUTION MINDSET

Startups tend to succeed by building a product that is so compelling and differentiated that it causes large number of customers to adopt it over an incumbent. This large customer base becomes a major asset for the company going forward. Products can be cross-sold to these customers, and the company's share of time or wallet can expand.

Since focusing on product is what caused initial success, founders of breakout companies often think product development is their primary competency and asset. In reality, the distribution channel and customer base derived from their first product is now one of the biggest go-forward advantages and differentiators the company has.

This pattern of distribution as moat and competitive advantage was used ruthlessly by the prior generation of technology companies. Microsoft bought or built multiple franchises including Office (Word, Powerpoint, Excel were all stand-alone companies or market segments), Internet Explorer, and other products and then pushed them down common business and consumer channels. Cisco has purchased dozens of companies that were then repositioned or resold to their enterprise and telecom channels.[54] SAP and Oracle have exhibited similar patterns of success.

Of the most recent crop of technology giants, Facebook and Google realized the power and importance of distribution early in their respective lives. While Google's reputation is that of organic growth, in reality the company bought placement on the Firefox homepage, as well as paid hundreds of millions of dollars per year to have Google search toolbars distributed via download with other applications and also paid laptop manufacturers to set Google as the default search engine. Google then used its search customer base to bootstrap other products and distribute Maps (Where2 acquisition[55]), Gmail, Chrome, Docs (Writely and other acquisitions), and other products. Similarly, Facebook invested heavily in growth efforts and acquired multiple companies for email scraping to be able to find people you should invite to the service (Octazen), low end feature phone distribution (the Snaptu acquisition allowed Facebook to acquire 100 million feature phone users onto its platform who they would not have gotten on the desktop alone), and other approaches. It then used this distribution to help accelerate acquisitions like Instagram to the global market.

---

[54] See eladgil.com for a link to a comprehensive list. [*https://en.wikipedia.org/wiki/List_of_acquisitions_by_Cisco_Systems*]

[55] See "The untold story about the founding of Google Maps." Link on eladgil.com. [*https://medium.com/@lewgus/the-untold-story-about-the-founding-of-google-maps-e4a5430aec92*]

In all cases, the steps to success have been:

1. **Build a product so good that customers will use you over an incumbent.** Build a large user base on the back of this first product.

2. **Be aggressive rather than complacent about customer growth early.** Outsized companies like Google, Facebook, and Uber were aggressive and calculating about growth from their earliest days. In contrast, non-metric-driven, less aggressive companies failed to reach the next level of success. Too many companies get complacent about distribution if their core product "just works."

3. **Realize your customer channels are a primary asset of the company.** Build new products or buy companies and push them down your sales channel. Uber has been trying to do this more recently with Uber Eats and its Jump acquisition.

4. **Realize that your company will not be able to build everything itself.** Buy more companies and push them down the channel. Most companies need to overcome internal resistance to buying companies. A common set of arguments are made about how easy it would be to build something in house instead, or that integration challenges will be too hard. In reality, breakout companies never have enough resources to do everything and should buy more startups. In general, most companies buy too few, rather than too many, companies as they scale.

The smartest companies realize they are also in the distribution business, and will buy (or build) and then redistribute a range of products.

CHAPTER 8

Financing
and valuation

CHAPTER 8

Financing and valuation

MONEY MONEY MONEY

For the first 40 years of the technology industry, high-growth, breakout companies would go public (IPO) much earlier in their lifecycle. Intel went public two years after incorporation, Amazon when it was three years old, Apple at four, and Cisco at the ripe old age of five. Microsoft was an outlier and long in the tooth when it went public after ~10 years in 1986 (largely on the back of its 1980 deal with IBM for MS-DOS.)

In the 2000s, the timeline to IPO lengthened significantly with some companies taking up to a decade or more to go public. With this shift in time horizons has come a shift in financing strategies and capital sources to fund them. Investors who used to invest in young public technology companies have been forced to invest in private companies instead. Long time horizons to liquidity has created large secondary markets for common stock. And finally, the shrinking number of public breakout companies (and public company founder role models) has created a founder generation skeptical of going public.

In this section we cover new sources of capital for late stage financings, secondary stock sales and tenders, and initial public offerings. I am not a lawyer and this is not intended to be legal advice so talk with your attorney about these topics.

LATE-STAGE FINANCING: WHO SHOULD YOU BE TALKING TO?

As your company grows, the range of investors who can fund your next round shifts. While some venture firms (such as Benchmark, True Ventures, and Upfront) focus largely on series A financings, many traditional venture firms have either expanded their scope to include later stages or raised stand-alone growth funds to fuel later-stage high-growth companies. This includes funds such as 8vc, Accel, Andreessen

Horowitz, Bessemer, CRV, DFJ, Felicis, Foresite, Founders Fund, General Catalyst, Greylock, Google Ventures, Index Ventures, Khosla Ventures, KPCB, Lightspeed, Matrix, Maverick, Menlo, Mayfield, NEA, Norwest, Redpoint, Scale, Sequoia, Shasta, SignalFire, Social+Capital, Spark, Sutter Hill Ventures, Thrive Capital, Trinity, USV, Venrock, and others.[56] In general, the larger the fund the more likely they are to do late-stage investments.

In parallel, there is a whole class of later-stage funds that have traditionally focused on the growth stage such as Capital G (Google Capital), GGV, GCVC, IVP, Insight, Meritech, Summit, and the like. Newer funds, like DST, Tiger, VY have also emerged to take an entrepreneur-friendly approach to late-stage investing.

A more recent development over the last few years is the emergence of public market investors, or family offices, as direct investors in later-stage companies. This includes firms like BlackRock, T. Rowe Price, Fidelity, and Wellington, as well as hedge funds like Point72 and TriplePoint Capital. Some hedge funds, like Viking and Matrix, have focused on life sciences and digital health investments at the later stages. Sovereign wealth funds like ADIA, EDBI, GIC, Mubadala, Temasek, and others have also done direct investments in companies, while Softbank has emerged as an investing giant fueled with capital from Saudi Arabia and other sources. Private equity or crossover funds like KKR, TPG, Warburg Pincus, Blackstone, Goldman Sachs, JP Morgan, Morgan Stanley, and others have set up private tech-specific funds or efforts. A number of billionaires have also started to write large checks from their family offices to invest directly in exciting technology companies.

Finally, you have additional options later in the company's life such as strategic investors and angel-led special-purpose vehicles, which are one-off funds raised specifically to invest in your company. The proliferation of late-stage capital sources suggests now is one of the best times for an entrepreneur to raise late-stage rounds.

---

[56] Note: I've made an effort to include usefully representative lists of investment firms in this section, but I must warn readers that these lists are not comprehensive—and they may soon be out of date in any event. Do your research and don't rely solely on lists of investors that you find in books. Also, I offer my apologies to any firms I overlooked.

TYPES OF LATE-STAGE INVESTORS

Type of investor: Traditional VC
Individual check sizes: Up to $50M in a single round (bigger numbers usually out of a growth fund)
Valuations for investment: Traditional VCs will not usually lead rounds above mid-hundred-million-dollar valuations. However, a number of funds have now rolled out growth funds that will invest at $1B plus.
Benefits: May be able to provide operating or scaling advice, depending on VC partner.
Drawbacks: More likely to ask for a board seat (which can also be a benefit, depending on the VC). If you have already raised money from VCs, may not broaden network much.
What they will look for: While traditional VCs will be interested in underlying business metrics, they will often be more focused on macro market trends, unit economics, and broader company strategy and differentiation. These investors will often focus on the "moat" the company is building as a point of strategic defensibility and ongoing sustainability.

Type of investor: Growth/mezzanine fund
Individual check sizes: $25M to $500M
Valuations for investment: $100M to $10B.
Benefits: May be hands-off investors. Depending on investor subtype, may bring different network to the table.
Drawbacks: May be less operationally inclined, even though emphasis is later stage. May be very numbers driven, so will spend a lot of time focused on financials, long term moats, and the like.
What they will look for: These types of investors tend to be very numbers-driven. They will focus on growth rates, margin, user adoption, costumer acquisition costs, and other key metrics around unit economics and core company metrics.

Type of investor: Hedge fund
Individual check sizes: $10M to $500M
Valuations for investment: Mainly later-stage rounds in the $500M-plus range, although a number of hedge funds have done series A or even seed rounds.
Benefits: In some cases, may have a great understanding of the industry or market based on their investments in public companies in your space. For example, Viking is a savvy genomics investor. May be valuation insensitive, although this is not always true and depends on the hedge fund. May care less about taking a board seat, which can be helpful if you already have multiple investor board members.
Drawbacks: Usually don't understand the challenges and uncertainty of a startup. May send a "low quality" signal to later investors if a hedge fund comes in early (this depends deeply on the hedge fund and how much they have invested in the industry in the past. Some are known as quite savvy).
What they will look for: Leaders in large markets. These are often financially driven investors who focus on underlying numbers and longer-term cash flows. More likely to think (and assess investment opportunities) like a public market investor rather than a venture one.

Type of investor: Private equity fund
Individual check sizes: $10M to $500M
Valuations for investment: Mainly later-stage rounds in the $500M-plus range, although some private equity funds have done series A or series B rounds.
Benefits: May have broad or differentiated networks. May be able to provide introductions to other late-stage portfolio companies if doing enterprise sales.
Drawbacks: There are many great, supportive, private equity firms investing in private technology companies. However, one private equity fund in particular is known to wrap a nasty set of terms into financing rounds or act badly once a term sheet is signed. Others, such as banks with private equity funds (e.g., Goldman Sachs or Morgan Stanley), are known to value the longer-term banking relationships and are more company-friendly. Be cautious when selecting a private equity partner to work with, and make sure to do diligence by checking with other technology company entrepreneurs they have funded.
What they will look for: Private equity firms tend to invest based on numbers and a large revenue stream. They will take a close look at margin structure, growth rates, topline revenue, as well as the overall macro market dynamics and defensibility of your business.

Type of investor: Family office
Individual check sizes: $5M to $500M
Valuations for investment: Any valuation, although typically family offices get involved in later-stage rounds.
Benefits: May have a strong network to help company, depending on market and who they represent. May or may not be valuation-insensitive depending on how professionalized their investing is.
Drawbacks: Often do not understand early-stage or startup investing and can get uneasy if things get tough. In general, it is better to work directly with the person whose money it is then the family office staff. Alternatively, look for family offices who have done a number of private market investments in the past and understand the dynamics.
What they will look for: Typically family offices look for signals from other institutional investors for round quality. They will look for startups in large markets and typically prefer high-margin businesses.

Type of investor: Angel SPV (Special Purpose Vehicle)[57]
Individual check sizes: $1M to $50M
Valuations for investment: Anything from series A on up.
Benefits: Usually this is an investor or angel already on your cap table who raises money for you as part of a large venture round. This is a way for angels or small funds to increase ownership in your company with your permission. This may also be a way

---

57 An SPV (special purpose vehicle) is a one-time fund set up to invest in a particular company. Just as a venture fund raises money from limited partners to invest in multiple companies, an SPV is a one-off fund that raises money from LPs to invest in only one company. Recently, a number of funds (early-stage as well as traditional VCs), as well as individual angels, have raised SPVs to invest in specific companies.

to increase time spent or deepen the engagement by an existing investor, or to raise money for the company in a way that ensures additional equity/preferred stock votes go to someone the company trusts.

Drawbacks: Your VCs may push back on an angel making a large investment this way. May have issues actually raising or delivering the money. You need to make sure to define the process they are allowed to follow and what information they can or cannot share with their potential LPs.

What they will look for: SPVs can either lead a round, or be part of a syndicate. If they lead a round, they will act like any other venture capital lead. If they are part of the syndicate, they may be a little more momentum-driven. For late stage round and large check sizes, expect an SPV to do full diligence on the company, its team, financials, and overall market trends, defensibility, and growth rates.

Type of investor: Public market investor
Individual check sizes: Up to $500M
Valuations for investment: Usually in the hundreds of millions to billions.
Benefits: Large source of trusted capital. Typically seen as "smart money." Tend to hold on to stock post-IPO and send signal to public markets that your company is legitimate.
Drawbacks: May publically mark down your stock and affect future fundraises or secondaries.[58]
What they will look for: Tend to assess company through the lens of what an IPO and beyond will look like (e.g., core financial metrics, competition and defensibility, etc.).

Type of investor: "Strategic" investors [59]
Individual check sizes: Typically range from tens of millions to a billion or more
Valuations for investment: Usually in the hundreds of millions or more. Strategic investors may ask to invest earlier, but you may want to save them for later rounds and decrease the risk of signaling in early rounds.
Benefits: Valuation insensitive and more likely to pay a premium. May have core ties or knowledge that can dramatically help your company. May be able to wrap a broader "strategic" deal around investment that can accelerate your company.
Drawbacks: For early round, may cause "signaling," in which other strategic investors avoid buying or partnering with you. For example, if you are a digital health company and Pfizer buys a stake in you early, other pharmaceutical companies may be less likely to partner with or try to buy you. Once rounds get later this signaling tends to decrease. Strategic investors may also try to use their investment to get information and learn about your business so they can eventually compete with you.
What they will look for: Strategic value of your company in their industry. Ability to learn from your startup about how their market may get reshaped. In some cases a strategic investment is a prelude to an acquisition offer, so strategics view it as a way to get to know you better.

---

58 See eladgil.com. [*http://fortune.com/2015/11/12/fidelity-marks-down-tech-unicorns/*]
59 Strategics are large, cash-rich companies in your industry who may want to invest in order to (1) cut a broader partnership with your company, (2) learn more about how software and technology may impact their industry, or (3) try to acquire you later. For example, Roche was part of $100 million round in Flatiron, GM was part of a $1 billion round in Lyft, and Intel was part of a major round in Cloudera. [*http://arstechnica.com/cars/2016/01/general-motors-bought-sidecar-gave-lyft-millions-now-its-launching-maven/*]

Type of investor: Large Foreign Internet company
Individual check sizes: Up to $1B
Valuations for investment: Huge range, from early-stage to multi-billion-dollar range.
Benefits: Less valuation sensitive. May help you enter China or other markets or simply be a source of capital. Tencent, Alibaba, Rakuten, and others have invested aggressively in tech startups over time.
Drawbacks: May try to tie investment to joint venture or other structures in their home market. May be trying to learn from your company so they can launch competitor in their own market.
What they will look for: Strategic value of potential investment upside, depending on firm and individual objectives.

Type of investor: Sovereign Wealth Fund
Individual check sizes: Up to a few billion
Valuations for investment: Huge range, from early-stage to multi-billion-dollar range.
Benefits: Some are less valuation sensitive (others are quite sensitive). May help you enter new markets depending on the country they represent or sell to large state-owned enterprises. Have enormous scale of capital. In a subset of cases some sovereign wealth funds may invest for strategic reasons—for example they want to understand or get closer to technology that may impact companies in their country, or to trade petro dollars for tech assets to diversify their economic holdings.
Drawbacks: Some may be slow to move or have multiple hurdles in place for investment. Some funds newer to direct investment may lack savvy or misunderstand how startups work.
What they will look for: Strategic value and potential investment upside, depending on fund and individual objectives.

HOW TO EVALUATE LATE-STAGE FUNDING SOURCES

As a later-stage company, you will have a broader set of investors to choose from than you did in the early days. If you are a high-growth company choosing from a strong crop of investors, consider the following factors when selecting a later-stage funder:

Follow-on capital. Some late-stage funds can deploy hundreds of millions or billions of dollars. Is the fund able to follow on as you raise larger rounds?

Public market impact. Some public market investors, such as T. Rowe Price and Fidelity, send a strong positive market signal, as they are known as long-term holders of public equities. As you go public, they may hold your stock over the longer run, and this may impact your post-IPO perception and performance.

Note: At least one public market investor recently began publicly listing month-by-month changes in value in their private market portfolio (which makes no sense—can you really change a public company's valuation on a monthly basis?). This has caused issues for these companies in follow-on fundraises, secondaries, and employee morale.

HOW DST REVOLUTIONIZED LATE-STAGE INVESTING

The three biggest innovations in venture investing in the last 10 years include (in no particular order) (1) Y Combinator and the early-stage revolution, (2) AngelList Syndicates and distributed angel networks, and (3) DST and late-stage investing.

Yuri Milner and DST revolutionized late-stage investing by taking large stakes in a number of companies, starting with Facebook in 2009, with the following characteristics:

• Investments could be primary, common stock secondary, or a mix of the two.

• Investments were entrepreneur-friendly, with no board seat taken.

• Investments were typically large in nature and could total $1 billion or more over the lifetime of the company. A company could effectively do a private IPO.

While this style of investing is now more commonplace, at the time DST entered the market with its Facebook investment its approach was quite radical. In those days, later-stage investors typically asked for complicated preferences, board seats, or other ways to control the company. A number of funds have since copied DST, but the firm seems to always be a step ahead of the rest with its global diversification and ability to cherry-pick some of the best companies and investments.

Strategic value. Late-stage investors may have specific industry knowledge, partnership/introduction potential, or country-specific knowledge. For example, when entering the Chinese market, Uber originally set up a stand-alone subsidiary through which money was raised from Chinese funders who can help with government relations and other aspects of entering China. An investment from a strategic investor can also solidify a key partnership. For example, when Google signed the deal to power Yahoo! Search (at the time a company-making move), Google took an investment round from Yahoo!

Simple terms. Some late stage private equity firms or hedge funds ask for complex structures or extra liquidation preferences when doing investments. Terms may include additional issuance of shares under an IPO price, extra clawback of value during a sale under a certain price, and the like. If you are able to keep terms simple that is often worth the trade-off of also getting a lower valuation.

Board seats. A number of late-stage investors are willing to invest without taking a board seat—something DST pioneered. Avoiding a bloated board may become challenging as the number of rounds a company completes grows.

Ability to buy secondary stock or drive tenders. Some companies will couple a primary financing event (buying preferred stock) with a secondary sale or tender (allowing employees, founders, or early investors to sell part of their stake). Depending on the fund they may or may not have the appetite or the SEC registrations to buy significant amounts of secondary.

KEY TERMS

Late-stage financings are not that different from earlier-stage rounds for the key terms to consider. However, at the later stages the two most important items you'll weigh tend to collapse down to preference and board membership.

Preference. While top-tier early-stage investors tend to have a clean preference structure (i.e., non-participating preferred[60]), private equity firms and family offices may ask for unusual preference structures that effectively convert an equity round into a debt round. For example, if the company and investor cannot agree on valuation, the private equity fund may ask for a 2X or 3X preference, as well as a ratchet on the next round. Similarly, later-stage investors may put in special provisions around IPOs (e.g., if the IPO prices under a certain valuation, or takes longer than six to nine months, the investor gets extra stock), future fundraises, or other aspects of the company's life cycle. In general, you should avoid these special terms if you can, although you may not have the chance to do so, especially if your valuation starts to exceed your core business metrics or capital is scarce.

Board membership. As with all financings, a key element to think through is whether or not to add a board member as part of the round. In general, larger boards are harder to manage. However, late-stage investors may bring a perspective to the board that has been lacking up to this point—around financial discipline, for example, or the state of the public market. This perspective can be helpful or destructive, depending on the board member and broader company context. On average, later-stage investors will be more numbers/revenue/margin driven, and this can drive a company down either a very good or a very bad path.

Additionally, later-stage investors may not be as used to dealing with the many "oh shit" moments that a startup typically faces in a rapidly evolving market, with a shifting product road map, and a changing org structure. Some late-stage investors are notoriously hands-off/founder-friendly (e.g., Yuri Milner and DST). However, many are used to "safer" late-stage investments and can cause trouble for a high-growth startup that's still rapidly evolving.

Choose your board members carefully! And consider avoiding new additions altogether, unless your late-stage investors can help in unique ways. Depending on the dynamics around your fundraise, you may not have a choice—e.g., if the investor requires a board seat and you do not have a good alternative option.

Before adding anyone as a board member, make sure to (1) do due diligence on her past investments and board seats; (2) have frank conversations about company direction and expectations; and (3) decide if there are other ways to give late-stage investors meaningful impact and access to company information—without adding a board seat. Alternatively, a late-stage investor may be able to add enormous value to your board and even help to clean out poorly performing early-stage investors. See the section on Removing Board Members for more information on this.[61]

60 See eladgil.com. [*https://www.forbes.com/pictures/fiii45hlf/participating-preferred-vs-non-participating-preferred/*]
61 Related post on eladgil.com [*http://blog.eladgil.com/2012/11/how-to-choose-right-vc-partner-for-you.html*]

ONE WORD OF CAUTION

One downside of dealing with private equity investors is their tendency to throw around their weight or act in ways not aligned with the traditional Silicon Valley venture capital ethos. One PE group in particular is known for signing a term sheet, then three weeks later trying to renegotiate those terms (after the company has told other investors it has selected a lead and lost leverage on negotiation). This firm got kicked out of at least one "unicorn" round recently and is known as a bad choice. However, their shenanigans are not fully public, so tread carefully when dealing with PE firms. There are some perfectly good actors in the private equity world (e.g., KKR) but also a small number of bad actors when it comes to venture.

DON'T OVER-OPTIMIZE YOUR VALUATION

A common temptation for founders is to raise money at the highest possible valuation. High valuations may help with employee recruitment and compensation, generate positive PR for a company, provide ammunition for M&A, and stoke founder egos. Unfortunately, too high a valuation can lead to a host of problems down the line. For example, for many of the unicorn companies, their ability to raise their next round has less to do with whether they are viable businesses, and more to do with the valuation at which they previously raised money. [62]

Too high a valuation relative to the overall market can cause the following issues:

1. **Follow on fundraises become hard.** Investors typically expect a 2–3X increase in valuation with each round. At very high valuations (e.g., billions) this decreases to a 50%–100% markup with each round. Nonetheless, adding $1 billion in market cap is actually a lot of value creation (revenue, user growth, etc.). The higher the valuation, the harder it is to grow % market cap.

2. **Investor mix may shift.** At high valuations the time horizons of the investors who will become involved may shift. Many of the non-traditional late stage investors who have entered private equity venture markets have a short time horizon of 18 to 24 months, and they may push for liquidity or progress in ways that may not be aligned with a company's ultimate goals.

3. **Internal pressure to hit a target valuation causes bad behavior.** This is a biggie which I will mention more below: The pressure a founder puts on herself with a high valuation may distort her behavior and cause her to lead her company down the wrong path.

---

[62] Of course, there will be a number of these companies that are not worth $1 billion plus and will simply flame out. However, we will also see a number of companies that, two years from now, will look cheap in hindsight.

"In general, a $500 million to $1 billion valuation is usually where founders and/ or employees might start to consider selling stock."

—Elad Gil

4. **Employee expectations.** People who join the company due to the perceived value and upside of the stock will be upset if a down round occurs or the valuation does not grow in the next few years. This can also occur if the company valuation slides flat for three to four years while waiting to catch up to its valuation.

The above are all fundamentally issues of expectations. The higher your valuation, the higher the expectations. The worst manifestation of this is the pressure founders put on themselves when valuations are high.

FOUNDER PRESSURE

When a founder has a multi-billion-dollar valuation two challenges arise: (1) the founder may push unsustainable growth at all costs to hit the valuation and (2) a lot of distractions arise that may not help the business (e.g., press, speaking opportunities, investments, etc.).

The pressure to increase revenue or growth at all costs to meet rising expectation valuations is where companies can often go wrong. For example, doubling down on money-losing customer acquisition in order to show growth may accelerate market share, but also flip your company from default alive to default dead.

This pressure to grow may be self-imposed by the entrepreneur, but more often than not it also comes at the board level. Later stage investors may aggressively push for growth, especially if the projections that the startup company used in its fundraising deck are not being met. Late-stage investors may not always understand the uncertain nature of a startup, even one on a high-growth trajectory.

As an entrepreneur raising a round you should ask yourself the following questions:

- Will the money I am raising get me to a healthy multiple on my last valuation? If not, should I take a lower valuation so that this multiplier may be more feasible?
- What milestones will this fundraise get me to? Will those milestones fundamentally change the perception of my company's worth?
- What sorts of exits are possible for my company? Are there likely acquirers above the valuation I am raising at? Do I plan to go public? If not, is it wise to raise at this valuation? If so, will my IPO be at a higher valuation then my private market fundraising?

SECONDARY STOCK SALES

As your company's valuation continues to rise, early employees or investors may want to sell a subset of their stock in the company. A "primary" investment in a company is when you give a company money in exchange for its shares. A "secondary" investment is when you buy shares from someone besides the company (basically a previously owned share). In both cases, the shares could either be common stock or preferred stock. In other words, secondary stock is defined by who you are buying shares from versus the type of shares themselves.

For current or former employees, selling stock they hold may be driven by personal issues such as an expensive hospital bill for a family member, wanting to buy a house for themselves or their family, or an interest in diversifying what may be most of their net worth.

Early investors may be motivated to sell stock early by a need to return money to their funds' LPs (especially if they are in the process of raising another fund and want to show returns), or they may simply be looking out for their own financial interests and the need to generate "carry" on their funds.[63]

Founders may also want to sell secondary stock to diversify their net worth, which is likely dominated by company stock. For that reason, founder sales, if done correctly, tend to align founders to focus on the long-term success or outcome of the company by taking away worries they may have about their personal financial future.

---

[63] Carry is the percentage of a fund's return on investment that a VC earns in exchange for managing that fund. No capital returned = no carry, which greatly limits what the individual VC takes home.

$500 MILLION TO $1 BILLION TENDS TO BE A TRANSITION POINT

In general, a $500 million to $1 billion valuation is usually where founders and/or employees might start to consider selling stock. This shift in behavior is due to three factors: (1) It take two to five years to get to a $1 billion valuation. During that time life events (children, family illness, and the like) may have occurred and there is a financial need; (2) the market cap of the company is large enough that most of an individual's net worth is tied up in the company, 1% of the company may be worth $5 million or $10 million, diversifitcation starts to be meaningful. (3) Employee belief in the remaining multiple upside to the company may start to diminish. Almost all high-growth companies are chaotic and messy, and competition always increases when something is working well for a startup. Most early employees interpret this as a limit on the upside of the company, which increases their interest in selling. Moreover, the value of small amounts of stock at that valuation is sufficient to motivate employees to sell.

FOUNDER SALES

Founder secondary sales have become increasingly acceptable as a way to ensure that leaders continue to focus on the long-term potential of their companies, rather than sell early.

As an active founder, you may want to sell up to 10% of your holdings (or up to $5 to $10 million, whichever is lower) in a secondary transaction, as part of a round, a stand-alone sale, or a tender (more on each of those below). If you sell more than 10% (especially if you're still operationally involved with your startup), it will be perceived as a negative signal about your belief in the future of the company.

Most founder secondary sales occur once a company reaches a multi-hundred-million-dollar valuation. (There are some circumstances where smaller sales occur in the mid-to-high tens of millions if there is a specific founder need. In general, these earlier-stage sales amount to sales in the hundreds of thousands of dollars in order to pay off school debt or provide a small financial cushion for founders.)

Most founders I know are happy they took some amount of stock off the table to relieve financial pressures as the time to IPO keeps lengthening.

IF YOU DO NOT REGULATE SECONDARY SALES EARLY, IT MAY BACKFIRE ON YOU

There are a number of issues that can come up if you do not create a framework for secondary sales for your company: large transactions impacting your 409A valuation, misbehaving investors ending up on your cap table, or even the random dentist buying stock from an employee at a premium and then harassing your company for information. (The "random dentist" is real—I saw this happen at one company.) There are also secondary funds that may act badly in these opaque markets—for example, Facebook ended up with an SEC inquiry into their company stock sales due to issues with Felix Investments.[64]

Ways to get ahead of these problems include modifying your charter or other agreements to prevent secondary sales, ensuring you have a ROFR on all shares, and in some cases contractually preventing people from selling without board approval. Having a preferred buyer or tender program will also help create liquidity while ensuring stock doesn't actively trade in a secondary market.

TYPES OF SECONDARY SALES

In general, secondary sales begin as one-off sales—for example an employee needs to quit the company to take care of a sick parents and wants to sell some stock to pay for better medical care. As market cap grows and with it the demand to sell stock, the company realizes that random people are buying their way onto the cap table, or the demand to sell grows to significant levels as the company gets older and more employees and investors hold illiquid stock for multiple years. At this point, many companies switch to a "preferred buyer" or "tender" approach. I review the different types of secondary sales below:

1. One-off sales
In this scenario, the seller is executing a one-time transaction with either an existing cap table investor (i.e., someone who already owns company stock) or a new entity that is not already involved with the company. In general, the company has an incentive to push the stock seller to a buyer it already knows well.

There are ways to incentivize a seller to work with a known buyer. That includes everything from a simple request (especially if the seller is still active with the company as an employee or investor or wants to maintain a good relationship with the company) to making life difficult for the seller via the exercise of rights of first refusal (ROFRs) or other moves that delay the transaction and may destabilize it for the buyer and seller.

---

64 See article linked on eladgil.com. [*https://www.law360.com/articles/516967/sec-settles-with-firms-over-pre-ipo-facebook-trading*]

In general, one-off sales can backfire on a company as new, non-savvy, or potentially badly-behaved investors come on board. It is beneficial to the long-term health and stability of the company to establish a set of "preferred buyers" early to soak up secondary sales and demand for selling stock. This may be an informal relationship with trusted investors already on the cap table who want to buy more secondary. In parallel, the company should start to institute programs detailing how much employees or early investors can sell, and under what circumstances. Holding out the promise of a tender or other program will often cause potential sellers to wait for the company to initiate a formal secondary program. Most people want to do the right thing for the company, and are willing to wait 6–12 months, or more, for the opportunity to sell in a company-sanctioned manner.

2. Selling as part of a funding round
A straightforward time to sell—as a founder, early employee, or early investor—is during a funding round. Most financing rounds for late-stage breakout companies tend to be oversubscribed. The extra demand for company stock means that an investor who could not get a full primary allocation may be willing to take in a blend of preferred (as part of the round) and common stock (acquired from an employee or founder), or early-stage preferred stock (from an early investor).

Most late-stage investors will be okay with buying some secondary common stock alongside a preferred funding round, as the preferred stock helps protect the overall investment in a blended manner. Alternatively, investors who could not get a piece of a round may be willing to buy only common stock instead, depending on the structure of their funds. (Some funds cannot have a large portion of common stock in their portfolios due to LP agreements or the need for additional SEC filings.)

Most investors tend to discount common stock 20% to 30% relative to the preferred stock price—i.e., they will want to pay less for common stock since preference does not exist and will not protect them in a downside scenario. For example, when DST purchased secondary stock in Facebook it did so at a $6.5 billion valuation—a 35% discount on the $10 billion preferred price at the time.[65] However, if the company is hot enough, or the buyer hungry enough, investors may pay the same amount for common and preferred.

The company will likely want to take an arm's length approach to the common stock sale to avoid 409A implications (more on this below). A large, company-sanctioned stock sale (and 409A re-analysis) could cause a repricing of common stock for the entire company (and future employee options), which is worth avoiding if possible. Talk with your lawyers about this.

---

[65] See eladgil.com [*https://beta.techcrunch.com/2009/07/13/dst-to-buy-up-to-100-million-in-facebook-employee-stock/*]

Usually no more than 20% of the funding round will take place as secondary. The venture capitalists may not want to take the risk of buying too much common stock (which lacks the financial and control protections of preferred stock). There are also regulatory limits on the percentage a venture capital fund can invest in secondary versus primary stock.

3. Preferred buyer programs

In a preferred buyer program, one or more funds are given preferred access to purchase secondary stocks. These programs may be informal (e.g., the company suggests that potential sellers talk to a small number of funds) or formal (e.g., the company assigns a secondary ROFR, or right of first refusal, to these funds).

In a formal preferred buyer program, a fund may sign a term sheet, LOI, or binding agreement with a company to provide dedicated funds to soak up secondary stock. As part of this agreement, the fund can generally purchase stock in a pre-defined range (e.g., at a 10% discount to last round) and may be assigned a ROFR by the company.

The ROFR may become important: In many cases, the company has a 30-day right to purchase stock from a seller at a price the seller has negotiated with another buyer. When a ROFR is assigned to a fund, this may add a second 30-day period; if the company passes, the fund has another 30 days to purchase stock at the price the buyer has agreed to. The net effect is a 60-day—or more—delay between the statement of intent to sell and the time when a transaction can actually occur. This two-month timeframe can make buyers and sellers quite nervous, as market and other conditions may change during this time, destabilizing a secondary transaction.

In addition, a ROFR provides a source of sanctioned liquidity for a stock under a certain valuation, driving certain buyers out of the market: they cannot close a transaction, as the preferred buyer will take the sale from them. Effectively, the ROFR creates too long a wait and too high a price for many sellers, driving down market demand for secondary. You should talk to your legal team about ROFR assignments to preferred buyers.

Preferred buyer programs can be of special help when acquiring other companies. In this case, the founders or investors of the acquired company may want to sell a subset or all of the stock they receive in the transaction. A preferred buyer may help facilitate this transaction (and hence the actual acquisition) without the company itself needing to pay out cash as part of the purchase. This can also be handled via a tender, where the acquired company's investors can sell into a tender instead of a preferred buyer program.

4. Tender offers

A tender is basically a large coordinated event in which one or more buyers buy secondary stock in your company at a preset price.

Tender offers typically follow this pattern:

1. **The company tries to estimate demand for a secondary stock sale.** This determines the rough size of the tender. The company may also put in place paperwork to further restrict stock sales by people who participate in the tender.

2. **The company signs a term sheet** with a buyer or set of buyers to purchase stock in a tender offering. The buyers set a single price for all sellers.

3. **The company determines who can sell into the tender.** Often, prior and current employees, investors, and founders can participate in tenders. In some cases, the size of the tender is preset, and who can sell is set in an order determined by the company. For example, if there is a $50 million tender offering (in other words, $50 million of stock is sold in aggregate), the company may say that current and past employees get first dibs on selling up to 20% of their holdings each. If there is enough demand from employees to cover the full $50 million, then investors and founders do not get to sell into the tender.

4. **An administrative institution is hired to administer the tender,** as there may be hundreds or thousands of eligible sellers. That institution will deal with all the mechanics and paperwork to cover the sale of the stock by employees and other sellers. Banks or other institutions, such as Deutsche Bank, are often hired to run tenders, even though they are not the actual buyer of the stock. The cost of hiring these administrators is typically at least partially covered by a transaction fee paid by the sellers into the tender pay (e.g., 1% of their sale).

5. **The set of people who can sell into the tender is notified that the tender is open,** and told the price set for the stock purchase. They are also informed of the window of time in which eligible people can notify the administrator how much they want to sell and fill out the paperwork for a sale. The selling window may be open for 20 or 30 days.

6. **Once the selling window closes,** the transaction occurs and the stock and cash change hands.

Typically, buyers in a tender are large institutional buyers from the hedge fund, private equity, or late-stage VC worlds, such as BlackRock, Goldman Sachs, DST, Fidelity, and others.

Tender offers may range from the tens of millions into the hundreds of millions or billions of dollars in size.

INFORMATION SHARING AND SECONDARY BUYERS

In general, you should share basic financial information with large secondary buyers who are on your preferred buyers list or who run tenders for you. All of these types of buyers will be willing to sign an NDA at this stage. These buyers are making large investments in the company and in some cases will be long-term shareholders. Treating them well and providing them with basic information to make their decisions is important.

For small, random additions to the cap table (especially ones without strong company sanction), you can restrict information access unless it is something you are legally obligated to share with every shareholder (e.g., some changes to your legal documents).

If you end up with a $5 billion valuation or higher, that's the point at which you will need to hire someone whose job (at least part-time) will be to regulate secondary transactions and the secondary ecosystem, unless you are able to lock it down up front and early.

HOW MUCH STOCK SHOULD EMPLOYEES BE ABLE TO SELL?

There are three common models for secondary stock sales by employees: (1) a percentage limit, (2) a dollar limit, (3) hybrid approach.

Percentage limit on secondary sales
Some companies choose a percentage of total holdings that employees can sell—e.g., up to 10% to 20% of each individual's holdings. This range is typically chosen so that most of the employees stock continues to be held—incentivizing them to focus on the long term value of the company and its stock. For companies that have truly broken out and are worth many billions, or for very early employees, these amounts may add inWto the tens of millions of dollars. Sales of this magnitude create a potential disincentive for employees to continue to work. Moreover, they can lead to a two-class system within the company before a true liquidity event occurs (e.g., an IPO or large sale). This two-class system can be culturally jarring.

Dollar limit on secondary sales
Alternatively, some companies allow employees to sell up to a certain dollar amount. For example, Facebook allowed employees to sell up to $1 million in stock. This meant that, irrespective of the overall net worth of the employee due to Facebook stock, all employees could cash out a common amount that was life-changing but not distracting. In some cases a dollar limit may cause some early employees to leave the company if doing so unlocks their ability to sell larger amounts of stock. In reality, people who leave solely to sell may not have stuck around much longer to begin with.

Hybrid approach: percentage up to a maximum dollar amount

A recent middle ground is to take a "whichever comes first" approach—that is, employees can sell up to 10% or 20% of their holdings or $1 million in stock, whichever comes first, over the course of their secondary sales. If an employee holds $20 million in stock, they can sell up to $1 million, even though that does not trigger their 20%. Alternatively, if an employee holds $1 million in stock, they can only sell 20%, or $200,000. This ensures that employees continue to hold the majority of their stock as a motivator to keep building the value of the company.

Whichever model they choose, companies generally place the following limits on employee sales:

1. **Employees need to be with the company at least one year and/or hit their cliff.** If an employee has not hit her vesting cliff, she does not yet truly own her stock. It is very hard to try to claw back cash if that employee leaves before her cliff date.

2. **The amount of secondary sold is limited to, at most, what the employee has vested.** Companies can alternatively limit secondary sales to a proportion of what the employee has vested (e.g., "no more than 20% of what has vested") in official programs such as a tender.

In general, refresher grants that occur later in the lifetime of a company are a fraction of the grants employees receive upon joining (with rare exceptions for true outlier performers or people who, for example, advance from an individual contributor to a VP and get a larger refresher grant to reflect this heightened position and impact). This means that most of the value employees get in stock tends to derive from the earliest grant; that will be their primary financial incentive to contribute to the long-term success of the company.

Obviously there are a lot of non-financial incentives to working for a startup: making their team and friends successful and contributing to the company's mission, for example. However, it is always striking how much the financials matter, even if people claim otherwise.

INVESTOR SALES: AN OPPORTUNITY TO RENEGOTIATE

As your valuation rises, early investors may want to sell all or a subset of their stock in your company. For example, an early angel may want to diversify or sell her stake, as your company's stock may be her biggest financial holding. Alternatively, a venture fund may want to sell part or all of its stake to return money to LPs, especially if they are raising their next fund and want to ensure the participation of those same LPs.

An investor's interest in selling stock also presents a key opportunity for you, an opening to renegotiate prior terms with that investor. Some key items you may want to revisit include:

Information rights. As an investor's stake diminishes, you can argue that they should no longer receive information rights if they have them. In some rare cases I have seen the biggest sources of leaks for companies have been early investors, rather than employees, trading favors with TechCrunch. Cleaning up early investor information rights can make a difference.

Board participation. Board representation is supposed to reflect ownership. Further, some early-stage investors are great advisors for a small ten-person company, but have no operating experience or insights for later-stage companies. As part of a secondary sale by a venture fund, you can ask that their board member step down, or you can convert her board seat into an independent seat from a preferred one. This returns control to the company and its founders and allows you to remove people from your board who are no longer helpful (or, in some cases, may be actively destructive). A large secondary sale to a preferred buyer or a tender is a unique opportunity to clean up the board, at least partially.

Cleaning up your cap table. A secondary tender may be an opportunity to clean up your cap table. For example, you can go to all your small, early angels and offer an "all or nothing" sale, where they can sell their entire stake or none of it. This may allow you to remove multiple line items from your cap table at once and consolidate them by selling their stock to a single investor with a bigger ownership stake.

In general, you should view investor secondary sales as an opportunity to claw back rights and clean up governance in a manner that is positive and mutually beneficial for all parties involved. The funds get to sell part of their stake and return money early to LPs, and the company gets to remove board members or information rights that have existed past their prime.

LOCKING UP FUTURE SALES

Any secondary sale is also an opportunity to prevent that same individual or fund from selling again without explicit company say-so. This is most important for the many companies that had sloppy initial structures in place for secondary sales (in some cases having no restrictions at all on early employees, not even a ROFR—Fenwick & West is notorious for leaving this out of their standard docs).

Whenever any party sells its stock, you should ask them to sign a contract that will prevent future sales without company sanction. Similarly, you may change your bylaws and general employee docs to create a situation that still allows for employee sales, but avoids long-term harm to the company via random cap table additions or bad actors buying stock. Ask your legal team to draft documents that help with both approaches.

"In general, you should view investor secondary sales as an opportunity to claw back rights and clean up governance in a manner that is positive and mutually beneficial for all parties involved."

—Elad Gil

409A AND RSUS

The key balance in secondary sales is to allow for such transactions to occur without impacting a company's 409A valuation for common stock strike price. The 409A is an analysis you do to set the price for your stock options. If large, company-sanctioned common stock transactions occur at high prices, you will need to reset your common strike price upward, impacting your ability to reward employees.

You should talk to your legal team about the right approach to secondary sales and 409A. In addition, you should consider moving to restricted stock units (RSUs) instead of options once your valuation is over $1 billion and you are within 18–36 months of going public.

MOVING TO RSUS

At some point it makes sense for most companies to move to RSUs. Early on, RSUs tend to be less tax efficient for employees than early exercise of options and holding stock for capital gains tax treatment. However, once your strike price is high enough, the early exercise cost to an employee is so high that most do not do it—or it wouldn't be wise for them to do so. (The '90s saw a number of examples of stock options that were exercised, followed by a big tax bill, and then there was no upside on the actual stock. As a result, employees paid all the downsides of taxes without the upside of stock valuation increases, or in some cases without the cash to pay the tax bills.) Or, they will need to do a secondary sale just to generate enough cash to cover the exercise of all their options.

Eventually, when your company valuation is high and you are within a few years of an IPO, RSUs have equivalent tax efficiency to options. RSUs allow both the company and its employees to avoid the complexities of trying to cover the exercise price of stock, as well as avoid the potential loss if the stock price drops over time.

RSUs also are never "below water," because they are effectively equivalent to shares of stock, not just options to buy that stock at a certain price. While a stock can end up trading below the option price an employee received, RSUs always have a value equivalent to the value of the stock. This means that "equity" granted to employees as RSUs will always have some value. Stock options, by contrast, may end up with zero value for very late-stage companies, if the strike price is at or below the current stock price.

THE SECONDARY STOCK SALE: THE EMPLOYEE'S PERSPECTIVE

The previous few sections have focused on how to regulate secondary sales from the company perspective. The focus of this section is the employee perspective: How to sell your stock on secondary markets.

1. Understand if you can sell stock.
Check your stock option plan, company charter, or other company documents to see whether you can sell secondary stock. If your company has a general counsel, you can also ask her about the details of what you can or cannot do. Alternatively, some later-stage companies have a person on the finance team dedicated to secondary transactions; even the CFO may be the right point of contact.

From a process perspective, most companies will have a 30- or 60-day right of first refusal (ROFR). This means that once you've negotiated a price with a potential buyer, the company can decide if it wants to purchase your shares at that price, instead of the buyer. If the company declines, existing investors in the company may also have a ROFR and will be asked if they want to buy your shares. If everyone passes, then the original buyer can purchase the shares from you. If the company or its existing investors want to exercise their rights of first refusal to buy the shares, they will pay you the same price you negotiated with the buyer. So even if a ROFR is invoked, you will be able to sell your shares.

It typically takes about 30 days for your company (and investors, if applicable) to waive their ROFR. But in some cases it can be longer, so you need to plan for this when selling stock.

Remember, right before an IPO, a company will often halt trading in its shares—which means you may not be able to sell for a few months before the IPO and then another six months after the company is public.

2. Decide how much to sell.
The decision on how much to sell may be driven by a few factors including:

- **Employment status.** Most companies require you to exercise your stock options within 90 days of leaving your job with the company, or you lose all the options you worked years to obtain. In this case, you need to start thinking of how to do a secondary sale shortly after leaving the company. You will need to decide whether to sell enough to just cover taxes on the full set of options you exercise, or if you want to sell more to take some money off the table as well.

- **Diversify your portfolio.** If 99% of your net worth is tied up in company stock, you may want to take some money off the table to protect yourself from a black swan event that would cut your net worth dramatically all at once. I know a number of people from, for example, Zynga who saw their net worth drop 70% with the stock price.

- **Cash needs.** Even if your company is close to going public, you may want some short-term liquidity to buy a house or car, pay for your kid's school, or the like. Remember: Just because your company files for an IPO does not mean it will quickly go public, and even after it goes public you will probably be prevented from selling your stock for six months, which means half a year of uncertainty.

- **Taxes.** There may be large tax considerations to selling your stock, depending on the timing. For instance, a number of people sold secondary stock in 2012 to avoid the tax hikes of 2013. Talk to an accountant before making any sales.

Many people end up selling 20–50% of their stakes pre-IPO for the reasons above. If you really need the cash or just want security, you may be able to sell your entire stake in a secondary transaction. Of course, that limits your potential upside if the stock does go up after the IPO. But that's the trade-off you are making with an early sale: the security of cash now, or the possibility of a larger return later.

3. Find a legitimate buyer.

Buyers of secondary stock are diverse. There are dedicated secondary funds, hedge funds, family offices, angels, dentists, and a random assortment of yahoos (aka individual investors) who operate in this opaque market. (See the previous section on secondary sales for more on this.)

In general, you want to find a buyer who:

- **Has the funds available.** If you are doing a large transaction, ask for proof of funds or make sure the person or entity is a well-known investor.

- **Will move quickly.** Avoid situations where there are multiple decision-makers between the purchaser and the person offering to buy the shares. For example, some secondary funds will have a decision-making committee that only meets periodically.

- **Has invested in private securities before.** If you are dealing with high-net-worth individuals (versus funds), make sure the buyer understands the secondary process, the risks involved, and the various steps needed to close a transaction quickly.

- **Won't be a pain in the butt to the company.** Adding a dentist from Ottawa to the company's list of shareholders may do your employer a disservice. The dentist may be willing to pay more for your shares than a professional buyer would. But random buyers may also have volatile properties (e.g., they may sue your company for no good reason). This can hurt the value of any remaining stock you don't sell, and it will certainly hurt your relationship with your employer. Only transact with random people if you don't mind burning bridges with your employer.

- **Your company will approve quickly.** Optimally, you want buyers your company knows or is willing to add to the cap table quickly. Some funds have had problems with the SEC in the past around secondary purchases, which means your company may not want them to buy your stock.[66]

4. Figure out the price you want.

Private market transactions are highly illiquid and volatile.[67] There are always rumors that somebody got higher or lower prices on their stock. Or, illegitimate buyers may suggest prices for stock that they can't or won't really pay to test the market. Often these transactions don't go through, and they muddy perceptions of real market prices.

---

[66] See link at eladgil.com. [*https://dealbook.nytimes.com/2012/03/14/charges-filed-against-brokerage-firms-that-trade-private-shares/?_r=0*]

[67] There are always rumors that a stock is selling for much higher and much lower prices. In my experience, these rumors often turn out to be false. Focus on closed transactions, where money actually changed hands, versus "a friend of a friend was offered $X but did not sell."

To get a sense of the market for the stock, ask colleagues what they are getting for their shares in transactions that have actually gone through. That means transactions that actually closed, versus offers they have received. Unclosed transactions are often meaningless.

Don't be too greedy. Focus on speed of closing at a price you are comfortable with. Unless you are selling a very large block, a difference of five cents a share won't make much of a difference if the stock is at $18 a share.

A few rules of thumb:

- **Common stock is often discounted from the last preferred stock price.**[68] This is on the order of 30%. For example, if your company just raised at a $240 million valuation, you can expect to sell your common stock at a price based on a $160 to $200 million valuation. If the round took place many months before your sale, and the company has made progress since then, you can typically sell at the preferred stock price.[69] You should by all means ask for the last preferred valuation, but investors may not be willing to pay that much. As the company matures and gets more valuable/later stage, the spread between common and preferred stock will disappear.

- **IPOs breed volatility.** There is typically a sharp run up in secondary prices in the weeks before a company halts secondary transactions, which is directly before an IPO. In some cases, those secondary prices will be higher than the post-IPO stock prices (see, for example, the first year of Facebook's public stock price[70]). If you want to sell, don't get overly greedy during this period. Prices are rising so quickly that you might be tempted to hold out for an even better one. Remember, though, the price is moving quickly because the company is about to stop all secondary trades. If you over-optimize and don't sell, you may be prevented by the company from doing so for an uncertain period of time.

  The root of this uncertainty is that not every company that intends to go public will do so immediately. After filing for an IPO, a company may wait for many months (or quarters) before going public, due to market conditions. Once the company does go public, you will be locked up for another six months. If the IPO gets delayed, you can end up with a bunch of illiquid stock and ongoing market risk.

---

[68] The reason for this discount is that preferred stock gets paid out first if the company exits at lower than its last round's valuation. So while preferred stock has "insurance" that makes it more likely to get paid in full, common stock does not, hence the discount. As a company gets more valuable and has more traction, the risk of a low exit goes down, and the gap in price between common and preferred shrinks and eventually disappears.

   In some cases, as part of a financing round, a venture firm will buy common shares from founders at the same time it buys preferred stock from the company. In this case, the venture firm will pay the same price for preferred and common, as (1) it wants to help the founders partially cash out, and (2) the percentage of common stock it owns is low enough to not be material versus its preferred stock position.

[69] If you work for a super-hot company that has made a ton of progress since its last round, and a lot of time has passed since the funding, then you can demand a premium to the last round of funding. Companies also track their own internal valuation at board meetings and via 409As, so you can ask the company what price they think the company is now worth in order to set a price.

[70] I know a number of investors who stopped buying secondary shares after they got "burned" by speculating on Facebook pre-IPO.

- **Expect things to move up and down in a semi-random fashion.** In a market with limited numbers of buyers and sellers, prices may move all over the place. For example, if one of your company's founders dumps a large block of stock at a low price to diversify, it can depress prices for everyone.

- **Don't forget taxes.** Talk to an accountant. Selling in one year versus another may impact the taxes you pay. Similarly, if the company was a qualified small business when you bought your stock/exercised your options, there may be very large benefits to holding the stock longer, or there may be future tax breaks depending on how you reinvest the money you just made.

5. See if the company wants to have their legal counsel run the transaction.
Many companies will have a stock purchase agreement (SPA) they want you to use to sell their shares. If not, you can use one of the major Silicon Valley firms to put together the paperwork.

Regardless of who does the paperwork, you will need a stock purchase agreement. Sometimes, you may need additional paperwork such as a third-party legal opinion that you legitimately own the shares you are selling. (This is usually only needed if there is a large secondary market for a company's shares, with lots of buyers and sellers. At some point you can get people acting badly in the market and selling shares that don't exist, which creates the need for this extra layer of legal work.)

6. Terms to include.
You want to make sure the paperwork for your secondary transaction includes basic items such as:

- The buyer is obligated to fund the shares within X days of being able to do so. For example, if she does not wire money to you within a week of the sale closing, you can void the transaction.
- The seller is obligated to sell the shares and can't back out.
- If the company blocks the transaction or exerts its right of first refusal (ROFR), the contract is voided.

I am not a lawyer and am completely unqualified to give legal advice. So talk with your lawyers about this.

7. More complex transactions.
Some secondary funds will offer more complex transactions that allow you to benefit from the upside of your stock in the future while cashing out today. In some cases, you take a loan out against your shares and then split the upside of the stock with the lender. Alternatively, you outright sell them the shares, but have a contract in place that if the stock goes above a certain dollar amount you split the upside. For example, you might sell your stock for $25 per share, but then split any appreciation of the stock above $30 per share. So if the stock sells for $32, you end up with $26 a share ($25 plus ($32–$30)/2).[71]

IPOS: TAKING A COMPANY PUBLIC

A common characteristic of companies from the 2007–2012 period is that many of them are focused on taking as long as reasonable to go public. While there are some drawbacks to being a public company, there are also a number of benefits.

BENEFITS OF GOING PUBLIC

1. **Employee hiring, retention, and conversion.** Compensation packages at companies sometimes go down after an IPO, with a higher conversion rate of candidates to employees. In general, this is due to the employees valuing stock as a liquid currency, as well as the perceptual de-risking of the company. Retention goes up on newer employees (who have more future value in the company) and often will go down for old-timer employees (who may have made millions or tens of millions and are now liquid and able to leave). In general, the old-timer contingent will be small and likely to leave eventually anyway.

2. **M&A.** A liquid currency provides the ability to buy companies without haggling around what the acquirers stock is really worth.

3. **New capital sources for the company.** Public markets can provide outsized funding for companies after an IPO. For example, Tesla's ongoing rise may have been difficult to support without the broader based global capital flows of the public market. In a lose capital environment this seems like a minor point. In tight capital markets this can be the saving grace for a company. For example, Opsware went public in 2001 as private market sources had all dried up.

4. **Ability to partner or sell at scale.** A public company tends to be taken more seriously for partnerships, sales, and other business activities.

---

[71] Thanks to Naval Ravikant for reviewing and providing feedback on this chapter.

5. **Fiscal & business discipline.** When Facebook went public, monetization was viewed as a low priority for the company. After the first serious drop in stock price after an earnings call, Zuckerberg moved engineering and other resources into the ads team to scale monetization. An argument could be made that Facebook would never have reached a $500 billion as a private company. Public market pressure forced Facebook to re-examine its own priorities and led to a highly valued, liquid currency that could be used to acquire Instagram, WhatsApp, and other potential competitors.

CONS OF GOING PUBLIC

1. **Larger, more complex board of directors.** Once you are public there are a number of committees you need to staff at the board level. This increases board size and complexity. Small boards tend to be more nimble.

2. **Financial and other controls.** As you prepare for the IPO a number of financial and process controls need to be instated. Some of these are actually a net positive for the company, but many don't help support the core business and just slow things down.

3. **Employee mix shifts.** As your company scales from 10 to 1,000 people, the risk profile of the people who join also changes. In general, the later stage the company the more risk averse the cohort of employees. Once a company goes public the hiring profile hits another transition. In general you will have the same overall caliber of people joining, however their risk profile will shift to more conservative. This can be actively managed or augmented by acquiring entrepreneurial companies and integrating them in culturally. Alternatively, the executive team and founders will need to encourage risk taking and rule questioning as part of the new culture.

MARKET CYCLES

Many first time founders running high-growth, private companies today have not lived through a major economic and capital cycle. When the public markets collapse private markets tend to overreact. This is due to a few reasons:

1. **Comparables.** If public market valuations drop by 20–30%, private market valuations tend to follow. This is the difference between a billion dollar valuation and a $700M valuation. If companies raised at a high price while the markets were strong, they may need to do a down round when markets rebalance.

2. **Venture and growth fund LP rebalancing.** Many of the limited partners (endowments, family offices, pension plans) in venture and growth funds have a set limit on the percent of their capital that can be in venture capital. If there is a large public market shift, they need to reallocate capital out of venture capital—which means that funds can raise less money to invest in startups. This usually takes one to three years to take place as the typical venture fund lifecycle is two to three years.

3. **Fear replaces greed.** When people get scared they sit on their wallets.

In general, it is best to go public during an ongoing bull market. You can raise large amounts of capital and have a liquid currency by which to make acquisitions. The capital you raise in an up market allows you to survive, and act more aggressively in a down market. Amazon took advantage of being a public company masterfully. During the bubble in the 1990s they used their market cap to make a large number of acquisitions. As the bubble collapsed they used the large amounts of capital raised from public markets to sustain the company through the dark periods of the early 2000s.

As founders wait longer to go public, they may end up with extra hurdles or obstacles relative to their IPO price. This may include drops in public markets, unusual private market terms (for example needing to clear an IRR or IPO price hurdle in order to raise private capital), or simply raising at too high a valuation and then spending a few years hopefully growing into it.

While the 1990s were characterized by companies who went public too early, the 2010s perhaps had many companies that waited too long.

IPO PROCESS

As you approach your IPO you should appoint an IPO team and a directly responsible individual (DRI) to project manage that team with the CFO overseeing the overall IPO. In parallel, you can reach out to other CEOs and CFOs who have taken their companies public to learn more about tips and tactics for a successful IPO.

An interview with Keith Rabois

Keith Rabois is an investment partner at Khosla Ventures. Since 2000, he has been instrumental in driving five startups from their early stages to successful IPOs, with executive roles at PayPal, LinkedIn, and Square, and as a board member with Yelp and Xoom.

At Khosla Ventures, Rabois has led investments in a broad array of startups including, DoorDash, Stripe, Thoughtspot, Affirm, Even Financial, and Piazza. While working as a VC he simultaneously cofounded Opendoor, a startup in the real estate tech world.

In this second part of our interview, Keith and I spoke about taking companies public.

Elad Gil:
You've been involved with a number of companies, either as an executive or board member, which have gone public: PayPal, LinkedIn, Square. Yelp and Xoom as a board member. A lot of founders today don't want to go public. What is your view of the pluses and minuses of being a public company?

Keith Rabois:

My view is pretty simple, which is companies should go public as soon as they can. Increased transparency and accountability is always a good thing. It's something we always teach and proselytize through our organizations, to our executives. And being prepared to go public creates a discipline, a focus, that most other processes don't.

It's also very binary. Once you are public, you have a lot of tools and levers at your disposal, about incremental financing, acquisitions, M&A. It unlocks a lot of potential that you may not otherwise be able to take advantage of or avail yourself of.

For example, Facebook tried to acquire Twitter. You know, there was a lot of debate about a $500 million offer. Had Facebook—at the time it was still private—had liquid currency, Facebook might have been able to acquire Twitter, which I think would have changed history. Twitter is a very successful independent company that actually has more influence in the world than Facebook, at least in my view. And that acquisition couldn't happen because there was a big debate about the value of Facebook's currency. There are a lot of examples like this.

I think the reasons why people don't go public are basically excuses. For example, people frequently talk about innovation. Well, ask anybody in Silicon Valley what the top five most innovative companies on the planet are, and inevitably you get some version of the following answer: Google, Facebook, Tesla, SpaceX, Apple, maybe Amazon. Five of those six are large-market-cap, publicly traded companies, and they're innovating at a pace that's clearly better than private companies. With the right leadership, you can innovate on the public stage better actually than on the private stage. So I think that's an excuse.

Second thing is people talk about the distractions of stock price and things like that. The truth is, when you run a company, people are distracted by lots of things: gossip in the office, the food you serve, these days their cryptocurrency holdings. At least when you're public, you as an executive have the same perspective as your employees, and you can tell when they're going to be distracted. You have knowledge and then you can countersteer against that. Whereas when they get distracted because you're taking away their bacon or some perk in the office, you actually don't have a lot of visibility into that. It also lags. I think countermanaging against distractions is part of the job as a leader or an executive or a CEO.

In addition, people talk about the cost of going public. Truthfully, that's overrated as well. You have a year post going public to implement most of the compliance burden. By the time you actually have to put in place the SOX compliance measures, you've already been public for a year and clearly have the resources. You probably raised several hundred million dollars to a billion dollars in going public. You can pay for four or five more accountants and some software at that point. I think that's another excuse.

Discipline around financials and reporting is also good and healthy to start as early as possible in the company's history. Doesn't mean you have to be profitable. I think lots of companies go public that are not profitable. In fact, I suspect most technology companies went public, historically, when they were unprofitable. I don't think that's a gating factor.

I think some people learned the wrong lessons from earlier companies. PayPal, for example, had a pretty searing experience of going public. We filed to go public the day before 9/11. We had a state regulator sort of attack us on the precipice of our IPO. And I think Peter Thiel learned from that lesson that going public is kind of a pain in the ass, and I think he's proselytized a little bit too much about that. Because it was an unusual set of circumstances that affected PayPal. That said, we did eventually go public, and I think everybody thought it was a good thing.

Yelp went public and it really boosted retention. A year before going public, everybody was motivated and excited about the opportunity to go public and create a permanent stand-alone company. And post going public, the company's retention of engineers and general employees actually went up by double digit percentages. So I think it was very healthy, even though Jeremy had originally been hesitant.

Elad: I think people in general underestimate the impact on employees in terms of retention and the ability to attract and compensate great employees. I was talking with one recruiting firm, and their data shows that after a company goes public they close a higher proportion of people with lower offers.

Keith: That doesn't surprise me. I've never rigorously analyzed it. But based upon the Yelp data where that was true, it wouldn't surprise me if that's true globally.

Elad: What do you think is most unexpected to first-time founders about having a public company?

Keith: Well, there is some incremental drag in board meetings. You wind up having a more process-oriented board meeting. I think both of us would probably advise startups having a smaller board, three to seven members max. Probably five more typically. When you go public, because of the committee requirements—audit committee, nomination committee—and various structural requirements, you wind up with a larger board, which does create disadvantages in having dialogue and debate, versus just presentations.

Now, there's ways to countermanage around that. Obviously you don't have to make the formal board meeting your only strategy session. So that can be solved. But it is different.

The type of employee that you attract is a little bit different, too, more compensation-focused definitely. More of the market is compensation focused today because the cost of living in the Bay Area is so high. Even people who might in other eras have been more willing to take more upside and equity and less cash are focused a bit more on their cash compensation.

I think the ability to attract younger colleagues that are recent graduates goes up. The recent graduates from CS departments at Stanford, CMU, other top universities are starting their careers, and they're looking for a place to learn. Now, some of those will become founders and go to YC and other escape ramps. But a lot of the meat-and-potato software engineers want to go to a stable company for at least two years. And once you're public, parents and significant others think of it as a stable entity. So candidates run into a lot less resistance from people that are important to them in their lives in accepting those offers.

And I think you can learn something from a large company. There are some practices that are very destructive for people who want to start their own company and that you wouldn't want to adopt. But there are a lot of things you can learn from large companies, too.

"I think of money, of capital, like oxygen. Imagine if we all had to live our lives and pay for every breath."

—Keith Rabois

Elad: You mentioned that you think companies should go public as soon as they can. What are signs that a company is ready? How do you know that it's time?

Keith: I think predictability is one. Meaning you can easily forecast your next quarter, your next six months. That means that, underneath that, you understand the levers of your business. There's a business equation of X x Y x Z, and you have precisely mastered that equation. You know exactly how what you do in one part of the company affects the next part which affects the final result, which is, let's say, your contribution margin.

Once that's well understood and the N is large enough so that the variance is rare, then I think you're ready to be a public company, assuming you're at some level of scale, which probably means about $50 million in revenue.

Elad: A lot of private company founders don't think the public market cycle itself is important. They say that it doesn't matter if the S&P or NASDAQ is at an all-time high. They can go public at any time. What do you think about the macro market cycles relative to time frames for going public?

Keith: I think that's somewhat naïve, and it's a function of having probably grown up in an environment that was very stable. If you think that since the global financial crisis of 2008, we've basically been in a hot market for the last ten years. Most founders have grown up, professionally and psychologically, in a fairly stable, attractive market.

Whereas if you started your career when the bubble collapsed or in the aftermath of the bubble, in 2000–2003, you understand what happens when there isn't liquidity in the market. For example, a lot of our companies use debt as an oxygen to grow. It's part of the business model of Opendoor, it's part of the business model at Affirm, it's part of the business model at

Upstart, as examples. The price of that oxygen can change very radically and very quickly. Bill Me Later and Zappos famously had to sell, even though their businesses were performing quite well, because their access to debt was affected. Just as access to debt is affected by general macroeconomic changes, the ability to use money as a resource to grow can be completely changed overnight.

I think of money, of capital, like oxygen. Imagine if we all had to live our lives and pay for every breath. We might live our lives differently. Like we might not work out as much; maybe we couldn't afford to run or sprint. But because oxygen is free, we don't even calculate it. In a hot market, everybody thinks that capital is sort of free, but that changes really fast. The price of capital has moved many, many times over the last hundred to two hundred years. And the virtue of having lived through various cycles is you're always calculating that in the back of your mind.

Elad: Are there any IPO process tactics that you'd recommend?

Keith: I think the canonical advice isn't too bad in this case, which is the earlier you have a CFO on board, the easier it is. That doesn't mean you should prematurely hire a CFO, but insofar as opportunistically you can find a great CFO, that will definitely help.

Secondly, I think that it can be done faster than people realize. The canonical advice again is that it'll take about a year. I've seen it done in three to four months. That's definitely pushing the envelope. Going from zero to sixty in three to four months would require incredible focus, energy, and probably some experience in the CFO or general counsel. So let's say six months to nine months being more reasonable. But about a year of preparation is a good idea.

Elad: One other thing I've seen people do that I think sometimes helps is create an IPO team. They'll pull either executives or mid-level managers from different teams and create a work plan. So they'll treat it like any other project.

Keith: Yeah, I think having a DRI or directly responsible individual can be a great strategy. We did that at PayPal. We took one of our corp dev directors or VPs, and he became the DRI. He quarterbacked everything. So treat it like a major initiative. Assign somebody who you trust and who has credibility within the organization to the task, so they can stitch everything together and motivate people. ■

This interview has been edited and condensed for clarity.

PART 2: HACKING LATE-STAGE FUNDING

An interview with Naval Ravikant

Naval Ravikant is the Chairman and a cofounder of AngelList. He previously cofounded Epinions (which went public as part of Shopping.com) and Vast.com. He is an active angel investor, and has invested in dozens of companies, including Twitter, Uber, Yammer, Stack Overflow and others.

As one of Silicon Valley's most respected angel investors and entrepreneurs, a veteran of some of the Valley's biggest startup success stories, and an investor in many others, Naval has a uniquely broad perspective on startups.

In this second part of our interview, Naval and I spoke about late stage funding.

Elad Gil:
There is a lot published (including on venturehacks.com) about early stage funding, but very little about later stage rounds. What are some of the key hacks for a
late stage funding round?

Naval Ravikant:
First I don't think all companies need large rounds anymore. The internet
makes it possible for many kinds of companies to be built a lot more cheaply. Obviously that's not true when you're doing hardware or when you have
local expansion issues. But overall, I think you can build companies a lot
more cheaply than people used to.

But if you're going to raise a late-stage round, what are the hacks? Frankly,
late-stage rounds used to be done by venture capitalists. And now they're
done more and more by mutual funds, by other companies in the space,
strategic players, even family offices often want to go direct. In those kinds
of situations, I think companies can create custom bundles where they can
keep control and can even sell common stock—which is the ultimate hack.
They can make sure they don't give up board seats, they don't give up vetoes
on M&A and option pool issuances and future fundraising. (On non-arm's-
length transactions, or insider self-dealing, though, you always do want
investors to have the veto.)

We used to have a saying at Venture Hacks: "Valuation is temporary. Control is forever." Whoever has control can effectively end up controlling your
valuation later. Never give up control. And control is given up in subtle
ways: A lot of term sheets will have so-called protective provisions that
originally existed to protect the preferred shareholders, because they were
minority shareholders. But effectively they give those shareholders control
over the company. So, for example, if your preferred investor has the right
to veto future fundraising, they effectively have a lock on your company. If
you ever need more money, you have to get them to agree, which means
they run the place. Same for expanding your option pool and issuing more
shares to new employees, or to keep existing people. Same with M&A.
That's probably the big one, where the biggest fights happen. Sometimes
the founders want to sell or don't want to sell the company, and then the
preferred shareholders try to control them for an opposite outcome.

So, in my ideal world, if I had a hot, late-stage, high-growth company, I
would essentially sell common stock.

Elad: What would be the argument? A lot of times the investors are saying, "I really
need the preference in order to protect my investment on the downside scenario."

Naval: The preference is there for a very specific reason: Imagine that my company was raising at a pre-money valuation of $9 million. And then you came in and you invested $1 million in the company, so the post-money valuation is $10 million. And now you own 10% of the company. Suppose I try to take the million dollars and say, "Hey, we're just going to divvy up the million dollars to all the shareholders." Well, if you didn't have a preference, I would get $900,000, and you would get $100,000 back. Not what you expected.

Elad: I see, so it's really to protect in a distribution, versus to protect against some future downside.

Naval: Correct. That was the original theory behind liquidation preference. But as it's gotten stacked on later and later, it's become this giant freebie. And the easiest way to see that it doesn't make sense for later-stage rounds is by seeing that it doesn't exist in the public markets. The public markets are all common stock. Why? For exactly that reason—it doesn't make sense anymore. If I have a $900 million company, and you come in and invest $100 million, well, presumably a $900 million company is really a $900 million company. I'm not going to turn around, shut the company down, and distribute the $100 million, because I'd be throwing away $900 million of real value.

The preference is really, really important at the early stages. You'd be a fool to do a seed round buying common stock. But it makes no sense at the later stages. And at the public stages, it's gone.

If I had a high-growth, high-performance company with multiple bidders—and obviously these kinds of negotiations are only possible when there are multiple bidders—I would be selling common stock. Or, if that opportunity wasn't available to me, I would be selling common plus liquidation preference. That's it. I would be leaving out all the other junk.

Elad: I see. So they still get the liquidation preference, but they don't get the protective provisions, they don't get all the control provisions.

Naval: Right, that's all left with the earlier rounds. Then the next hack you can do—suppose you can't even get that—is to give them the protective provisions, but only for non-arm's-length transactions. That means transactions that are not happening at a distance with other people. So if I'm issuing myself more stock, sure, I need your approval. If I'm issuing stock to a friend of mine or if I'm selling the company to my brother, then I need your approval. But if it's an arm's-length, bona fide transaction, I do not need your approval.

The next hack down from there is, okay, I need your approval, you have the veto, but the veto belongs to the preferred class as a whole. It doesn't belong to each series individually. Because that way, if I can get the other investors to go along, then you have to go along. Presumably my earlier-stage investors are people that I trust more. I've worked with them longer, they're friendlier, I chose them more carefully. They're more understanding of how startups work. Whereas my later-stage investors are more likely to be people who just showed up yesterday into the business. So that's the series of strategies that you would fall back on.

Another thing that entrepreneurs obviously do is create founder shares, which have extra voting power. That works up to a point. There are rights that preferred shareholders have that you can't take away from them legally, no matter what contract they sign, under Delaware law and California law. So you always have to be aware of that.

Elad: What are some examples of that?

Naval: I believe that under California law, for example—this was true in 2003 when it was relevant for me—every series has to separately approve an M&A, even if it says that preferred as a class can do it. That's one example. Another one is inspection rights. So when you have a shareholder on the books and you're a Delaware company, they can demand your financials. Even a small shareholder can, which a lot of people don't realize.

Elad: How do you think about the secondary component of late-stage rounds? When should founders do it, should they not do it, how should they think about it, how should they think about other early investors relative to secondary? At what stage does it become okay?

Naval: It's becoming more and more common. As the markets become more liquid, the industry becomes more hit-driven. So the odds of your thing working out all the way get lower. The incentives of founders and investors are starting to diverge more and more. You can have a $100 million exit as a founder and you're really happy, but your investors may not be, because their funds are getting larger and larger. The incentives are diverging more and more, so it makes more sense to do early founder liquidity.

Maybe in 1999, if you started a venture-backed business, your odds of success were 1 in 10. Today they might be 1 in 50.

Elad: Just because there are that many more companies?

Naval: There's a lot more companies. We're going after hugely winner-take-all markets. The new entrants keep coming up, the platforms keep shifting faster and faster, the half-life of the winners is shorter. It's becoming a much more competitive atmosphere.

A friend of mine described incubator graduates as the locust swarm of startups. And you just don't know—with every graduating class, here's another hundred locusts. And who knows which one is coming after you and what tack they're taking? So every business is constantly under more and more sustained assault.

As a founder, you get a couple of shots on goal in your life. And you might even only have one for that thing you're really super passionate about. I think good VCs now realize that if they're going to ask you to go for the billion-dollar exit, then they have to be willing to let you take some off the table along the way. So I think the secondary component is becoming more and more common, and it will become more and more liquid. Secondary markets are here to stay.

Elad: Is there a specific valuation before which you don't think a founder should ask for liquidity? Or alternatively, is a founder unwise for not diversifying before a certain point?

Naval: The situation you don't want to be in is one in which you took substantial liquidity but your investors lost all their money. Once you're convinced—almost beyond a shadow of a doubt—that the value of your company is greater than the stack liquidation preferences of your company, then I think it's legit to start asking for a secondary. You want to know that you're generating enough revenue or cash flow, or that you've built something that's getting acquisition offers at a price that exceeds the liquidation preference value of your company and will make the investors some money (and they want you to keep going).

The most common way the secondary conversation starts internally is with an acquisition offer. The investors want you to turn down that acquisition offer, and you probably want to also—but you're tempted. And a smart investor at that point will say, well, let's let you take something off the table.

That's why secondaries probably shouldn't happen for seed and A and B companies. But generally it's C and up now where you're starting to see it quite commonly. Even in B-round cases, you'll see it if the company's made substantial progress.

Related to that, I think the single most important elephant in the room is that companies don't need that much money anymore. It's become a lot cheaper to build a company. All your software is open source. All your hardware is sitting at Amazon, in Amazon Web Services. All your marketing's done on Google, Twitter, Facebook, Snapchat, App Store, contact lists. Even the people that you need—you need mostly engineers, and even half of them are outsourced. A lot of your customer service is happening through the community.

So, companies just don't need that much money. Slack is a great example right now. Slack is raising money, but I don't even know what they're doing with it—probably secondary. Stewart famously said in the last round that he had, what did he say? Fifty or something?

Elad: Fifty or a hundred years.

Naval: Yeah, fifty or a hundred years of money, and he's still raising more. Why? Because these funds have a lot of money and they can just put it in. You can raise it for acquisitions, which might be a good reason, and you can raise it for founder liquidity. But these are not the classic reasons.

Our heroes today as entrepreneurs should be [Bitcoin creator] Satoshi Nakamoto, who built a multibillion-dollar enterprise single-handedly, or just two people, whoever he or they are, anonymously. Or WhatsApp, 50 or so people, bought for $19 billion. YouTube, when it was bought, was probably under 60 people. And most of those people were working in datacenters and doing servers. In an AWS world, I'm not even sure they would have needed that many people. Instagram, when it was bought, was just a few people. So it's possible to build something of huge value today with very few people.

Elad: I think the commonalities of all the things that you mentioned, except for Bitcoin, is that those were large, network-based consumer applications. But in general, when you're thinking about an enterprise company—and there are some counterexamples, like Atlassian—people still believe that you should build a sales force, they still believe that you need some scale in other areas beyond the engineering side.

Naval: Although I think that Slack doesn't really have much of a sales force.

Elad: Yeah, that's fair. And that feels very much like a consumer model.

Naval: Exactly. Even the enterprise companies are starting to head that way. So yes, a company like a Slack or an Uber is going to need a lot more resources. But it's still going to need less resources than the five-year-older version of it would have. And that's less than the ten-year-older version would have. So the trend line is very, very clear.

Elad: Do you think people are raising too much money? And if so, why?

Naval: I think they're raising money because money is cheap and available. The Federal Reserve and central banks of the world are printing money like crazy to fight deflation. Money is just cheap. Money is available. So why not? It's insurance. It's a scorecard. It's a tool that you can use for acquisitions. You can hire a few more people. It's brutally competitive to hire people, so you can pay them better—Google and Facebook are paying through the nose.

But the downside, the subtle difficulty of raising money, is that when you raise more money you do spend more money. There's just no way around that, no matter how disciplined you are.

And what's worse is you move slower. You get less stuff done. The meetings are bigger, the groups of stakeholders that have to be coordinated are larger. You're less focused as a company; you take on too many projects because you have all these resources.

So it's just human nature that when you have money you will spend it, and not always for the better. I think it takes your eye off the ball. In that sense, it is true that companies that are at least somewhat cash-constrained do better.

Pierre Omidyar is a famous example—this is back in the old days, from eBay. He had a lot of competitors, and he actually credited his success to being the only one who didn't have much outside financing for a long time. So when people were trading on his site, doing auctions, he came up with a rating system, which was very novel at the time. It seems obvious in hindsight, but his was one of the first sites to have automated ratings. Everybody else wanted to have a better customer experience, so they had individuals getting in the middle of every transaction. Which meant that as the whole thing spiked, he scaled much, much, faster than them and ran away with the market. By not having the headcount, he was forced to build scalable processes from day one.

Elad: There are all these different types of new investors who have come into the market or whose presence has grown: family offices, hedge funds, private equity firms, foreign funds, either sovereign funds or alternatively pools of capital that are raised externally. How should people think about those new sources of capital, and what do you think are the trade-offs?

"Valuation is temporary. Control is forever."

—Naval Ravikant

Naval: I actually think it's a positive development for entrepreneurs. I know VCs like to bash on them as dumb money. But you have to keep in mind that that's like your local laundromat owner getting angry that a new laundromat opened up down the street. They don't like competition. So you always have to filter venture advice through venture incentives.

As far as an entrepreneur's concerned, more people vying to give them capital is good. More competition for something that they have to buy that's normally expensive and painful is good.

Fundamentally, venture capital is a bundle—it's a bundle of advice, control, and money. The more options you have, the more you can unbundle those three things, and get the advice from the people you want and the money from the cheapest source of money, and leave the control behind. So I think it's good.

Now that said, a lot of these people who are newcomers—what are the downsides? The downsides are that these new types of investors are hot money, so they might not support you in a future round. They may not be smart money. What that means is not that they're not going to add value, because almost nobody adds value as an investor in a later-stage company. It's just that they might screw you up in a future round by not doing their pro-rata, by trying to veto something they shouldn't. The way you solve that is by not giving them control in the first place, and not expecting more money out of them in the future.

And then finally, money has karma too. You cannot take someone's money without having a moral, ethical obligation to them. You can't do it without committing your time. And you don't want to get sued by them, because that makes you untouchable later on. So you do want to make sure that you have a good relationship with the people you're getting the money from.

Especially with a lot of these later-stage players, they tend to swap people out a lot more. Venture capitalists are very stable—they raise money in ten-year partnerships, they own and run their partnerships. It's very unlikely that your venture investor is going to get switched out on you, and if they do it will probably be with somebody else who's an experienced venture investor. But if you take money from a corporate investor and whoever is the head of corporate development gets sacked the next day, the company's CEO's brother comes in and might be a nightmare.

If you give them a board seat or there's a relationship person, you do want to have some control over who that person is. But I think more options are good, more choices are good.

Elad: Yeah, I've seen good and bad situations—and this is from either my own company or companies I'm involved with. The bad has been that some of those sources of capital are a little bit jumpier. Some are not. Some are very stable and smart. But every once in a while you'll have the random billionaire who's never invested in tech and then freaks out. Or I should say their office freaks out, because the people who manage their money may or may not be savvy about tech.

The positive for my startup has been working with people who come from finance backgrounds or from the New York network. And they've been amazingly helpful in a variety of ways. They're very good strategic thinkers; they're at the top of their game. But they also just have a different network from the traditional Silicon Valley group.

Naval: Yeah, it used to be that you would go to a VC for their network. But most entrepreneurs these days are much better networked than they used to be, thanks to accelerators, thanks to blogs, thanks to just being savvier about it. Different investors can be good for bringing out-of-market networks.

But exactly as you said, you want to interview your investors. And you really want to look for the subtle signals—I think people's true motivations and behavior are revealed, not said. If somebody spends ten minutes telling you how honest they are, I can guarantee you that's a dishonest person.

You should reference-check the hell out of them, you spend time with them, and you see how they treat you during the negotiation process. If they're relatively easy during the term sheet negotiation process, if they're quick to respond, if they're no hassle, if they say smart things, they're probably going to be good people to work with. If they give you an exploding term sheet, if they're difficult to work with, if they're inflexible, intransigent, they're going to be ten times worse once the money is in.

By the way, that's true of VCs too. You can learn everything you need to know about a VC during the term sheet process before the close. And don't be afraid to call off the close if you're getting negative signals. I've done it and I've never regretted it. The moment you know that you're working with someone that you would not work with for the rest of your life, stop working with them right there. Save your time. Because you get married to investors, with almost no possibility of divorce. And your dating period with them ranges from a week to a year. A year if you're really lucky, but it's usually just a few weeks. So you really have to look for the subtle signals.

This is actually where your early-stage investors can be super helpful, because they've seen it all. So you can use the nose that your early-stage investors have developed to help pick out later-stage investors. You do have to be a little careful, because early-stage investors can be brand obsessed— either they want to get a big markup, or they want to get a markup from Sequoia, so they'll say or do whatever just to ingratiate themselves. But you will have somebody within your circle who has a good nose, has a high bar, and speaks truth. You'll know it from the way they say it; they'll say the unpopular thing. Get that person to make an assessment for you.

Elad: I want to get back to your earlier point, about how companies today don't need to be as large as they used to. How do you know when to stop hiring? Because there's always that impulse, if you have the capital and you want to keep going.

Naval: The nature of human beings is that you come into a company, you work like a dog, you work really hard, and then you get tired and hire someone to do your job. And it always takes two new hires to do your job. Just repeat that ad nauseam, and you end up with five thousand people sitting around at a web app company. And everyone from the outside is like, "What are all these people doing?" That's a simple web app. Why do you need thousands of people to do it?

Then, sure enough, the new CEO comes in and knows that they have to fire half these people, but they don't know which half. That's the dilemma that everybody faces, because they're all politicking, so nobody knows who's actually doing the work. And once you're in that situation, you're in trouble.

So I think you should hire extremely slowly. Hire only after there's a burning need for that person. I think you have to be ruthless about firing and trimming the ranks. And I know that's not popular—I know people don't like that model—but it's worked well for me and for us. The founder just has to keep a very, very tight eye on waste. And there's always waste.

"You cannot take some-one's money without having a moral, ethical obligation to them."

— Naval Ravikant

Naval: I think it's better than the other model, which was no stock. But I do believe it's outdated. So we do six-year vests. Venture capital firms do ten-year vests. So I think in a rational model you would not only do longer vests, but you would also probably not have permanent issuances of value. Maybe you would have stock for the early people, because they're creating scaffolding that then turns into a big company. But the older a company gets, the further along it gets, the more your grants should shift to profit sharing.

Elad: I guess RSUs don't quite capture what you're saying.

Naval: RSUs are basically a tax-efficient way to give out more compensation that's somehow lightly tied to the overall performance of the company. If you're a multi-thousand-person company, though, one person can't affect performance that much. So I view it as a very diffuse kind of thing. When you look at true "eat what you can kill" kinds of businesses, where the human capital is really important—like go to Wall Street, where it's kind of cutthroat—those are all bonus-based.

Profit sharing can be very tax inefficient. AngelList is set up as an LLC, so for us it's actually more efficient to do that because we only have one layer of taxation. But I just think that as companies get larger and larger, and get further and further along—you can hack it even before you're profitable—you can do revenue sharing. Or you can give very outsize grants. So you do small grants for everybody starting out, a standard grant that everybody gets. But then next year you either increase a person's grant substantially or you let them go.

Elad: It almost reminds me of McKinsey's "up or out" model, where it's a partner-ship and people either advance and get more and more pay or they're out.

Naval: Exactly. Peter Thiel put this well in Zero to One: how are you going to sell your 21st employee? Because you can't give them enough stock that they own 5% of the company. So at that point you have to be on track to building a huge company. Or, I would argue, you can build a great company with a very small number of people, and you can incent them heavily.

Right now is the lowest-risk time ever to be a founder. You can go into an accelerator and roll the dice, see where it goes. You can get some money, see where it goes. There's very little risk to being a founder. But early employ-ees are asked to take founder-level risk, because the companies often don't have product/market fit, without getting founder-level equity.

Elad: Well, I don't think that they end up working as hard as founders, or dealing with the stress and the bad issues most employees never hear about.

Naval: Absolutely true. But there used to be a very steep decline, where the founder would own 40% and the first employee would own like 0.15% or 0.25%. I think those days are ending.

I think future companies, especially those that haven't raised money yet or haven't raised substantial capital or haven't gotten product/market fit even loosely, when they're hiring early employees, they're really just hiring late founders. And so they should be giving 1, 2, 3, 4% of the company, instead of giving 0.1, 0.2, 0.3, 0.4%.

The issue with hiring engineers into early-stage companies today is not that there's a shortage of engineers, it's that there's a surplus of founders. And so you have to basically treat them more like founders, because there's opportunity cost for these early engineers who could go start a company, join YC, whatever.

Elad: Although I think that the one thing that people tend to both overestimate and underestimate is the risk associated with a startup. There's a whole class of people that think startups are incredibly risky, and if they blow up your career is over—which is of course false. But on the flip side, too many people assume that 90% of startups have an exit of some sort. Which is also not true. Most startups completely fail. Their founders have lived on very low salaries, and they make nothing after that.

Naval: And they've been so stressed beyond belief that they've lost their health and sacrificed their family.

Elad: Yeah, they're ten years older than they should be in some sense. And they haven't made salary for three, four years.

Naval: Yeah, actually the most successful class of people in Silicon Valley on a consistent basis are either the venture capitalists—because they get to be diversified, and at least used to control a scarce resource, although it's currently not a scarce resource—or people who are very good at identifying companies that have just hit product/market fit. They have the background, expertise, and references that those companies really want them to help scale. And then those people go into the latest Dropbox, they go into the latest Airbnb.

Elad: It's the people who were at Google, and then joined Facebook when it was a hundred people, and then joined Stripe when it was a hundred people.

Naval: When Zuckerberg is just starting to scale his company and panics, he's like, "I don't know how to do this." And he calls Jim Breyer. And Jim Breyer says, "Well, I have this really great head of product at this other company, and you need this person." Those people tend to do the best risk-adjusted over a long period of time, other than the venture investors themselves. ■

This interview has been edited for clarity and length.

"The most successful class of people in Silicon Valley on a consistent basis are either the venture capitalists, or people who are very good at identifying companies that have just hit product/market fit. They have the background, expertise, and references that those companies really want to help them scale."

—Naval Ravikant

CHAPTER 9

Mergers & acquisitions

CHAPTER 9

Mergers & acquisitions

M&A: BUYING OTHER COMPANIES

As your valuation increases, your stock may suddenly become a valuable currency with which to buy other companies. Many first-time CEOs or executive teams tend to shy away from acquisitions due to a lack of familiarity. If done right acquisitions can accelerate a company's product and hiring plan, as well as enable key strategic or defensive moves against competitors.

When I was at Twitter, the M&A team reported to me. I saw firsthand both the value of M&A as a strategic tool as well as the sheer number of startups that flounder and are looking for an acquirer (the failed startups no one ever talks about). While at Google, I was involved with the diligence, integration, or post-merger product management of a number of companies including Android (which became the well-known handset platform), Google Mobile Maps (originally a company called ZipDash), and the first Gmail client application (originally a company called Reqwireless).

M&A was a powerful tool for both Google and Twitter to add new products and key people as well as make major strategic moves. Similarly, Facebook has stayed at the leading edge (and acquired major market share) via its acquisitions of companies such as WhatsApp and Instagram, but also less famous companies like Snaptu, which drove major adoption of Facebook as a mobile client to over a hundred million people in the low- and middle-income world.

Most companies wait too long before making their first acquisition or are hesitant to use their stock as currency. Hopefully the information in this section will spark your M&A interest—and facilitate your ability to buy companies—early, rather than late, in your startup's growth.

WHEN SHOULD YOU START TO BUY OTHER COMPANIES?

Each CEO and board needs to decide when the time is right. Strategic acquisitions may be necessary early in a company's life. For example, when Twitter acquired Summize (which became Twitter Search), Twitter was just about 15 people in size and worth only around $100 million itself.

By the time a given company is worth $1 billion or more, the CEO and board should start to think of M&A as a serious tool for accelerating the company's progress and valuation. For example, at $1 billion market cap, a $10 million acquisition is just 1% of your startup's equity. If the acquisition can increase your valuation by just 10%, then it is clearly ROI positive. By the time your company is worth $5 billion to $10 billion or more, M&A can become a central part of your overall company strategy.

For revenue-generating companies, the potential value of an acquisition may be directly quantifiable. For example, when Twitter M&A worked for me, it was easier to assess the potential value of advertising-related acquisitions because of the direct revenue impact they would have. If Twitter could generate, say, $50 million more revenue than it had a year earlier, the potential dollar value of the acquisition was clear and therefore the range of prices we were willing to pay became a simple math problem.

You can also translate revenue + margin into potential market cap. If your valuation (or your public market comparable) is at 10X earnings, then an extra $10 million in margin may equate to another $100 million in market cap for your own company. This sort of math allows the M&A team to present ROI-based arguments around ad-tech related acquisitions, and allows you to start prioritizing the purchases you want to make on the product side.

THREE TYPES OF ACQUISITIONS

For a high-growth company, acquisitions fundamentally boil down to one of three types: (1) team buy, (2) product buy, or (3) strategic buy. There is actually a fourth type of acquisition companies can make, often called a "synergistic" acquisition. Most high-growth technology companies do not do "synergistic" buys—that is, those made for market share and cost-cutting reasons—like more mature companies do, so I will not discuss that type of acquisition here.

Type of acquisition: Team buy, aka "acqui-hire"
Valuation range: Anything from small signing bonus for the founders to $1M to $3M per engineering/product/design employee acquired.
Reason for purchase: Increase pace of hiring. Hire key talent the company would not be able to otherwise acquire. In most cases, the product the purchased company was working on is discarded and the acquired team reassigned to a new area.
Examples: Drop.io acquisition by Facebook was largely to acquire Sam Lessin.

Type of acquisition: Product buy
Valuation range: $5M to $500M. Most are in the range of several million to $100M in size.
Reason for purchase: Fill a product hole or reposition an entire team to work on an area that is already in a company's road map. Sometimes the original product survives as a stand-alone product, sometimes it is integrated with other products, and sometimes it is discarded in favor of a new, similar product to be launched by the acquiring company.
Examples: ZipDash, acquired by Google and repositioned to form seed of Google Mobile Maps. Android purchase by Google. Acquisition of Summize by Twitter to create Twitter search.

Type of acquisition: Strategic buy
Valuation range: Up to $20B
Reason for purchase: Purchase of a non-reproducible asset that has strategic value. For example, while Facebook could have launched a photo app, it could not reproduce the active and dynamic community using the Instagram social network.
Examples: Instagram and WhatsApp purchases by Facebook. DoubleClick, Motorola, and YouTube acquisitions by Google.

How you approach the negotiation and execution of each of these three types of purchases will differ wildly. The large, strategic buys tend to be heavily negotiated and often involve the CEO of the acquirer. They may be more about connecting with the founder of the target company and painting a big picture of why they would want to join forces with one another. These can be very emotion-driven sales. On the other end of the spectrum, small team buys may be desperation moves by founders shopping for a "soft landing" for their startups as they run out of money or realize they lack product/market fit.

M&A ROAD MAP

You should have a member of the corporate development, product, or business development teams (depending on your organizational structure and resources) develop an M&A road map. That individual should get input on that road map from *(i)* key hiring managers on the types of people or teams they would most like to acquire, *(ii)* product and engineering leaders on product road map holes, and *(iii)* the executive team on key "big picture" strategic buys the company should consider.

If I were to imagine the M&A road map at Facebook circa 2012, it speculatively may have looked something like this:

- Hiring M&A. Facebook needs to build out its mobile team, and is being pressured by Wall Street to increase its ad business. Therefore, we should buy teams of 3–10 people with strong backgrounds in (1) mobile engineering/product/design or (2) advertising products. Teams will be broken up and added to the areas of greatest hiring need. We should also buy machine learning or data science heavy teams as we can not hire enough of them.

- **Product M&A.** Buy Snaptu to enable mobile clients in LATAM/ASIAPAC, an email-scraping company to help with international growth efforts, and an IM-focused team to reposition for Messenger.

- **Strategic M&A.** Build relationships with founders of the top five social apps on mobile and the web. Set up quarterly 1:1s for Zuck to meet with the CEOs of WhatsApp, Instagram, Pinterest, Twitter, and Weibo. Determine when to pull the trigger and make a bid on each.

Building your M&A road map is a crucial first step. Next, we'll take a look at how to assess what your prospective acquisitions are worth—so you can move forward on an offer.

General considerations when buying a company:
- Can we absorb a team of this size without screwing up our culture?
- What will the org chart and reporting structure be?
- Will the leadership of the team we buy have an impact more broadly in our company? Are there areas we are struggling with that the incoming entrepreneur can own?

MANAGING INTERNAL STAKEHOLDERS

Internal pushback to M&A

It is common for employees or executives at a company to push back on M&A. Pushing back on acquisitions may reflect a strategic or tactical insight. Alternatively, pushing back may reflect a lack of understanding or pragmatism about the inability of the company to do everything with the limited resources it has. Or, it may reflect jealousy around the acquisition price and financial outcome for the founders of the company you are buying. In general, more junior employees or company old-timers tend to push back more on M&A than experienced executives who have seen the value of doing acquisitions well at another company.

The set of companies you are looking to buy should be considered an internal secret and not something widely discussed with the entire company at an all-hands. This should be kept quiet because:

1. Word may leak. This can cause a number of bad scenarios including *(i)* competitive bids on the startup being acquired *(ii)* disruption of that company's operations—for example if one of your employees tells their friend at the company that you are thinking about buying them *(iii)* lobbying of regulators by your competitors to block the acquisition.

2. Most employees won't have context. Many of your employees may lack the broader strategic context, or experience, to understand how M&A may be used as a tool. They may also not understand that you may talk to ten companies but only buy one, and there is the potential for employees to get upset or worried about acquisitions that will never happen. Why cause organizational churn or questioning for no reason?

3. It makes it harder to bid on the same company again later. If you publically try to buy something, and then publically pass, it may become harder to justify to your team another attempt on the same company. Strategic imperatives, financial models or other items may change and it is best to maintain flexibility.

4. Members of your team may try to inappropriately block the acquisition. See below for common objections.

DEALING WITH OBJECTIONS

Common objections from the internal team may include:

1. Couldn't we just build this ourselves for cheaper? Why buy a small team with a nascent product for $20 million when that same $20 million could allow us to hire 100 people for a year?

Answers may include:
- In reality there are lots of things your company could do but it is limited by resources (including the ability to hire that many people quickly). If you do not buy the company, this strategic objective will not get done or will be delayed dramatically.
- You are also buying a team that has thought deeply about the area and will not need time to ramp on it, as well as brings it own unique insights to bear.
- The company being bought will bring its own leaders that will help drive this initiative forward.
- The financial value if this team succeeds and gets things done a year earlier may be worth much more than the $20M being paid for the company.

2. We are going to crush this competitor! Why would we buy them? In some cases it does not make sense to buy any competitors and to indeed outcompete everyone in the marketplace.

Your answers to this objection may include:
- This competitor has been driving down margins by competing for every deal. By taking them off the market we make back the value simply by having less competition.

- This acquisition is accretive, e.g., we are trading for 10X revenue but only paying 5X revenue for this competitor. So we gain market share, grow our market cap for more than the stock we spent to buy the company, and may also lower our costs or get efficiencies via scale.
- This buy is defensive. Buying this competitor will block large-scary-co from entering this market. If large-scary-co cannot get a toe-hold via acquisition, this market is ours long term. If they decide to buy this competitor and put resources behind it, we will have real competition for once.

3. Does the team really meet our bar? There are concerns on the engineering team that this team does not meet our hiring bar. A friend of one of our tech leads says the team is not very good.

Response (for a team acquisition):
- We will continue to maintain our high bar. We will be taking the team through our interview process and will make the acquisition contingent on us bringing on board a big enough subset of the team. We will not add (or will give a short trial period to test out) employees that we are uncertain about.

Response (for a strategic acquisition):
- We are buying this company for its core asset and market share versus just the team. Once we start the integration we will assess each individual team member and decide where, how, and whether to slot them into our organization. If anyone on their team wants to switch teams after the acquisition, they will need to do a full interview circuit with the team they want to switch to. This will ensure our high bar is maintained.

4. It will take a long time to integrate. Don't we need to port over their stuff? It will take a year or two to rewrite their code for our stack! We could have our own team build the same thing faster.

Response:
- We do not, and will likely not, have the headcount for this project in the near term. Given that this team has a live product we can distribute, we think it is faster to buy this team and either *(i)* let them continue on their own stack or *(ii)* have them port over to our infrastructure.
- In parallel we will have a product in the market and will attract customers or scare off or block competitors.

5. What if the acquisition fails? All new projects can fail and some will certainly do so. What if this acquisition is one of those failures?

Response:
- We do not have a 100% success rate for our internal new products and that is by design. If nothing fails it means we are not taking enough risk. Similarly, for acquisitions some will work out and some will not. However, if enough of them work

out they will more than pay for the acquisitions that do not. No matter what, we will also end up getting talent into the company that might be hard to hire directly otherwise, simply due to the risk profiles of the people involved.

M&A INTERVIEW PROCESSES

One of the key areas that matters to your employees (outside of price, which may cause its own gripes) is whether new acquired employees meet the bar (particularly in the case of a team buy or small product buy). This gets complicated if your team is largely composed of more junior, less experienced people whose only professional experience (outside of internships) is your company. In general, less experienced employees may not do a good job of interviewing senior people. If the company being acquired is a team of very senior engineers from, for example, Google or Facebook, it is possible the senior engineers will not pass the interviews with your more junior team. There are a few ways to ensure that the company being acquired gets a fair shot. For example, for engineering interviews:

1. Standardize interview processes and questions per the "Recruiting, Hiring, and Managing Talent" chapter of this book. If you do not have a consistent set of questions hiring feedback may be arbitrary. Make sure your interview questions work well for senior as well as junior engineers—sometimes coding questions can reflect recency of a computer science degree (more emphasis on certain aspects of theory for example) versus ability to code.

2. Put mainly senior engineers with cross-company experience on pre-set panels for M&A. This ensures your employees will have the context and bar to interview and assess more senior hires.

3. Remind the interview panel that most of the people who are interviewing were just told that their company is for sale, and may not have had time to prepare for interviews.

4. Do references (if it makes sense to do so) and weigh them highly. The employees of the company being acquired do not have a say in where they are going (their company's founders are driving the acquisition) and they are unlikely to have interviewed recently. As such, they are unlikely to have prepared for interviews with your team and they will also lack context for the acquisition. As such, discount some standard interview items like "do they have passion for our company" that you may have if you hired someone off the street.

You can do the analogous situation for other company functions.

M&A: HOW TO SET A VALUATION FOR COMPANIES YOU BUY

Setting the right valuation for a company you plan to acquire is more art than science. Each type of acquisition comes with its own set of considerations as you set a valuation. However, there is also a common set of things to look at when determining your willingness to pay.

VALUATION FACTORS TO ASSESS FOR ALL THREE TYPES OF M&A

- **What is the "target's" cash position?** If they only have 3–6 months of cash left, they will not have a lot of time to negotiate, raise more money, or find other buyers.

- **How desperate are the founders or management team to sell?** Founders and management teams can get tired. Do the founders want to exit? This was famously the motivation behind Flickr's exit to Yahoo!

- **Is the acquisition competitive?** Who else might be bidding and what would they pay for it? If your stock is perceived as having more upside (e.g., if you are Airbnb at a $1 billion valuation), then you should be more financially convincing as an acquirer than Google (which is unlikely to increase its value by 10X again anytime soon).

- **Is the acquisition defensive?** Is it important that you block someone else from buying the company, so you avoid their entry into your market? For example, Google's purchase of Waze may have been in part defensive, to prevent Facebook or Apple from entering mapping well.

- **How truly unique is the target you want to buy?** If you are looking to buy a mobile team and there are a dozen of them running out of money, it is a different scenario than trying to buy Instagram, which is a one-of-a-kind asset.

TEAM BUYS OR ACQUI-HIRES

Team buys have a range of potential valuations depending on the following factors:

- **Team quality.** How strong is the team? Do they come out of brand-name companies or schools? Have they launched or built awesome products in the past?

- **Unique expertise.** Right after the iOS App Store launched, the value of mobile client developers was high and companies would pay a lot to buy these teams. Similarly, today Google and Facebook appear to pay large amounts for deep learning expertise. What expertise is your team missing that could move your company forward?

- **Acquirer desperation.** Google paid through the nose to acquire "social" product managers, designers, and engineers during its Google+ heyday. Are there skill sets that your company desperately needs?

- **Celebrity cofounder or engineer.** Does the prospective team have any well-known engineers, designers, businesspeople, or entrepreneurs on board? These "celebs" can help your company recruit exceptional talent once they are on your team. They may also have an outsized impact on your company due to their own personal networks or skill sets.

In general, on the low end, an acqui-hire means a 20% signing bonus to founders and standard salaries and packages for everyone else, with the cap table (i.e., the company's investors) getting no money back. This is more common than people think, and many touted and tweeted acquisitions turn out in reality to be hiring a subset of a team and shutting their company and product down.

For a true "team buy," companies will typically pay $1 million to $3 million per engineer, designer, and product manager who ends up getting an offer to join. Businesspeople, operations, etc., are typically viewed as anything from a marginal bump in valuation to a potential negative if severance packages need to be generated for them.[72] Depending on how the acquisition is structured, much of the per engineer value may go to pay off the cap table (e.g., the $5 million invested by VCs in the company) or to retention packages for the team.

Most companies ask to interview the employees of a startup before making a team buy, and reserve the right to cut team members who do not meet the bar. This could reduce the final acquisition price further. In other words, you may drop the price on an acquisition if the target company's engineering talent is inconsistent in caliber and you only want a subset of the team to join your company. This is, as expected, a tough conversation to have. See more in the section on interviewing teams you acquire.

PRODUCT BUYS

Beyond the generic valuation considerations mentioned above, you may also want to assess the following factors when considering a product buy:

- **How much time will this save us?** What product hole will this purchase fill? Can the team be repositioned to fill this hole?

---

[72] Note that in some cases companies may pay an enormous price per engineer for key talent areas. For example, Google paid large sums for deep learning teams in 2015, and before that for "social" experts during the Google+ heyday/fiasco.

- **What is the estimated quantifiable impact of this purchase?** For example, how many more users will this get us and what is the expected value per user we have? Or, how much more revenue or cash flow will this generate at what margin?

- **How will the strategic market landscape change if we make this purchase?** Do we block a competitor's ability to do something? What does this enable us to do?

General rule of thumb for a product buy: You want employees of the target company to get at least a 20–50% bump in their compensation packages over what they could have gotten if they walked in off the street to interview with your company. Since they do not have a choice on where to go, paying them a little more up front discourages them from leaving your company two months later. Some of the early employees from a product or strategic buy may actually make dramatically more than this, so this is meant more as a "worst-case" scenario.

STRATEGIC BUYS

True strategic buys accomplish one of the following for your company:
- Change the overall market structure in your industry.
- Provide you with a key, non-reproducible/defensible asset.
- Block a competitor from a major action, market position, or the like.
- Dramatically change some aspect of your business (cost structure, distribution channel, etc.).

In most cases, a strategic buy will involve multiple potential acquirers with deep pockets bidding for the same asset. For example, Google, Facebook, and Apple all supposedly bid on AdMob as a way to increase their market share and capabilities in mobile ads. (It eventually went to Google for a reported $750 million in 2009.)

Key questions to ask for a strategic buy:

- **How does this purchase change fundamental aspects of my business?** Does it consolidate a key market? Allow me to cross-sell products? Enter a new business area?

- **Is there a way for me to otherwise reproduce this asset on my own** or via an alternative set of purchases?

- **Will a competitor buying this asset cause an existential crisis** for my own company or product line?

- **Can this company become a major competitor to me in its own right?** Can I buy it before it competes with me directly or gains more traction?

- **Is there unique talent at this company, or a unique team,** that can change the trajectory of my company?

- **What is the P&L of our combined entity?** What revenue do we project this purchase will generate? How can costs be cut?

- **What is the set of metrics I can use to set a purchase price?**

M&A: CONVINCING SOMEONE (AND THEIR MAJOR INVESTORS) TO SELL

There are two sorts of founders: those that want or need to sell and those that don't. In general, founders sell either due to fear and exhaustion (because they are tired, have run out of money, or are about to get crushed by a competitor) or conversely due to ambition and excitement (because they are excited about the impact they and their team will have, or about the financial payday).

CONVINCING PEOPLE TO SELL: TEAM AND PRODUCT BUYS

For team and product buys, you need to convince both the entrepreneurs and the investors that selling to your company is a good idea. There is a different strategy to getting each on board.

Convincing entrepreneurs. If a founder is burned out or running out of money, not much convincing is needed—they will even try to sell you on the sale. If the entrepreneur does not need to sell, your main levers are:

- **Compensation.** There are different "levels" of wealth in people's minds. They might include, for example, the ability to pay off school debt, the ability to buy a house, and the ability to never work again. In general, founders will react different-ly to $1 million in stock ("Wow, that's a lot of money! I can work for your company for a few years and then try again at a startup"), $5 million ("I can afford real estate in the Bay Area and not worry as much in life!"), and $10 million ("I probably do not need to work ever again").

  Depending on the entrepreneur, her financial status to date, and her personal history, different levels of wealth may be sufficient to convince some founders to sell irrespective of other factors. In general, stock and even cash payments will vest over one to four years, and in some cases stock the entrepreneur already earned will be re-vested.

---

73 Some investors (especially large VCs) may have the ability to block any acquisitions of the company. This means you will need to convince them to go with your offer. Some investors may behave poorly when you are getting acquired. One of my investors at Mixer Labs, while we were being acquired by Twitter, was an enormous pain in the butt and kept trying to negotiate more deal value for himself.

"One of the biggest causes of early exits are founders' spouses, who are typically less risk-seeking."

—Elad Gil

- **Impact.** What impact will the founders and their company or product have on your product and direction? Since you are starting to buy other companies, you are probably reaching millions or even hundreds of millions of people with your product. Can their product or vision overlap with yours so that they can influence the lives of millions of people?

- **Role.** What role can you offer the founders and/or CEO? Will they have a larger team or even more influence than they did at their startup?

- **Threats.** While I am not a big fan of this approach, some companies are famous for threatening startups they want to buy. They may file a lawsuit claiming IP infringement, or mention casually that they plan to enter the market, so the two companies may as well join forces. In most cases these are idle threats.

Convincing investors. In a team or product buy, you will also need to convince investors to allow the sale to go through (assuming they can block it). Most investors want to see at least a 3X return on their investments on average. Of course, that means they need to do better than 3X on the "winners" to offset companies that shut down or return nothing to the investors. If your offer returns less than 3X their investment, investors may fight against the acquisition.

Things to mention to investors:

- **"You are trading low-appreciation stock for high-appreciation stock."** The basic argument is that the company you are buying is not on a high-growth or breakout trajectory—but your company is. By selling now, the company you acquire (assuming you are using stock to do so) will have a multiple on this outcome, as your own stock should appreciate dramatically. In contrast, even if the startup doubles in value over the same time period, selling to you is a much better return. For example, my startup Mixer Labs sold to Twitter in 2009, when Twitter was worth about $1 billion. This means we've seen at least a 10X return, on top of what we were acquired for, since that time.

- **"We plan to buy someone in this market. If it is not this company, it will be someone else."** This means the door may close on the opportunity for the company to exit to you in the future. It's now or never.

- **"Our relationships are important to us, and you are in our ecosystem."** You see certain VCs involved in exits to the same set of companies over and over (e.g., Google, Facebook, Twitter, etc.). These VCs will want to maintain a good relationship with your company so that if they need to help sell one of their portfolio companies, they will have a direct line of access to your corporate development team. This is another way of saying that Silicon Valley is a long game, not a short one.

CONVINCING FOUNDERS TO SELL: STRATEGIC BUYS

Assets that are truly strategic and breaking out themselves are much harder to acquire. This means longer-term relationship building will make a big difference in the likelihood that you will be able to purchase the next hot company in your market.

Once your company hits a certain scale, you should start meeting with the CEOs of companies you may want to buy every quarter or two. This relationship-building may eventually pay off in a competitive strategic situation. Mark Zuckerberg at Facebook was notoriously focused on building relationships with the founders of WhatsApp and Instagram, leading to pole position for them to acquire both companies over time.

When convincing people to sell a strategic asset, there tend to be a few large levers:

- **Autonomy.** Many founders started companies so that they could drive things themselves. They do not want a lot of overhead and bureaucracy. A promise that you will leave them alone to run their company, while providing financial and Sales, General & Administrative (SG&A) resources to help support scaling, can be attractive to founders. For example, Android and YouTube both ran autonomously, with their own hiring processes and criteria, for years post-Google purchase. In parallel, Google supported these acquisitions financially, and provided headcount and resources for the messy business areas (operations, sales, etc.) that product-centric founders often don't want to deal with.

- **Support.** Some founders just don't want to do the extra work of building a stand-alone public company. They want to focus on product and design, not building out a sales team. Or they hate sitting in meetings to discuss employee ladders and accounting. Pitching autonomy plus the support to focus on the stuff they care about can convince founders to join you.

- **Impact and role.** In some cases an incoming founder will be given a larger role than she had in her own stand-alone company. You often see startup founders take on broader divisions of the acquiring company or key strategic roles. For example, John Hanke from Keyhole (which developed the software behind Google Earth) ended up running all of Google Maps.

- **Competitive dynamic and/or fear.** YouTube exited to Google in part due to the threat of lawsuits from the media industry. Some founders/CEOs can be convinced that they are about to get crushed by third-party forces, lawsuits, or other external threats.

- **Money.** Financial outcome can cut both ways—i.e., if a company is going to do well no matter what, founders may think a certain amount of money is a high enough baseline and not be tempted by the immediate exit. However, in some cases you can convince a founder that the safe road is to sell now and never have to worry again. One of the biggest causes of early exits are founders' spouses, who are typically less risk-seeking. Often they push for the safe exit so that they and their children are set for life.

M&A: NEGOTIATE THE ACQUISITION

Negotiate the sale: team or product buy

All negotiations are about relative leverage (or the perception of leverage). In order to understand more about the company you plan to acquire, you should ask about cash position/burn rate, cap table, team size, product growth rates, and other factors. This will allow you to determine how desperate the founders are to exit.

Some additional rules of thumb:

1. **If a company closed a funding round in the preceding 3–6 months, you usually need to pay at least a 50% premium on the valuation.** In some cases their investors will try to push for a 2–3X valuation bump. However, if the overall market has shifted dramatically, the founders are desperate to exit, or the company has poor future prospects, you could trade at the last-round valuation or a discount.

2. **The typical value per engineer, product manager, or designer is between $1 million and $3 million per person.** Business, operations, or community managers tend to have low-to-negative value for a team buy (since in some cases they will not be part of the acquisition and you will need to pay severance). For special or outsized talent this may go as high as $5 million. Note this money is often spread across the cap table (mainly investors and founders) and retention.

"Entrepreneurs should always talk to a small subset of their investors or advisors when they receive an acquisition offer."

—Elad Gil

3. **Get a range of valuations to offer from your CEO or board, and then anchor as low as you reasonably can.** A board typically approves an "up to" price for an acquisition, with an agreed-upon likely range (e.g., $15 million up to $20 million). If the situation is not super competitive, the deal team may anchor on the lower side (e.g., $12 million) to provide some room to move. If the situation is competitive, the deal team is more likely to open with an aggressive offer (e.g., $18 million).

4. **Many corporate development teams quote total deal value in their opening bids without mentioning what part goes to the cap table (i.e., preferred and common stock) versus retention.** This can materially impact value to founders, investors, and employees. Bids usually also ignore cash on hand.

   - As an example, say you offer a $10 million purchase price to a six-person team with $1 million still in the bank. Since you are buying the company, you also get their cash, making the real purchase price $9 million. (Some people even use part of the company's cash to pay bonuses to the team in a manner that does not impact the acquirer's cash holdings.)
   - In reality this offer may mean $6 million to the cap table and $3 million in retention. So, if a founder owns 20% of the company at this stage, she will receive $1.2 million, not the $2 million she likely expected when you quoted a $10 million offer. The remaining $3 million may include additional retention for the founder, but is likely to also be split among the other five employees (i.e., $500,000 in four years of retention each, including the founder).

- In many cases, once an entrepreneur decides to exit and is excited by an initial offer, she will not walk away once she fully understands the nuances of the deal. At that point, she has already seen the light at the end of the tunnel ("I don't need to wake up in a cold sweat in the middle of the night anymore!") and has mentally spent the money ("I can finally pay off my credit cards and buy a condo!"). This is why entrepreneurs should always talk to a small subset of their investors or advisors when they receive an acquisition offer. They need experienced people, who have seen this happen a bunch of times, to help them avoid the common traps laid by savvy corporate development people.

In general, it is important that the person negotiating the deal with the founder not be the same person that the founder will eventually report to or work with day-to-day. There are often bad feelings between a deal person and at least some of the entrepreneurs who get acquired. Letting go of your startup baby is hard to do, and negotiations can be tough on first-time entrepreneurs.

NEGOTIATE THE SALE: STRATEGIC ASSET

When buying a strategic asset some key principles are:

1. **Buying strategic assets is also a sale by your company.** Facebook's ability to buy Whatsapp and Instagram was a reflection of the relationship Zuckerberg had built with each founder in advance. Over time he sold the other CEOs on the benefits of joining Facebook and built a trusted relationship. Effectively, Zucerkberg sold Facebook to Whatsapp rather than the other way around.

2. **The CEO needs to get involved.** As CEO, you will need to be part of the relationship building leading up to the acquisition, and some aspects of the actual deal itself. If your counter party CEO feels they have a relationship to you, they will trust you with their, and their company's, future. It will be easier to negotiate and close the deal.

3. **Move quickly.** Especially if there are multiple parties bidding on the asset, moving quickly to a conclusion may benefit you enormously by creating time pressure or a sense of inevitability that you are the right choice. It will also show professionalism and a lack of dickering on minor items. Google famously bought YouTube in less than a week for $1.6 billion.

SCALING RESPONSIBLY, FOR YOUR USERS AND THE WORLD

An interview with Hemant Taneja

Hemant Taneja founded the Silicon Valley operations for General Catalyst in 2011 and made a series of successful investments, including Snap, Stripe, Gusto, Color, Grammarly, and Livongo. He also cofounded Advanced Energy Economy, a nationwide nonprofit for advanced energy, and serves as a board member for Khan Academy. Hemant has five degrees from MIT.

Hemant has become an outspoken advocate for responsible innovation, calling on fellow tech leaders to embrace their influence and wield it responsibly. He published a book called UNSCALED, which describes the 30-year secular shift in society where we are rewriting all major parts of the economy.

I sat down with him to hear his thoughts on where we are in Silicon Valley's evolution, how startups can position themselves to scale successfully, and why a winner-take-all mindset is often counterproductive. Along the way, he also shared how founders can embed social responsibility in their processes from day one.

Elad Gil:
One of the points you made is that we're in the midst of a large, secular shift around organizing content, community, and commerce online. I'd love to get your view on what's happening.

Hemant Taneja:
The big shift that we're in the midst of is around scale. For 100 years we used scale as a metric of success. We scaled core services like healthcare, education and finance so everyone in America could have baseline access. And this was a net positive for a long time. Childbirth became safer, we got really good at dealing with trauma injuries and infectious diseases. Through scale, more kids were educated and more people had access to financial services. We created a vibrant middle class with economies of scale in the past century. China moved over 300m people into middle class within two decades using the same principles of scaling.

But today, I am convinced that scale has run its course.

Let's take healthcare for example. In the old days, healthcare was only available to the affluent members of society. They used to have a family doctor who came to their home, knew them intimately, and took care of their health with great empathy. In order to bring basic healthcare to everyone, we started building hospitals across the country. We figured out how to control infant mortality rates, infectious diseases, and trauma, among other things. Today, if you visit a hospital, you barely get a few minutes with a physician, they barely know anything about you, and they are busy typing notes into their electronic medical records (EMRs) instead of making eye contact. This experience is a far cry from the experience a family doctor provided.

We could go similarly go through education, finance, energy, and other core sectors.

We've literally taken every one of these important services in society and scaled them to the breaking point. The banks have failed small businesses and large segments of consumers. The health care system is bankrupting us. We are not preparing our kids for the twenty-first century. The power sector has contributed significantly to climate change.

Fortunately, over the last twenty, twenty-five years, we have been engaged in this secular shift to organize content, community, and commerce online. It has given us, for the first time, an opportunity to rethink how we provide these basic services that are fundamental to our society.

It has also brought the role of technology and technology entrepreneurs front and center. We're in the hot seat. We're building modern education, modern health care, modern financial services. When I think about my own work over the last decade, I've been drawn to founders who are trying to take advantage of this secular shift and taking on these extraordinarily large markets.

Elad: I'd love to hear your perspective on first principles around focus on customers versus focus on regulators. As companies are scaling in these big, regulated markets—health care, education, finance, etc.—how should that focus shift?

Hemant: Take health care. I recently convened a working group of healthcare executives, who lead the most forward-thinking health systems in their use of technology. The conversation focused on use of software standards to interoperate with EMRs for improving healthcare quality and costs. And they were going on about standards and the various issues of EMR for four hours. I was shocked that their dialogue didn't include any focus on either the patient or the physician at all.

In my closing remarks, I said that to them at the end of the dinner. "Gosh, if you think that by thinking so incrementally you're going to go impact healthcare quality and costs, it's never going to happen."

One of the companies I helped create, Livongo, is an example of rethinking healthcare for consumers with chronic diseases from first principles. Today, a majority of the more than 30 million consumers who have type 2 diabetes check their blood sugar regularly and visit their primary care physician or endocrinologist a few times a year. In between those visits, their health deteriorates and they have seizures and development of co-morbidities. Most solutions, including use of software, in a traditional sense has been to get consumers to follow this regimen of engaging with their health. Silicon Valley created dozens of diabetes management apps for consumers to capture data around blood glucose and nutrition more efficiently. Meanwhile, the prevalence of the disease and cost of delivering care keeps rising.

At Livongo, we took a consumer-centric view and created a service that allows them to "disengage" from their disease as much as possible. They want to be healthy. Livongo gives them a connected glucometer, monitors their data with machine learning, and intervenes if the consumer needs to make any adjustments in diet or exercise to remain healthy. This approach, in my estimation, will save us over $100 billion a year at scale in managing diabetes. Also, as we collect more data about consumers' metabolic patterns, we are recognizing that there are many types of diabetes that we previously thought of in the "type 2" bucket. Highly impactful.

Taking a persona, like the type 2 consumer diabetic, and thinking about product mechanisms that are going to deliver experiences that consumers need, across industries, is an enormous opportunity.

Elad: Is that the common thread—that customer exploration and focus—that is causing these companies to break out? Are there specific tactics that these companies have in common where, you know, it doesn't matter if you're working in health care or financial services, you're basically doing these three things?

Hemant: One thing these companies have in common is that these markets are so large. Arguably these are all markets that are $100 billion or more. And companies tackling them, the ones that get it right, have the potential to be $100 billion market-cap companies, something that used to be crazy to think about in venture capital ten years ago.

I think the commonality between all of them has been that they identified their target customer persona precisely at the beginning. So, for Stripe, it's the developer trying to do online commerce and who needs an API for accepting payments online. For Gusto, it's the modern HR person in a small business that is on social media and can be reached in new ways. For Livongo, it was a diabetic who always checks their blood sugar and is employed by a self-insured employer.

I think taking these massive markets and narrowing product focus down to a specific persona to start has been a core reason why these companies that have gotten it right.

Elad: How does that change as the company scales? You start dealing with product complexity. You start adding additional product lines. Maybe you want to broaden your scope because your first market was very high potential but a niche, which is often how great companies start. How do you think about that transition? Are there specific examples that come to mind of people who've navigated that well?

Hemant: That's a great question.

If you look at how Stripe has scaled, providing the online payments API globally is a massive opportunity. While they have built an "AWS for commerce" stack for their customers to deepen their product stack, the traction of their core offering just dwarfs everything else.

And you want to take advantage of that. I think for them it was, "We want to make sure the majority of the new companies that start today start with us," because that represents the future. By focusing on that, they have secured their future. Only when the organization became great at doing so did they start to focus on going upmarket to also serve companies that have been around for a while.

"We're in the hot seat. We're building modern educa-tion, modern health care, modern financial services."

— Hemant Taneja

For Livongo, the playbook for scaling is different. Their objective is to keep consumers with diabetes healthy. Those consumers have many co-mor-bidities, like hypertension and obesity, and Livongo needed to deepen its offering much sooner in its lifecycle despite having a similarly large mar-ket to serve because it was the right thing to do for its customers to be truly impactful.

In general, it's different for every company. But if a company has a large market to go after with your initial target persona, it should maximize scaling there before diversifying and diluting the organizational focus.

Elad: What are the common failure modes or patterns there? One could imagine either being too focused on the core markets and never broadening into something else. Or, to your point, getting distracted by new add-ons when you should really be doubling down because your market is so large and singular. How do you know which of those situations you're in, or how do you navigate that situation?

Hemant: These are not winner-take-all markets. So first of all, the empha-sis on "market leadership" becomes hard. The companies, instead, need to focus on charting a course with aggressive but manageable growth rates over a long period of time.

There is an optimal growth rate that is unique to each company. It depends on the physics of the operations: What is the pace of hiring that's required to service their initial customer versus expanding to the next market seg-ment? How complex are the logistics in delivering the services? What is the capital intensity required to diversify? Those questions start to become paramount in figuring out a growth plan that makes sense.

Good founders have done it. They've remained fiscally prudent. But a lot of companies have tried to do too much and diversify too much because lot of capital was available for cheap, but then they often had had difficulty raising money or growing into their valuations because they just couldn't maintain focus on the unit economics.

Elad: That's a really interesting point about winner-take-all markets. Because in the early 2000s, mid 2000s, a lot of the emphasis was on the fact that markets are winner-take-all and that investors should only invest in the winner-take-all companies. I think that's because you were dealing with a lot of truly network effect–driven businesses. Do you think most venture-scaled businesses are winner-take-all? Or do you think you have more complex oligopoly or other market structures? In other words, how important is winner-take-all?

Hemant: First of all, I think it depends on the market. But for a lot of these large markets that have been regulated and are just opening up, I think it's hard to think about being winner take all. Gusto is an example of that. There are millions of small businesses that they can serve with a modern people platform. Should Gusto focus its product and sales on companies that are 1 to 10 employees, or 10 to 100, or 100 to 1,000?

You have to carve out your niche and become really great at it, and not worry about what other companies are doing. Figure out how to build a business that is foundationally designed to grow at what you think the optimal growth rate is, and don't worry about how you take the disproportionate share.

Elad: That's super interesting. Because the canonical view would be: Google was winner-take-all, Facebook was largely winner-take-all. But to your point, if you're dealing in health care or fintech, that same characteristic doesn't seem to apply as much due to market size and structure, and fragmentation.

You've also been a big advocate for building responsibly, and I'd love to hear some of your thoughts on that notion.

Hemant: Tech companies spent decades focusing on creating software to deliver efficiencies across every sector, including health care, education, and finance. Now we're rethinking how those services are delivered from first principles. New companies often begin around profound ideas: What does it mean to recommend to a diabetic how they should spend their day and what they should eat? Or what does it mean for teaching behavior in a classroom full of high school kids?

Those are big responsibilities. The traditional mindset has been to grow at any cost, right? Silicon Valley has been obsessed with this idea of backing the hacker-entrepreneur who moves fast, breaks things, and iterates. But that mindset and growth at all costs is not well suited to building responsibly in areas that greatly impact people's daily lives.

So for me, there's this notion of the empathetic entrepreneur who understands their customers' needs deeply, figures out what's the responsible way to serve them, and makes sure that is represented in their MVP, even if it comes at the expense of some growth.

Traditional large corporations that serve these markets have this idea of corporate social responsibility. I think startups building in Silicon Valley today need to have their own startup social responsibility. In my opinion, that is met by being transparent about how algorithms and machine learning are being used to deliver services, and by building measurement systems to make sure that the company's success is not based on taking advantage of things like bias and discrimination that we want to avoid in society. I've generally looked for founders who truly understand this, respect this, and are building with those principles from the beginning.

Elad: As a company scales, how do you think it can reinforce those principles through the culture or the day-to-day work? What have you seen work well tactically?

Hemant: It really is about starting to build measurement systems around the impact that your products are having in society, in whichever dimension they're meant for—be it social emotional learning, chronic care management, fiscal literacy, media, or what have you. And being transparent.

Founders need to be prepared for the yet-unknown. It's not always going to be immediately obvious when you're deviating from your company's core values. Teams need to be thinking about building what I call "algorithmic canaries" into their products and metrics dashboards in order to catch unintended, negative outcomes before they become broadly adopted.

If algorithmically-driven sales optimizations lead you to excluding groups of people from even learning about your product, or managers in your company tend to review older workers using different language and criteria than with younger employees, algorithmic canaries should throw a red flag. The same is true for understanding how your product is being used: canaries should alert you to your product being used in ways you never intended it to be.

You can look at how some companies just abused practices to grow. Think about what happened with Zenefits. Think about what happened with Theranos. Think about what happened with Uber. They all took shortcuts to grow fast and put their employees, customers, and other stakeholders at risk.

"We need to think hard about how our collective work is coming together."

— Hemant Taneja

I think that you can have a team that values "responsible innovation" from the beginning. You can state that weaponization of technology is just not something you're going to use in your product development. Or else you can end up being one of these companies that eventually become kind of fatally flawed.

I am convinced that we are a decade into a thirty-year cycle. You know, we talk a lot about high valuations, or when's this bubble going to burst. I would pay less attention to that and think much more about the broader digitization that we're in the midst of, one that Silicon Valley is leading. I care deeply about embedding this thinking in our culture.

We need to think hard about how our collective work is coming together. For example, right here in the Bay Area, we have companies building self-driving trucks. We have companies working on longevity, including Spring Discovery. And we've got experiments going on in basic income. What if it all comes true? Some day we are going to have to talk to three million truck drivers in the country: "We've got good news and bad news. Good news is you're going to live thirty, forty, fifty years longer. Bad news is that you won't have a job. And oh, by the way, we're going to put you on a stipend and eliminate all your pride and self-esteem." That sounds terrifying.

Just thinking systemically about what we're creating as the technorati is also important. That needs to become more of the conversation in our tech ethos.

"I think startups building in Silicon Valley today need to have their own startup social responsibility."

— Hemant Taneja

Elad: To build on that, when do you think founders of breakout companies should get involved with either philanthropy or politics or thinking about broader societal issues? One argument would be that you should be solely focused on your startup. You should be focused on scaling it until you have the free time and money to help society more broadly—the Bill Gates model of philanthropy. The other argument is that as soon as you are seeing success you should really be engaging with society more broadly—immediately. I'm curious how you think people should handle that transition and when they should do it.

Hemant: I'm a believer that getting involved in philanthropy from early on is a good thing. I actually cofounded this organization in Boston called TUGG (Technology Underwriting Greater Good). The whole idea was to have the tech community help mentor social entrepreneurs.

In Silicon Valley culture, there's a lot of mentorship that goes around in helping each other build startups. I think that even if you can't afford to help others financially, whatever time you're spending mentoring other entrepreneurs contributes to the pay-it-forward culture that we have. Apply a reasonable portion of that time toward helping social entrepreneurs. Then over time, as you're successful because you have been deeply obsessed with your startup and things worked out the right way, start to get into philanthropy financially as well.

That's the continuum that I think about. So start with the "mentoring" time that you have today. And as you achieve financial success over time, contribute financially as well.

Elad: And how do you think about political activism and things like that in the context of a startup? Because on the one side, there's all sorts of examples where you want to create a balanced view within your company, because your company or employee base really represents all different types of people. But at the same time, Silicon Valley has been notoriously terrible at engaging in the political process in a way that is positive for society. Philanthropy is one part of impacting society. Politics and regulation is another. How should companies or founders think about that?

Hemant: I like the role of business to be in helping design the right policies, and stay away from politics. I've done a lot of work in the energy sector for the past decade, and it's always been about how to help create policies that lead to the adoption of clean, affordable, and secure energy.

Our bias should be to have more transparency in how we use software and data in our products and services. Engaging in a dialogue with policy makers, and demonstrating self-regulation via algorithmic accountability, is a way to productively engage with policy makers. Missteps by the companies in the social media sector around this make us take a step back in this regard. We need to learn from those experiences, because otherwise we run the risk of more regulation.

I think that it is a very worthwhile investment in time to bring regulators along with our use of data and AI. Because less regulation implies more innovation. But I think that only comes from investing in a trusting relationship with the regulators. ▉

This interview has been edited and condensed for clarity.

Things to just say no to

If you are in Silicon Valley long enough, you feel like you have seen it all. Here are some things to "just say no" to.

1. **Envelopes full of cash.** Google used to give out everyone's Christmas bonus as a thousand dollars in cash in a plain envelope on the same day in December. Urban legend has it as Googlers would disembark off the shuttle to San Francisco, they would get collectively mugged of tens of thousands of dollars by thieves who heard about the company's generosity.

2. **China.** Uber had come the closest to succeeding in China with its 20% ownership of Didi, but basically every other tech giant has been blocked and then cloned in China, with early operations shutting down. For most companies, a China strategy ends up being a painful, money-burning fail.

3. **Giant chrome pandas.** Dropbox bought a giant chrome panda at the height of its funding success. As time went on and the company focused on frugality, the giant chrome panda became a sign of its earlier wanton spending, and became a constant reminder that you should save money. You can instill that lesson without wasting a ton of money on a chrome sculpture—for example, one company I heard of recently put a Juicero machine in its office as its own version of a "chrome panda."

4. **Pool tables.** When I first moved out to Silicon Valley, I joined a Sequoia-backed startup that had 120 people. Within three months it grew to 150, and then shrank over the next 9 months down to 12 people over four to five rounds of layoffs. After the first round of layoffs, the company bought a pool table to "help employee morale." Unfortunately, anyone spotted playing pool tended to be laid off in the following round. Eventually shooting pool was a sign that the people playing would soon be gone. The pool players probably had the free time to play pool, so probably that was correlation rather than causation. Still: Not a good sign.

Stripe
Press